Displaced Person

2006

Emma E. Nielson

Displaced Person

A Girl's Life in Russia, Germany, and America

Ella E. Schneider Hilton

Assisted by Angela K. Hilton

LOUISIANA STATE UNIVERSITY PRESS

BATON ROUGE

*Designer:*Andrew Shurtz
Typeface: Trump Mediaeval Shadow display
Typesetter: Coghill Composition Co., Inc.
Printer and binder: Thomson-Shore, Inc.

LIBRARY OF CONGRESS CATALOGING-IN-PUBLICATION DATA:
Hilton, Ella E. Schneider, 1936–
Displaced person : a girl's life in Russia, Germany, and America /
Ella E. Schneider Hilton, assisted by Angela K. Hilton.
p. cm.
ISBN 0-8071-2878-3 (alk. paper)
1. Hilton, Ella E. Schneider, 1936– —Childhood and youth.
2. Russian Germans—United States—Biography.
3. Russian Germans—Soviet Union—Biography.
4. Refugee children—Germany—Biography.
5. World War, 1939–1945—Refugees—Biography.
6. Refugee camps—Germany—History—20th century.
7. Holly Springs (Miss.)—Biography.
8. Refugees—Mississippi—Social conditions—20th century.
9. Mississippi—Social conditions—20th century.
I. Hilton, Angela K. II. Title.
E184.R85H55   2003
940.53'092—dc22
2003016540

To Mama

Contents

Illustrations

Foreword

Displaced Person is a marvelous story in many ways. It is an inspiring rendition of the American dream: a young girl born to German parents in the USSR, caught in the maelstrom of the Second World War, assigned for seven years to a refugee camp in Germany, offered the chance to come to America, and, after some hardships in rural Mississippi, presented with the opportunity to go to college, marry a fine young man, live happily in American society, and become, as she describes herself, "the All-American Girl." *Displaced Person* is also a representative tale of post–World War II refugees, driven from their homes by competing social and political systems and mighty armies, fearful of the consequences of returning to those homes after the War's end, and seeking some place where they might feel wanted. Many millions shared this kind of experience in the twentieth century, a century perhaps best known for the great migrations of people uprooted from homes they and their ancestors had lived in for centuries.

Displaced Person is a cautionary tale for a world of such violence that entire populations seemed to suffer from post-traumatic stress syndrome. Children like Ella endured violence and fear, not just from bombs overhead but also from the brutality of their own parents, who had such difficulty coping with the turbulence and horror they experienced. Above all, however, *Displaced Person* is a tale of Ella's courage, persistent optimism, and wonderful powers of observation that give the reader insights into the Soviet Union under Stalin, war-ravaged and postwar Germany, and 1950s Mississippi. As in all societies and all experiences, her story includes good times and bad, and she presents them with compassion, humor, and insight.

Ella Schneider Hilton is a descendent of the Volga Germans, who emigrated from Germany to Russia after the end of the Seven Years' War (1756–1763). One of the first initiatives undertaken by Empress Catherine II (the Great, 1762–1796) of Russia following her accession to the throne was to encourage immigration of foreigners. At that time many political economists regarded population growth as the key to economic advancement and thus to political and military power. Catherine hoped not only that foreigners would augment the overall population of Russia, but also that they would provide the agricultural and manufacturing skills needed to modernize the Russian economy. To facilitate immigration, Catherine created the Chancery for the Guardianship of Foreigners and appointed as its head her then favorite, Gregory Orlov. The Chancery recruited primarily in western Germany, where there had been persistent problems related to overpopulation and where the Seven Years' War had caused considerable hardship.

Between 1763 and 1767 some 30,000 foreigners, mostly Germans, came to Russia and settled in the Volga region. The Russian government offered land for purchase, a generous loan policy to make property ownership possible, exemption from military service, religious freedom, reduced taxation, and considerable self-rule. The majority of these settlers were Lutheran, and Catherine the Great authorized the building of a church in each colony. The church became and remained the center of the Volga Germans' cultural world, which is reflected in Ella's recollections of her mother and grandmother. After initial hardships, the Volga Germans prospered and, by the late 1800s, had reached a population of about 1,750,000 residing in 192 towns and villages. As is evident from Ella's story, these people retained their German culture and their sense of separateness from the surrounding population.

In the late nineteenth century, the Russian government began a policy of Russification, which put the Volga Germans under considerable stress. Many of their privileges were revoked, most notably their exemption from military service. As a result, many left Russia, emigrating especially to the American Midwest and to Canada. Those who remained behind kept their German language and heritage but did not always stay in the original settlements.

The Russian Revolution inaugurated an even harsher period for the Volga Germans, especially since the new Soviet government banned religion. It labeled Lutheran pastors counterrevolutionaries, arrested many of them, and sent them to slave labor camps. In 1920–1921 the violence of the Russian Civil War and the harshness of the Soviet government caused widespread famine in the Volga region, and as much as one-third of the population perished as a result. Still, the Soviet government recognized the separate existence of the Volga Germans and in 1924 established the Autonomous Socialist Soviet Republic of the Volga Germans.

On June 22, 1941, Nazi Germany invaded the Soviet Union, and on August 28, 1941, the Soviet government, fearful that the Volga Germans would side with the Nazis, formally abolished the Republic of the Volga Germans.

Five days later the government announced the forced evacuation from their homes of over 400,000 Volga Germans. Although the Soviet government clearly regarded the Volga Germans as dangerous, it still drafted their young men into the Soviet army, so the question raised in *Displaced Person* regarding which army Ella's stepfather served is an interesting and unanswered one.

The fate of the Volga Germans remained largely unknown until 1955 when Soviet authorities revealed their whereabouts in Siberia and Kazakhstan and granted amnesty to the survivors. However, as a condition of that amnesty, the survivors had to sign papers that they would never return to their original settlements. In 1964 the Soviet government admitted that the previous decrees against the Volga Germans represented no more than oppression of an innocent people and called upon other Soviet citizens to assist it in restoring the Volga Germans to prosperity and cultural autonomy. In January 1965 the Soviet government declared all of the decrees of 1941 to be null and void.

In the autumn of 1943 the German army evacuated Ella and her family from their home in Kiev as the Soviet army approached. After staying for some time near Berlin, the family went to Bavaria, locating in various places until American soldiers took custody of them while they were staying in Passau, on the Danube River near the German/Austrian border. They were then counted as part of the great tide of Germans who had come from the eastern parts of Europe. During the last years of the war and in the first two years following the war's end, approximately 12 million *Volksdeutsche* (cultural and linguistic Germans living mainly in countries east of Germany proper) poured into Germany and Austria from Poland, Hungary, Czechoslovakia, and the USSR. Some, like Ella and her family, had fled, and some, like many in Poland and Czechoslovakia, had been expelled.

The Allied governments began discussing the growing population upheaval in Europe as early as 1943, especially after the appearance of *The Displacement of Population in Europe* by Eugene Kulischer, an officer of the International Labour Office. Kulischer identified "displacement" to apply to those foreign laborers who had been brought to Germany to work and those *Volksdeutsche* who had left or been expelled from their native countries. Kulischer acknowledged that many of the latter might not want to return to their home countries but argued that the best solution to the demographic upheaval would be to repatriate as many of them as quickly as possible. In April 1943 an Allied conference in Bermuda declared that persons "displaced by the war" would be returned to their home countries. Shortly after Allied military forces landed in Normandy, they adopted the term *refugee* to identify persons deprived of their homes within their own countries and *displaced person* to identify those "outside the national boundaries of their country by reason of the war."

When the war ended, American policy was to encourage the repatriation of as many displaced persons as possible, on the assumption that most wished to return home. Fortunately for Ella and her family, the Allies placed those persons of "ex-enemy nationality" at the bottom of the priority list for repatriation. At the top were Western European (French, Dutch, Belgian, Luxembourger), Czechoslovak, and Soviet foreign workers or prisoners, with Poles and Yugoslavs of secondary importance. It became clear to the Allies in the summer of 1945 that many Poles, Yugoslavs, Ukrainians, Jews, and people from the Baltic states were fearful of returning home, and General Dwight D. Eisenhower, commanding general of United States Forces, European Theater, changed army policy from compulsory repatriation to offering those who did not want to return refuge in Germany until resettlement to some other country could be arranged.

Who would care for displaced persons in the American zone of occupation was not determined as the war ended. For the first few months the care of displaced persons was in the hands of the United States Army, especially the commanders of the occupation troops and the United Nations Relief and Rehabilitation Administration (UNRRA, later the International Refugee Organization or IRO) teams assigned to the army under the supervision of Eisenhower's office. At the end of 1945 this authority passed to the military governors of the respective zones of occupation, then to the Allied High Commissioners, and finally, in 1951, to the newly established Federal Republic of Germany with the understanding that its representatives would integrate the remaining displaced persons into German society.

Until 1948 American policy toward the entry of displaced persons into the United States was based on the existing immigration laws. The quota for admission of all immigrants to the United States was 39,000, but no more than 3,900 could come in any given month. Of the 39,000, only 13,000 could come from Eastern Europe. On December 22, 1945, President Harry Truman sent a letter to the *New York Times* in which he announced he would do all that was within his power "to see that our established immigration quotas are used in order to reduce human suffering." That meant that the quotas would remain and that sponsoring agencies had to commit themselves financially to help immigrants (no immigrant could enter if he/she would be a ward of the state), but Truman would still do all that he could to make immigration officials available to displaced persons who wished to come to the United States. Truman ordered the secretary of state to join with the attorney general's office, the Immigration and Naturalization Service, and the surgeon general of the Public Health Service to create the necessary offices in Germany to process displaced persons for emigration. Preference was given to orphans and people with relatives living in the United States.

In June 1948, in response to the emerging Cold War and particularly the Soviet takeover of Czechoslovakia, Congress passed the Displaced Persons Act establishing the Displaced Persons Commission and allowing for the admission to the United States of up to 205,000 people per year for two years. In 1950 Congress amended the Displaced Persons Act and specifically provided for admission of "54,744 refugees and expellees of German origin." Undoubtedly Ella and her family came to the United States under this provision. Their sponsors were the Lutheran Church in America and, as she tells in her story, the Dean family of Holly Springs, Mississippi. This family arranged for their transportation from New York to Holly Springs, where they entered into one year of indentured servitude to repay the costs of their trip and maintenance.

Ella's tales of living in Mississippi in the 1950s provide insights into that society as important as the insights into the lives of displaced persons provided through her tales of living in camps in Germany. A true outsider in America, Ella encountered in Mississippi racial separation, class distinction among whites, harsh and backward living conditions for many, and considerable generosity and compassion. Having endured and described so many forms of prejudice, Ella forces the reader to wonder at the similarities and differences of discrimination toward a German in the Soviet Union, a *Volksdeutsche* in Bavaria, and a foreigner/poor white in Mississippi. While at times feeling sorry for Ella, the reader often admires her courage, persistence, and irresistible belief that things will get better as she confronts prejudice. Above all, one appreciates her straightforward efforts to understand her surroundings even if they cause her and her family discomfort or harm. That effort is the foundation for the insights she offers, and those insights are a treat. In short, hers is a marvelous tale. Enjoy it.

Karl A. Roider
Baton Rouge

Acknowledgments

First and foremost I wish to thank Theodor Puder, my step-father. When I was hungry, he fed me. When I was barefoot, he made shoes for my feet. When I needed shelter, he provided. And for *my* future, he moved to America.

God bless America for taking us in and for giving us homeless a home. Thank you to Joseph and Katherine Dean for giving this Displaced Person a start.

This book was completed in May of 2001. After reading the manuscript, my beloved husband Tom pronounced it to be very good. Within the month, he suffered a heart attack. Despite hospitalization and surgery, he went to be with the Lord on July 18, 2001. LTC (Ret) Thomas Gary Hilton, U.S. Army, QMC, who earned the Bronze Star (with Oak Leaf Cluster) in Vietnam, received a hero's burial with full military honors at Arlington National Cemetery. Thank you, Tom, my precious husband (mein Herz und meine Seele), my best friend and the love of my life, for showing me what love is and for participating fully in my wonderful American dream.

Erika, my firstborn, who girded me in prayer and showed me by her strong faith, that God is good, even in the worst of times.

Angela, my baby, heartbeat, and editor. It took me ten months of "stream-of-consciousness" to write, and Angela over three years to turn it all into an organized manuscript. Her gentle way of addressing me (not as mother but, "Ella, this doesn't flow," or "Ella, you are exceeding maximum verbosity") was an inspiration. I followed Angela's advice to "write whatever you remember, regardless of what other people remember." This book contains only "whatever" I remember. Without her guidance and loving patience, these recollections would never have come to fruition.

To my little family, Erika, Lydia, Otto, and Susan, words in any language would be inadequate to express my love for you.

Thanks to all the people at LSU Press, especially Sylvia Frank Rodrigue, Margaret Hart, and Gerry Anders. You are all amazing and gifted people who worked tirelessly to bring this work to print.

Vielen Dank Ilse und Paul Zaech, my precious Bavarian friends who adopted me into their family these past ten years.

To my friends who provided advice, encouragement and inspiration, Jim Gilfone, Betty Duree, Tommy Michalek, Jim Wilkerson, Gudrun Hanson, Astrid Hicks, Giesela White, Amie Oliver, Amy Edwards, Nicole Kerr, and Jaroslaw "Slav" Dubrowsky.

I thank God for the innumerable blessings He gave me in this wonderful land called America. I pray that God our Father will continue to bless this great nation and that it continue to be a blessing to all who are fortunate enough to enter her ports. I am convinced that:

"In all things God works for the good of those who love Him, who have been called according to His purpose" (Romans 8:28). God is good . . . all the time.

To all those countless people who touched my life . . .

Spasibo.
Dankeschön.
Thank you.

Displaced Person

Russia

Mama screamed. It was almost an inhuman shriek that sounded like it came from an animal in pain. It broke the stillness of the muggy Mississippi dawn and brought the whole family out of our beds and to our feet.

"Theodor! *Theodor!* Where are you? Hurry up! Oh dear God, what have I done in my life to deserve this? Oh dear God, take us back to Russia. Maybe Communism wasn't so bad after all. Take us back to Germany. Even under Hitler we lived better than this. Theodor, is there any way we can go back?"

My mama's pretty face was wet with tears. Her jet black hair was drenched from perspiration, her slip and underpants clinging to her stout, wet body as her begging, agonizing, wailing, and handwringing continued.

Mama had backed up from the kitchen into the bedroom/living-room combination where the six of us slept in three double beds. There the box Papa had made in Germany to carry our belongings to America served as our dinner table. We sat on our beds to eat. Mama always sat on the side of the bed that was nearest to the box/table so that she could serve each of us. The plates were old, mismatched, chipped, discolored, and dirty-looking. Was this broken-down two-room shack the answer to our prayers?

Full of sleep, I looked over Mama's shoulder. I could not see much because the single 60-watt bulb hanging from the ceiling seemed to cast more shadows than light. I could hear a strange rattling sound coming from the shelves lined with gallon jars of clabbered milk. Slowly my eyes focused on one particular jar. Something was coiled around it. Horrified, yet fascinated, I stared at the biggest snake I had ever seen in my life! Its head was raised about ten inches from the jar, pointing straight at us. The end of its tail was vibrating in a blur. Papa ran out of the front door. Within seconds he returned with a 2 × 4 and started hitting the snake with all his might. In the process, he demolished all the jars on the shelves, a week's supply of clabbered milk. The walls and window of the tiny kitchen were covered with broken glass, white yogurt—which now looked pink—and chunks of snake meat.

Mama, standing in the doorway with me and my siblings close behind

I

her, kept begging to be taken back to any camp in Germany. Although we had been dirty, hungry, infested with lice and bedbugs, at least we had lived in barracks fit for humans.

According to Mama, the snake was a bad omen. Our future in America would bring nothing good, what with poisonous snakes, red clay dirt, rain that dripped in from the leaky tin roof, and long-legged spiders that crept through big cracks in the floor to find refuge from the elements. The green creeping kudzu vine, taking over trees, buildings, fields, and anything else in its way, was threatening to swallow us as well. All this was the devil's creation. Our lives were doomed.

Later that day, needing quiet solitude, I walked on the side of the red-dust road to nowhere in the hot, humid Mississippi sun. At times like this memories always drew me back like a magnet to my childhood, visits to relatives in Stariska, USSR, Christmas and Easter celebrations, but most of all to our neighborhood, our home, our little apartment in Kiev, USSR, my birthplace.

1941

As the firstborn child I was adored by both my papa and my oma (grand-mother, in German). I was the apple of his eye and my oma's darling, tall and skinny for my age, plain-featured (taking after my papa's side of the family), with fine shoulder-length pageboy-cut brown hair and dark brown eyes. My only exceptional physical attributes at that time were my long, slender fingers. Mama always told her friends, "Ella will someday be a concert pianist."

Yet, with envy in my heart, I watched Mama pour all her affection on my two-years-younger sister, Sister Erika, who was the darling of Mama's side of the family. Much ado was made over her when we visited Mama's sister, Tante (Aunt) Rosalia, each summer in Stariska, a village near Kiev. As a child, she tended to be on the heavy side with a milk-and-honey complexion. Sister Erika had dark brown healthy short fine hair (not like Mama's, which was jet black with purple highlights). Her deep-set dark brown, almost black, eyes were surrounded by black eyebrows and shadows. Her heart-shaped face was complemented by full lips, straight teeth, and a dark brown birth mark the size of a pea that adorned the left side of her chin. Whenever Mama's family visited us, I stood by as my baby sister was fawned over as a beauty.

In our family, the words "I love you" were never heard from my parents or Oma. Our basic needs were met. We were provided with food, shelter, and clean clothing. Care amounted to love for that generation.

"Ella, go sit on your father's lap for a while so that I can sweep this place," Oma was saying.

"Papa, can I sit on your lap?" I asked.

"Come here, liebchen [darling], you can sit on my lap," he said.

I sat very still with my hands on the table watching Papa drink vodka out of a water glass.

Our two-room windowless basement apartment was on Budwarna Kudrawski Street number 30, in the better part of Kiev. The front room served as a workshop for Papa and the occasional visits by Opa, as grandfather was called. It was a dingy-looking place. The front room had a carpenter's workbench, with many tools placed against the wall and an even greater number hanging from the walls and ceiling. However hard Oma tried to clean it, it was always dark and damp. Sawdust was forever covering the floor and everything else in the apartment. Oma was sweeping both rooms while Papa took a break from his hammering, cutting, sawing, and painting.

"Papa, what are you making?" I asked.

"A Schrank." A clothes cabinet.

I liked the smell of the wood and occasionally joined Papa, only to be run out. His workshop was off limits for everybody.

"Ella, you can come off your father's lap. I've finished sweeping the sawdust. I don't want you kids dragging all the dirt into our living room," Oma said.

Since I could not go out to play unattended, I climbed on my bed. There were two beds, each a little larger than a double bed. The mattresses were sewn out of crude linen filled with matted-down straw. Before making our bed each morning Oma would take all the bedding and pile it on Mama's bed, then find the slit in the middle of the mattress, reach in, and loosen the straw. Two down-filled covers, rolled to look like sausages, took up half of each bed when it was made. The other side was used to sit on. Placed on top of the covers were four bleached-linen, down-filled white pillows with two of the four corners pointing straight up like rabbit ears reaching for the constantly dripping wet ceiling. The pillows and down comforters were wedding presents from Mama's family in Stariska. A single electric light bulb dangled from the ceiling. The only other light came from Papa's workshop. When not doing housework or cooking, Mama and Oma were sewing, mending holes in socks, crocheting, or knitting. Mama's busy schedule included daily shopping for groceries at the bazaar, visiting friends, sitting in the yard talking to neighbors, and taking Sister Erika and me to the park. When they couldn't sit outside to embroider or crochet, especially in the wintertime, Mama and Oma always complained that the apartment was too dark and they were ruining their eyes.

A cast-iron potbellied stove, on which our meals were cooked, stood in the middle of our spacious bedroom/living-room combination. Even in summer the stove gave welcome relief because the basement apartment was always damp and chilly.

"Oma, can I get the scraps of wood out of Papa's workshop?" The fire in the stove was losing its glow. I wanted to be helpful at every opportunity.

"Only if you ask Papa first," she said.

Oma used the leftover wood from Papa's workbench to rekindle the fire and then added a few chunks of coal. It was delivered once a week by a man leading a horse-drawn wagon. Oma kept the heat going night and day.

Four straight-backed wooden chairs, handmade by Papa, stood around a medium-size square wooden table. Papa was a heavy smoker. Whenever I got bored I counted, in German, the burned niches left by his hand-rolled cigarettes on the edge of the table. My counting only reached to ten. After I counted to ten in German, I started over in Russian. Our spoken everyday language was German. We spoke Russian only with our Russian neighbors or in public places.

A handmade china cabinet and wardrobe stood side by side next to a bench against the wall. I liked the wardrobe the best. Papa had painted its doors with beautifully colored flowers flying up and down. Two half-barrels made of wood stood under the bench.

There was no bathroom in our apartment. The rich family who lived above us had a toilet. I noticed it when I visited them a few times, during the winter months, to play with their daughter. Our family used an outdoor outhouse. "Oma, I have to go potty." She dried her hands on her beautiful white half apron, took me by my hand, and led me to the foul-smelling outhouse, actually just a few boards nailed together into an oversized box. It stood in one corner of the backyard. Fumes from the outhouse were overwhelming in the summertime. On rainy days and at night we used one of the wooden half-barrels. We called it a "Fass." Papa had built it as a waste-disposal pot with a lid that fitted securely on top and rope handles for carrying and emptying the contents into the outdoor outhouse. The whole family used it at night as a chamberpot. After emptying the Fass, Oma scrubbed it with a stiff brush, rinsed it, brought it in, and used it during the day for disposing of scraps and dishwater. In summer she kept the door open to air out the living area. The stench from the outhouse permeated the rooms, and an invasion of flies followed. The other half-barrel was used for washing clothes or for bathing.

During the warm summer months Oma bathed us about once every six weeks. My hair was cut short. Washing it more than once a month, or every two months, was bad for it and for my skin (per Oma). Oma's hair was pulled straight back, braided in a pigtail, and then rolled into a bun secured by long needles. I don't remember ever seeing Oma wash her hair.

One day Oma and Mama were preparing mushrooms that Mama had bought at the bazaar. Mama had bought two kinds of mushrooms. Oma worked on a big beautiful red mushroom that had white dots all over its head. The other mushrooms were a solid brownish yellow (Mama called them Pfefferlinge). Mama washed the yellow mushrooms in cold running water in the filthy-looking sink in Papa's workshop, the same sink Oma used to wash our hair and the dishes. She sliced those mushrooms and fried them with chopped onion in a cast-iron skillet on our stove for a delicious meal. We always ate bread with our meals. If the bread was at least a week old, it was broken into small chunks and used with the next pot of borscht (beet soup). When eating week-old bread you had to be very careful not to break your teeth while chewing a piece. The benefit of eating old, hard, dried black rye bread was that it removed the yellow from your teeth (per Oma).

Sister Erika and I sat motionless watching Oma place the cut-up red mushroom into an old bowl. With a spoon she smashed the mushroom into a paste and added a little honey. Then she cut strips of paper from an old, yellowing newspaper, spread the mushroom mixture on both sides of the paper, and hung the strips on nails permanently placed in the ceiling all around the living room and workshop. I wanted to help but Oma would not hear of it. Wagging her finger at me and Sister Erika, Oma impressed upon us not to ever touch or eat from this dish or we would surely die. Red in any mushroom means death. The flies must have loved it. They swooped directly from the open door to the flypapers and stuck there. If perchance they missed the flypaper, they buzzed directly to the bowl. I liked to sit at our table and watch in amazement the swarm of flies descending to partake of the beautiful red mushroom meal. The dish was covered with armies of dead flies. Whenever a flypaper was full, it was discarded and replaced with a new one. I wanted to know why I could not eat the brilliant red, white-dotted mushroom. Oma's explanation: "Because they are very poisonous. That is why Mama is fixing the edible mushrooms for us." Oma washed her hands often and thoroughly but still worried because "even a trace of poison can hurt you."

In the summer I wanted always to be outside. "I'm going out to play!" I would yell as I headed toward the basement door.

From the back room Mama would say, "Stick your head out of the door and see if there are any clothes drying on the line."

The backyard, surrounded on all four sides by three-story buildings, had no trees or even a sliver of grass. It consisted of rock-hard black dirt that the rain washed clean of dust. A few clotheslines ran from wall to wall where laundry was hung out to dry on a first-come basis.

"Yes, there are clothes on the line."

"You know quite well, Ella, you cannot go out when there are clothes drying."

No children played outside when anybody's wash was drying on the line.

Whenever we ran out of clean clothes to wear, Oma started a fire outside before dawn, boiling water in a huge metal pot placed between two well-used blackened rocks. Washdays were always on Mondays. Whites were washed first by hand in one clean Fass, then the clothes were placed into the boiling water for a while. The wash was brought inside to rinse in Papa's sink, then hung on the clotheslines to dry. Oma's washday prayers were always for no wind, so that the white bed linens especially would not get dusty and dirty before they dried.

After Oma brought in the dried clothes, I'd ask, "Can I iron today?"

"Let me get it all folded and put on the chair first."

She helped me climb on top of the heap of folded things. I sat there with pride until Oma thought the ironing was done. Ironing was easy. Whatever wouldn't fit on the chair was folded and placed under our mattresses. After a few nights everything was ready to be placed in our clothes closet, which was outfitted with shelves and nails.

During the fall and winter months we kept our door tightly closed because of the unbearable subzero temperatures. My girlfriend's windows on the second floor froze shut and could not be opened until spring. I visited her very few times in the winter. The stench in everybody's apartment was overwhelming. Winter washdays were rare. Oma washed our underwear and undershirts only. Clotheslines were strung from one end of our apartment to the other. During the winter months dresses, wet boots, socks, mittens, hats, shawls, and coats were a permanent installation around the potbellied stove after our daily outings. Surprisingly, the outhouse did not smell very strong in the winter.

I could not help but look into the outhouse toilet hole. In the wintertime all the deposits were frozen.

"What happens when it gets full and runs over?"

Oma assured me it would not run over. In the spring, the warm weather thawed the accumulation, and farmers came to collect it for use as fertilizer on their fields.

I liked wintertime. Even with the wind howling outside, our basement apartment was comfortable during the day. Oma entertained us with her many stories and songs. The stories sounded like fairy tales. I loved to hear about our family's fortune and misfortunes in years past.

Oma started off with a new story every time she was begged to tell one. "In our village, when I was your age," she began, "we had Christmas trees and a Christmas church service. We got together with relatives on Christmas Day to eat, drink, sing, dance, and exchange presents. All this was later forbidden by the Communist government. For the Christ Child they substituted Mr. Frost. He was the gift giver." After many repetitions by Oma of "Silent Night," I could sing it flawlessly by myself. Oma said, "I know, Ellachen"—an endearing diminutive form for Ella—"you are little, but the things that you memorize now you will remember always. You have to learn all the little prayers, and you must memorize the 'Our Father.'"

My interest was in the angels who came from heaven to see Baby Jesus. Did they have wings? I could never hear enough about Jesus and angels. Oma continued, "When I was a child we had a Lutheran church in our village. On Sundays we all put on our black Sunday dresses and the whole family went to church. Easter service was particularly memorable. We decorated our sanctuary in flowers. With a 'Christ is risen!' greeting, and a 'He is risen indeed!' reply, we exchanged hand-painted Easter eggs and braided yeast bread with our relatives and friends. The pastor made his rounds in the afternoons for a special blessing on the family."

"Oma, can I go to church?"

"No, we cannot go to church because there are no churches anymore. The Communists have closed all the churches."

"Who are the Communists?"

"You are too little to understand."

Cozy under my down-filled comforter, I could hear Oma from the opposite end of the bed murmur her prayers. Before Papa turned the light out, I lay staring at the ceiling, mesmerized by the condensation of the rainbow-colored beautiful drops that grew fatter and fatter until eventually they dropped on me or the bedcover. Finally, I fell asleep with angels dancing in my head.

Occasionally, on rainy or wintry days, Mama looked over Oma's shoulder and watched her preparing food. Sometimes, to Oma's delight, Mama asked for advice on life in general and how to do things in particular. When cooking borscht Oma would say, "Now Elsa"—Mama's given name—"this is how we did it in our family and this is how Jakob"—Papa's given name—"likes it, with lots and lots of cabbage. Watch me so that when I die you will know how to do it right. Make my Jakob happy. Be sure the girls know how to cook, wash clothing, crochet, embroider, sew, and knit. They will never go hungry knowing how to do all these things."

Mama smiled and said "Ja, ja."

* * *

"Jakob, can I get you to go to the bazaar tomorrow? Also, stop by the bakery and get us some bread. The snowstorm is really raging." I heard Oma's voice penetrating the darkness. It got so cold that the milk that Papa ventured out to the bazaar to buy froze in the metal container before he returned home. Oma dressed Sister Erika and me in double of everything. Our underwear was knitted out of wool and itched constantly, particularly after urinating. My underpants always smelled bad. I had two pair, and if I had an accident, there was an extra pair in the clothes closet. Our socks were likewise knitted out of heavy wool. When Mama, Sister Erika, and I visited Mama's family in her village Stariska, we brought back a bag of wool, which Oma spun into a thin thread. Then two thin threads were rolled into one ball. Never idle, Oma was always doing something: embroidering, crocheting, or knitting. Sister Erika's and my boots, which reached to our knees, were made out of heavy brown felt. Bought at the bazaar, they were always too big at first so that we could grow into them. The first year I had to wear two pair of heavy socks. The following year they required only one pair, and the third year Oma wrapped my feet in strips of material cut from an old linen sheet or dress. After that, the boots belonged to my sister. From time to time, the cold in our basement was so bitterly biting that Oma left our boots, coats, hats, and gloves on overnight.

Wintertime was always an ongoing challenge of trying to avoid sickness. To prevent a cold or the flu, Oma made sure that Sister Erika and I had our tablespoon of homemade vodka daily. Even so, I always had an ear infection.

The thought or taste of vodka reminds me of Papa and how he made his own out of pure alcohol. Many times I stood next to the kitchen table when I was just that tall. Papa had a container that he filled with cold birchwood charcoal and placed over a bowl. The bottom of the container held a linen rag. Papa then poured the pure alcohol over the charcoal. After the charcoal was saturated, I watched crystal clear drops drip slowly into the bowl. When the bowl was full, Papa poured the purified vodka into a clean water glass. It looked like plain water to me. When we had company, the other men did the same. Sometimes a few drops of vodka spilled on the table. Instead of wiping it with a rag, Papa put a match to it. The most beautiful blue flame danced across the table. It burned the wet spot dry without burning the table. One evening the men were discussing how to drink homemade vodka without dying. One of them said, "The trick is not to inhale the fumes from the alcohol. Drink it with one swallow not inhaling. If you inhale the fumes they will get into your lungs and kill you." Papa interjected, "When drinking it is always good to eat pickled herring, black, crusty, rye bread, and smoked fatback with sour pickles. If you follow this recipe you will not get drunk or have a headache."

During the times of drinking and remembering stories from the past with friends, I sat on Mama's lap. I had learned that it was a good time to ask questions. When we were alone my questions were often answered with, "Ella, you don't need to know. You will get old too fast." When we had company, I was more likely to get a real answer. "Mama, how did you and Papa meet?"

"It was at a dance. Your papa was tall and handsome. He was good-looking, fun-loving, and liked to drink vodka. He had a beautiful baritone voice and sang in Russian and equally as well in German. He liked to dress in the Russian peasant outfit, no collar on a white longsleeved fine linen shirt embroidered by Oma with sunflowers and little blue forget-me-nots. The neck opening came halfway down his chest, and the wrists were embroidered with the same floral design. The shirt hung down his thighs. He wore black trousers stuffed into black leather boots. Around his waist he wore a belt that looked almost like a rope. He was an excellent dancer and could do all the Cossack dances. It required a man to be physically fit, with all the jumping up and down and turning flips and cartwheels. Your papa and I got married and came to Kiev to live. No, he had no brothers or sisters. His mother, your Oma Katherine, lives with us now and takes care of you and Sister Erika. Yes, he has a father, who is Opa [grandfather]. He doesn't live with us. He comes to visit every day."

"What does Papa make with Opa in the other room?" I asked.

"He makes furniture and troikas [sleighs pulled by horses in the wintertime]. He also builds houses. But most of all he likes to take pictures of you and your sister."

"Why doesn't Opa live with us?"

"He lives someplace in Kiev. That is enough of your questions." And she sent me to bed.

Mama and Papa slept in one bed. Oma, Sister Erika, and I shared the other. Sister Erika and I slept on one end of the bed and Oma, with her long legs between us, had her head resting at the opposite end. Oma suffered with pain in her fingers, elbows, shoulders, hips, knees, and feet. It seemed like the moist cold of the apartment aggravated these symptoms. Some nights I could not sleep; Papa snored while Oma moaned and groaned. Frequently, I stayed awake and stared at the potbellied stove, where I could see a few slips of light peeking through the darkness. In the almost totally darkened room I squeezed my eyes shut and let my imagination take on terrifying proportions. Pictures of all kinds of wild animals that I had seen at the zoo were chasing me. I never dared to cry out, afraid to get everyone upset. Frantically, I clutched my handmade rabbit while spending many sleepless hours until I dozed. I awoke when Opa entered.

"Opa is here!" I yelled. No reaction from anybody. Papa kept working. Oma continued cooking. Mama crocheted. Opa was very old, I thought, half-bald and wearing glasses. He sat in Papa's workshop. They talked. I wanted to run over and hug him but was afraid of the reaction I would get from him. Oma was separated from Opa, but he regularly came to visit us.

When he came, Papa sat and talked, smoked, or worked at something with him in the workshop. Oma lived with us and ran the household as a matriarch with an iron fist.

* * *

My most incredibly terrifying impression of Papa occurred when we were, just the two of us, visiting friends. It was June 22, 1941—the day before my fifth birthday. He asked me to pose on their beautiful, new-looking sofa so that he could get a good picture of me. Photography was his hobby. I was his favorite subject. The grown-ups were drinking vodka. I was happy with my glass of milk. There were no other children present. In my beautiful, white-laced, finely woven linen dress that Oma had sewn just for this occasion, I was sitting on a straight-backed chair at a tablecloth-covered table. A bouquet of white daisies in the middle of the table kept my interest. From across the table Papa said in a very loud and commanding voice (very unusual for my papa to talk to me like that), "Ella, get on the sofa."

"Papa, I need to go potty."

"Get on the sofa."

Climbing onto the sofa, I begged again, "Papa, I need to go potty!" Holding onto the back of the sofa in order not to sink in, I was finally able to stand.

"You stand there and smile for me until I am finished taking your picture!" he ordered.

By now I was crying. "Papa, I must go potty." My crying became sobs.

Red-faced, he yelled at me: "Ella, do as you are told. You want to cry? I will give you something to cry about."

"Papa, I must go potty."

With two big steps of his lanky body he came flying across the room looking like a madman and spouting a string of profanities. Holding his camera in one hand, he smacked me across my face with the other. The pain was so intense I could not hold on any longer. I wet my pants—and our friends' soft new flower-printed sofa.

Papa flew into a rage. Putting down his camera, he beat me mercilessly with both hands in fists that felt like rocks. His friends, listening to my anguished cries, tried to calm him—"Jakob, she's just a child. We'll wash it and after it dries it will be like new again"—but the unrelenting blows continued to fall, whiplashing my head from one side to the other. All along, he was yelling, "I'll teach you! I'll teach you!" By now, I was rolled into a ball lying on my wet dress on the wet sofa. I don't remember begging him to stop. His beating frenzy continued until his strength was spent. All of a sudden, the blows ended and the room became very quiet. Apologizing for my behavior, he shook hands all around. Silently he took me—still sobbing and rubbing my swollen eyes—by my hand and we walked in darkness down the street back home.

When we returned home, my hair was matted from perspiration as if glued to my scalp, my face red, my eyes swollen almost shut. I was still crying but only in short sobs. The upper part of my dress was wet from tears.

The skirt was wrinkled, soaked, and permeated with the smell of urine. My legs were dry except for my socks and shoes.

Mama opened the door and screamed for Oma, "Katja"—short for Katherine—"come quick," wringing her hands, shouting over and over again, "Ach du lieber Gott! Ach du lieber Gott!" (Oh my God!) Within seconds Oma arrived in the workshop still drying her hands on her white apron, addressing Papa, "Jakob, what happened? Have you been drinking? Who beat this child?" Not waiting for an answer she gathered me into her long skinny arms and held me close to her bony chest. Taking off my wet shoes, socks, and dress, Mama inspected my body for more red swollen areas.

I had never seen Papa so angry and mean-looking. After seating himself at the table, he explained as best as he could in short sentences. "She would not cooperate. What was I to do? The sofa will never be the same. Can you imagine what our friends must think of us after this? It was all your doing, spoiling her," he said, pointing his finger at Oma. Mama sat across from Papa and never said a word. While Oma, after his explanation on how else was he to teach me a lesson, flew into a rage, turning red with the veins bulging and pulsating on the side of her head. Screaming and wagging her index finger in his face, almost touching his nose, "Jakob, what you have done to this child is unforgivable! Have you lost your mind? You could have killed her. Listen and listen well. You will never to your dying day touch this child ever again. Do you hear me?" This strong statement coming from his mother was written in stone.

Added sweetness and sweets from Mama and Oma with comforting words, they tried to make up for his brutality. Oma's efforts met with little success. I would not go near Papa out of fear. Since Oma was handling the affair, Mama had nothing to say. Even though we lived in Russia, we were raised in the German tradition of a regimented dictatorial matriarchal lifestyle. Oma's word was absolute and final.

* * *

While Papa and I had visited friends, Mama and Oma were busily preparing to celebrate my fifth birthday the following day. It was late when all the preparations for my birthday party were completed and we finally settled into bed. All of a sudden, I was awakened out of a sound sleep by a loud banging at the door. It sounded like someone was kicking with the back of a shoe or boot against the door. We all sat up in our beds.

Even before Papa made it to the light switch, he yelled in Russian, "Kto

eto?" (Who is it?) Not waiting for an answer he yelled, "Ja idu" (I'm coming).
Papa opened the door. I could not see the door from my bed, but I could hear
it squeak when it opened. Mama and Oma had jumped out of bed. I crawled
into my parents' bed in order to see what was going on since I had a direct
view through the workshop to the front door from there.

Two grim-faced men in dark clothing, hands in their pockets, were looking around the workshop. One said, "Vy Jakov Schnajdjer?" (Are you Jakob
Schneider?)

"Da." (Yes.)

"My NKVD." (We are the NKVD—the secret police.) "Odjevajcja i pojd-
jom s nami." (Get your clothes on and come with us.)

While going through the closet trying to find a bag to gather some items
for Papa to take, Mama said to the first man, who was doing all the talking,
"Pozhalujsta, skazhitje mnje kuda vy vozmjote jego. Ja pridu tuda zavtra i
voz' mu jego britvu." (Please, tell me where are you taking him. I will go
there tomorrow and take him a razor.)

His reply was simple, "Nje vol'nuitjes'. Kuda on idjot, nichjego nje
nuzhno!" (Don't worry. Where we're taking him, he won't need a thing!)

After searching the apartment and finding what they were looking for,
they left, confiscating a small radio. Oma was saying to Mama, "I just knew
that his radio would get him arrested. Someone must have informed on us.
But who? It had to be someone in the neighborhood."

Papa usually listened to the radio. But because of the birthday preparation, none of us had listened to it that night. The German army had attacked Russia and was moving east.

Mama was crying and so was Oma. I could not understand why. Later,
in the dark I overheard Mama whispering to Oma that the NKVD would
never send Papa back home alive. Mama started to cry again, and after a
while Oma joined her. I had never heard two grown women cry so hard before. It scared me to death.

Following a sleepless night, Mama dressed and left Sister Erika and me
with Oma. She went to the bazaar. She came back hours later looking very
tired and pale, with dried blood on her hands and a few red streaks across
her face. She took off her coat, then embraced Oma. Without saying anything, they both broke into heart-wrenching cries. Their grief-stricken bodies became one and were shaking in unison. After a while their sobbing and
wailing subsided. They sat on Mama's bed as Mama described the terrifying
scene she had witnessed at the bazaar. Trembling and between sobs she re-

lated how she and other German/Russian women were searching for their fathers, husbands, and sons. She had turned over one bullet-riddled body after another, into the hundreds. All were cold and stiff—the men had been executed during the night. The faces of many were unrecognizable because of wounds and blood. Some women recognized their loved ones only by their clothing. Women were crying, kneeling, and praying. "But I did not find Jakob," Mama said. "He was not among the dead."

Mama and Oma decided that Papa must still be alive and had probably been sent to Siberia. A carpenter and photographer could be of use in a labor camp. A flicker of hope kept burning in our hearts that he had survived the massacre, Stalin's purge of Kiev.

Nothing was ever said to me or my sister about why Papa wasn't coming home. I finally said to Mama, "Is Papa coming back?"

"Never," she replied. "You are not to ask questions or mention this incident to anyone, ever. You understand, Ella? If anyone should ask you about your papa, tell him you don't have one. From now on do not speak German until we get to Tante Rosalia's house."

Just as soon as the whispered conversation between Mama and Oma was over, still crying silently, they started to pack a few keepsakes. I sat on my bed observing this scene with much interest. Mama put our one and only suitcase on her bed. Oma took a plain bed linen out of the Schrank and said, "Elsa, do you think we need to take this?"

"No, only what we will wear."

They packed our prized possessions: pictures that Papa took of the family and friends; some handmade embroidered bed linens; Papa's embroidered Sunday shirt, just in case he came back; one hand-crocheted window curtain sometimes used as a tablecloth; a few things Oma had made by hand when she was a young woman; one aluminum two-quart soup pot; two oversized beat-up metal coffee cups; a small black leather-bound book, Oma's Bible; a cured piece of side meat wrapped in linen cloth that was already saturated by the oozing fat; and a loaf of bread at least three days old that was good and hard. Mama cut a small hole in the top of the loaf, removed some of the softer bread from inside, and replaced it with her wedding band, her gold earrings, a broach, and some money. Then she glued the crust together with thick flour paste, wrapped the loaf in a linen rag, and placed it in the suitcase. Closing the suitcase, she girded it with Papa's left-behind leather belt.

Oma was cleaning and putting everything in its place. "God forbid, Elsa, a friend or a neighbor should come in while we are gone and find the place in disarray."

Sister Erika and I had to get off the beds so that they should look newly made. Mama dressed us in double everything: a second pair of the itchy woolen underpants, woolen winter socks, and undershirts. My dresses barely fit and I could hardly move around or bend over. Mama kept reminding Oma that the nights were still cold, whereas the days were getting much warmer. This was June. She snapped back at Mama, "Then we can take some of the things off."

It turned out we weren't going straight to Stariska. But Mama and Oma thought we had to get out of the apartment. The NKVD might come back. So we were going to seek temporary refuge with friends, a Russian family who lived across town.

The streets were deserted and almost dark as we made our long, silent walk to the other side of Kiev. Sister Erika complained that her legs hurt, and Mama and Oma took turns carrying her while the other carried the suitcase. I tagged along behind both of them. Our Russian friends were happy but very surprised to see us. Of course, we could visit with them for a few days. No, they had not heard about the roundup the night before. After dinner they moved the table out of the kitchen, gave us blankets, and we found a resting place on the floor.

The next day Mama went back to the bazaar. When she came home she told Oma that she had run into a neighbor who said that the NKVD had come back to round up the rest of the family only hours after we left. They questioned the whole building, but none of the neighbors could tell them where we had gone.

Within a few days, Mama and Oma bid our benefactors and God-sent friends a tearful goodbye. Mama said, "We must not overstay our welcome. The authorities are probably looking for us." We had put our friends in jeopardy with the authorities—they might even be arrested if they were found to harbor German Russians (per Mama). So we headed for the bazaar, where Mama talked to farmers who were selling their goods. When all their vegetables, pork, fruits, butter, shoes, or linens were sold, they would return home.

Eventually she found a farmer who was headed toward Stariska, Mama's village. Could we ride with him as far as he was going? Sure. We piled into his wagon. After a while, my sister and I placed our heads on Mama's and Oma's laps. Empty potato sacks were our blankets. As we bumped along, we were lulled into a sound sleep by the clatter of hooves against the cobble-stone streets of Kiev. I awoke when the farmer stopped to water the horses out of a bucket from a nearby stream. We all had a good refreshing drink of water. My eyes brimmed with excitement watching houses change to landscapes.

It was pitch dark when we arrived at his farm. Since his family was already asleep, he offered us his barn, which Mama gratefully accepted. I was hungry and so was Sister Erika. Mama broke off a piece of bread very carefully so as not to disturb the end of the loaf where the jewelry was hidden. Sister Erika and I slept between Mama and Oma, covered now with two smelly horse blankets. The new straw felt like sleeping on a cloud. All too soon, the rooster, the manager of time, crowed. It was more like a shriek. Within a few minutes, more and more roosters joined him from far off in an uneven chorus. The animals were up now and making all kind of noises. We went outside next to the barn and relieved ourselves. The farmer's wife came and invited us in for breakfast; warm fresh frothy milk for Sister Erika and me, hot tea and honey for Mama and Oma. An unevenly baked loaf of dark black rye bread was already sliced on the table, accompanied by ham and boiled eggs. Mama asked the woman, "Where is your husband? We want to thank him again for giving us a lift."

"He'll be back. He has gone into the village to talk to some friends."

Mama and Oma exchanged a quick glance. Shortly after breakfast he returned. Sister Erika and I were playing with the kittens in the front yard. Seeing him, I dropped the kitten and ran into the house in order to hear the latest news. The farmer had found a man who was going toward Stariska to buy some materials. We could ride with him. Mama and Oma shook his hand and thanked him deeply for his kindness.

Mama and Oma took turns riding up front. On the back of the wagon we sat between sacks of flour, potatoes, poppy seed, red beets, eggs and other assorted items. One of the sacks contained a smoked ham. I snuggled the ham so that I could inhale the appetizing smell.

"Oma," I said, "why does the farmer want to sell his potatoes?"

"Because they are last year's crop, and they will be sold to other farmers for seed potatoes or to feed hogs."

Tired, my bottom hurting from the constant jerking, bumping, and jostling through deep holes, I closed my eyes pretending I was asleep. As darkness set in, the woods, which had such an inviting friendly look in the daytime, became black, frightening monsters. We were still a short distance from Stariska when I heard a loud, long, drawn-out howling.

"Oma, what is that sound? It scares me."

She said, "Don't be scared. That is only a lonely wolf that wants company. He is calling for his friends to come out and play."

The farmer butted into our conversation. "We have many wolves in this area. I don't like to take a trip in the wintertime because the wolves will attack the horse. If there is a whole pack, they will even kill and eat the people."

"Can't the horses outrun the wolves?"

"Not when there is a pack of wolves and they haven't eaten for days because of a heavy blizzard and deep snow," he said.

I was thankful it was not wintertime. To me it seemed like an eternity before we reached Tante Rosalia's home in Stariska.

Tante Rosalia was Mama's older sister and had raised Mama and three other siblings after their parents died. She and her husband had no children of their own. Mama came from a family of nine children. No one knew what had become of the other four. Tante Rosalia's husband had disappeared during the last roundup. We were welcome especially because she had been alone.

I enjoyed the wide-open spaces, skipping or running pell-mell through the village. Tante Rosalia's beautiful garden, with tall red and white poppy plants, fascinated me. Some of the flowers had already lost their bloom. After eating a few of the green poppyseed pods, Sister Erika and I became violently ill. When my stomach was not cramping, I slept and dreamed a lot. Since doctors were unheard of, home remedies were used on a trial-and-error basis. Tante Rosalia gave us a big glass of buttermilk (with little bits of butter floating on top) every time we opened our eyes. I obediently drank my glass of lukewarm buttermilk, used the outhouse, and went back to sleep. My stomach stopped hurting after a couple of days. When we finally got well Tante Rosalia gave us a friendly reminder: "You can only eat the poppies when the pods turn brown, and then you must shake the pods until you can hear the little seeds dancing around inside."

I had just got over the poppyseed treatment when I was bitten by the dog. Tante Rosalia had a big, fierce-looking dog chained to the barn door. Even after being told by Tante Rosalia, "Ella, stay away from the dog. He will bite you," I decided the dog needed water. He bit me. His teeth dug deep into my right shoulder. My screams brought Oma out of the house in a panic. Tante and Mama were working in the field. (Because there were no men left in the village, all able-bodied women worked outside.) Oma beat the dog with a broom until he turned me loose. The bite was deep, bloody, and painful. Oma was beside herself. She kept on saying, "Ellachen, Ellachen, what have you done?" After examining the wound, she cleaned it with vodka. My hair-raising screams must have been heard by our next-door neighbor, who was as old as Oma and stayed home to care for her grandchildren. She came running and advised Oma on what to do next. She said she had some herbs that were just the remedy for dog bite. While the neighbor ran back to her house, Oma put a rag on my wound to absorb the running blood. Hot water was always available on the wood-burning stove, which was made out of bricks and stood in the corner of the room. The stove was about six feet tall and flat on top. We had slept on it when we got cold during our previous wintertime visits. The situation looked very grim. My shoulder was by now double in size. Upon her return, the old lady deposited a handful of weeds into a pot of boiling water. She said, "Katja, the herbs have to boil, then we will drain them and place them hot on her shoulder." Over my screaming objection, my red swollen shoulder was wrapped in rags with the nasty-smelling herbs. The bitter taste of this brew was even worse than its odor. I refused to drink it, so they doctored it up with honey. I was in pain and delirious for days. From that day on I avoided dogs.

Whenever I became ill or injured, Oma was always concocting home remedies. The previous winter while visiting Tante Rosalia I had become ill. I was burning up with fever. Mama boiled onions. When they were done, she removed them and added honey and vodka to the liquid. After I drank it, I had to get into bed. Mama and Oma covered me with everything they could find, starting with the down comforter. The down comforters looked like huge pillows. Feathers were gathered when geese or chickens were slaughtered. When someone in the village got married, the women always contributed feathers to the wedding bed cover.

After just a few minutes, I got so hot and sweaty I could hardly breathe. I begged, "Please, please let me get out of bed." If that did not work I would say, "I am dying, please get me out of bed."

"Just a little while longer," was Oma's gentle response. The "little while longer" turned out to be forever. I begged, I pleaded, I promised to be good to no avail. Finally I dozed off from sheer exhaustion. After many hours of my sweating, Oma seemed to know when the fever had broken. Only then was I allowed to sit up. Everything I had on was soaking wet. They dried me off and replaced my sopping nightshirt with a dry, clean, cool one. Oma was telling Mama, "Elsa, look at this child and that red rash on her body. This looks like scarlet fever." Mama agreed. From then on when the conversation was about childhood diseases, I was told that as a child I had scarlet fever.

My ears hurt, the right one worse than the left. Ever since I could remember, my ears had given me great pain. A yellow liquid, the consistency of mustard, oozed right out of them and down my neck. Oma put plugs of cotton in them. When the old cotton was saturated, she replaced it with new. Particularly at night, the pain was almost unbearable. A hot brick— normally used to heat the bed—was wrapped in a rag and became my pillow. It seemed to make the pain worse. However, Oma knew best. "Ellachen, the pain always gets worse before it gets better, no matter where you are hurting." Summer was the worst time of all because I had to endure not only the pain but the smell. The pillowcase was always covered in yellow spots.

Oma knew a lady in the neighborhood who was nursing a baby. "Some women nurse their babies until they have a mouth full of teeth," she said. She took me to the neighbor's house. Dutifully, I lay down on the bed. The lady took out one breast, leaned over, and squeezed a stream of milk into my ear, sometimes missing the ear altogether and spraying my face and hair. Once the ear was filled, I had to lie very still in order for the milk to ooze into the ear canal and disappear completely. After this treatment my ears ran day and night and hurt constantly for weeks. Then the stream of yellow suddenly stopped. Now I could remove the plugs of cotton from my ears and hear what was being said—I didn't have to watch lips anymore.

* * *

"Oma, tell us a story." Instead of fairy tales, Oma told Sister Erika and me, time and time again, how our family got to Russia. I never got tired of hearing it.

"I came from Germany as a child, not much older than you are. Though we spoke Russian outside the house with neighbors and when meeting strangers, at home we always spoke German. We were different from the Russian peasants. We spoke two languages, always looked clean, and only spoke when we were spoken to. We are Germans. Many of our people immigrated to Russia during the time of Katherine the Great. The Tsarina promised Germans who would come and settle in Russia much land, no taxes, no military service, and animals and seeds to start farming. In turn, they would try to make a profit and, most of all, raise enough food to feed the people. We spoke our own language, constructed our own villages (always building straight roads), had our own schools, and continued to live, through the decades, our German way of life. We became known as the 'Volga Deutsche.' Through many years of hard work, we accumulated much wealth. We were resented by the Russian peasants. Not until the Czar was killed in 1917 and the eventual takeover by the Bolsheviks did we, the German/Russian–speaking people, begin to be afraid. Our fate was sealed. There was no way out of Russia for us."

Oma continued, "When I was a young girl, with my family and our whole village, I spent many years in Siberia. We were taken out of our villages and given orders to start east. German sympathizers could not be kept around. The Volga Deutsche took whatever valuables we could and made our way to Siberia. The weather was harsh and the living conditions were primitive. The next few years we were fighting for our very existence. Typhoid fever and dysentery were rampant. Starvation and disease killed many. Nevertheless, we banded together to build houses out of freshly cut trees. They consisted of two big rooms, one for the living quarters of the family, the other for the animals, separated by a thin wall made of small birch branches. A big stove of handmade bricks usually sat in one corner of the room. There was a half-moon opening built into the stove for heating, cooking, and baking bread. In the wintertime the children slept on the stove, as many as could pile on top. The room itself served as kitchen, living, and bedroom. Coarse handmade linen sacks stuffed with straw were used to sleep on. During the day they were piled in one corner of the room. In the adjoining room, the animals lived, and so we kept each other warm. Sometimes when friends came to visit from another village and could not make it home because of a blinding snowstorm, all the men and boys slept above the animals in the attic used for storing hay. The floor was dirt patted down with cow manure."

At this point, I always interrupted, "Did it stink?"

"Oh, no, it didn't stink. When the manure dried it had no smell but gave off a beautiful shine. My mama took the fresh cow manure from the barn after everyone had left to work in the field. She would smear it all over the room. By noon when everyone returned for lunch, it was dry. The floor was never washed, only swept, with a handmade broom of young willow branches tied together. Our people still lived their isolated existence, seldom intermarrying with Russians, while holding onto our German way of life. We were all waiting for the day when would return to our beloved farms."

She stopped, reached down to the edge of her skirt, turned it inside out, wiped her face, blew her nose, then rubbed the cloth together. Replacing her hands in her lap, she continued. "Eventually the government decreed we could return to our farms west of the Volga River. When we arrived, we found that our villages, farms, and homes had been taken over by the local Russians. So all the returned Volga Deutsche grouped together and started our lives over again, except now we worked for the Russians. The collective farms came into existence, and that actually served to foster some prosperity for us, the hard-working survivors. We built new homes again. Within a few years many families had achieved enough success to move into better houses or leave the village altogether. By the time you were born, Ella, the Volga Deutsche had reestablished small communities with our German language and traditions, but we lived in fear of our Russian neighbors. That is enough for today, I am tired and all talked out."

We lived with Tante Rosalia several months. During that time meetings or, rather, gatherings were held late at night in different homes. When it was Tante Rosalia's turn, I sat under the kitchen table and listened to every word. Questions by individuals, "What are we going to do?" went unanswered. Someone had stopped an old Russian farmer coming home from the bazaar. The old man had told how unbelievably heavily Kiev was being bombarded. Every day and every night the city was being attacked. From what they were saying, the city must have completely disappeared.

I asked Mama, "Where is my onkel [uncle]?"

The standard proverb I got as an answer: "If you know everything in your young life, you will get old too fast."

* * *

Katrina, our neighbor, came running and yelling, "Katja! Katja!" Once in the door, she stopped short. "Where is Katja? I have had a dream!"

Everybody in the village had great interest in dream interpretation. According to Oma, we should take heed of our dreams "because God is trying to tell us something. He foretells the future only He can see and He does it through dreams. When you get older, Ella, you can see for yourself in the Bible where God foretold the future in dreams all the time." Dream interpretations, like old treasures or heirlooms, were handed down in our family from generation to generation. Occasionally a dream came true and the whole neighborhood would talk about it as a spiritual event of great importance. Oma reasoned, "The Bible tells us about God sending dreams to all kinds of people, so why should He stop now? Of course you couldn't tell the Lutheran pastor back in our village because he would interpret it as the devil's work." Oma was quick to add, "Sometimes the Church or even the pastor is better off not knowing what is happening in our family."

"Oma, do we have a pastor now and where is he?"

"No, we don't have a pastor anymore. The Communists have done away with all the churches and the pastors."

I was always astonished to hear when a dream came true. Some examples used by Oma:

If you dreamed you lost a tooth, then someone in your immediate family would die.

A dream about snakes meant a friend would come to see you.

Dreams about manure meant that you would receive money.

Dream about flowers, you will get sick.

If you dreamed about an angel, you would die.

Dreams dealing with a date should always be written down. You must get out of bed and record the date, even if only with your finger in the dust on some piece of furniture or book cover. If you did not do this, you would not remember the date the next morning no matter how hard you tried.

The list of meanings went on and on. When I awoke, no matter what I had dreamed, Oma's interpretation was always, "Today you will get a spanking." And it always came true.

There were now German soldiers in our village. One day someone said the German army was in Kiev. Mama and Oma talked it over and decided to return there. We journeyed back the same way we had come. We had arrived in Stariska when the poppies were blooming; when we left, the women and children were out in the fields harvesting potatoes.

* * *

Kiev was dark when we reached it. We walked from the bazaar to our dingy basement apartment and found it just as we left it, except everything was covered with dust and pieces of ceiling. There was water on the floor. The next morning Oma mopped and took the bedding outside to clean off the dust. Mama made her way to register us with the occupational German authorities. When Oma took us out to play, everything looked awful. Our brick building was pocked with holes. Boulders of cement lay in our yard. Windowpanes were missing in almost all of the windows. What a shock to see most of our neighborhood in ruins, some buildings scorched, some gone completely. I did not find any of my friends to play with. Oma wanted to take us to the park, but we could not walk on the sidewalk: it had disappeared. We had to dodge big craters in the streets. After a block or two Oma decided it was too dangerous to walk in the street with army trucks and horse-drawn wagons going up and down. When we returned home the sun was still out, so the three of us sat in the yard for a while. That did not last long before it was time to go inside.

"Oma, I want to go out again." I said.

"Ella, it is windy. It is better to be inside rather than sit in the whipping wind," was Oma's reply. She was busy knitting. Sister Erika was napping on the bed. I sat on my hands thinking, What happened here while we were gone?

For dinner Oma cut off a piece of bread for each of us from a loaf Tante Rosalia had baked in Stariska. Oma rubbed the crust with a piece of garlic. We chased that with some hot mint tea.

Before dark, Mama returned from the registration office. She was accompanied by two German officers, who told us that by order of the German authorities we were to move into the beautifully furnished two-room apartment upstairs, with windows, a toilet, and a big balcony—the apartment where my friend used to live.

The windows were blown out, but one of the officers assured Oma that they would be repaired the following week. Meanwhile, Oma stuffed sheets and unused pillows into the broken windowpanes. In the corner of the front room stood a beautiful ceramic inlaid stove, a china cabinet, and a table and four beautifully carved chairs. Everything was left behind by the previous owners. We had dishes, bedcovers, towels, soap, and a completely furnished apartment. The adjoining room was furnished with two huge brass beds, an antique wardrobe, and long, white torn lace curtains gracefully moving with the wind.

Our building had not taken a direct hit during the fierce fighting for Kiev, but there were only a few families left in the three-story building. When Mama asked the remaining neighbors what had happened to the rest of the families in the building, no one knew, or at least no one would say. Oma was going around saying, "Ich kann das nicht verstehen. Wo sind denn die Leute geblieben?" (I don't understand. What happened to all the people?)

Mama and Oma were busy moving all our belongings upstairs, except Papa's tools. I was told to stay out from underneath their feet. My bed was right by the window. Fascinated, I would spend the whole day watching the traffic on the street.

The next day, Mama said she was going to the bazaar. Oma wanted to know what she planned to use for money, Mama said, "I don't know. I'll take some of the clothing out of the new closet, and Papa's pants, shirt, shoes, and underwear. Maybe I can exchange them for food." When she returned, she brought a head of cabbage, beets, onions, and a few potatoes. Adding a piece of fatback we had brought back from Stariska, Oma made the best pot of borscht. It lasted us three days.

We had unexpected visitors a few days later, the two handsome, beautifully dressed German officers who had accompanied Mama home after she had registered. Putting their hats on top of the wardrobe, they placed their packages on the table. One of the officers, after shaking hands with everyone, picked me up. Laughing all the while, he tossed me almost to the ceiling. No sooner had I come down to the floor again than I made my way to the windowsill, where I sat and watched as all were laughing and talking. Oma was making tea. One of the officers had Sister Erika on his lap. The other turned around and motioned for me to come to him. I did. He put me on his lap, asking me, "Wie heisst du, liebchen?" (What is your name, darling?) "Ella," I said. They showed us pictures of their wives and children and said how much they missed them. How happy they would be to return to Germany after this war was won. Mama and Oma were happy to see the men because they brought so much for us to eat that it seemed like a Christmas celebration. Since very little food could be found in the city, any meal was welcomed.

After the officers left, Mama said, "Ella, if any of our neighbors asks you why German officers come and go from our apartment, tell them Mama works for them and they come over to pick up or leave work. If they ask, 'Do the officers leave you cookies and candy when they leave?' say, 'No, never.'" However, they always did.

A few days later, Mama came almost breathless into our apartment. "Katja, I have a job. I am going to work for the German occupational forces because I am well versed in both German and Russian. So you will be taking care of the girls while I am gone."

"Do you know what kind of job you will be doing?" Oma asked.

"I am not sure." Mama never discussed what she did, even when talking with Oma.

I sat very quietly listening while Mama explained to Oma about the coaching and instructions she received from the German officers about filling out official German papers. Now it was time for Sister Erika and me to learn answers to questions that were being asked. The questions changed depending upon where we were and who asked. Since I was the oldest, I was grilled daily by Mama, "You will forget everything, only what I am telling you to say. You and your sister were born in Poland, not Russia. Germans will like you better if you tell them you were born in Poland."

"Mama, where is Poland?"

Her black eyes showed her dismay over my question. "Just do what I tell you or you will have all of us killed."

1942

In the months that followed, we took many walks through the seasons. I loved weekend outings to the Dnieper River just to sit with Mama and Sister Erika and watch the river flow by.

Now that we were living on the second floor, our Russian neighbors did not have much to say to us. They avoided us. Oma, who always chitchatted with them before, was mystified: "Elsa, why are our neighbors not speaking to us?"

Her reply, "Maybe they are afraid we will inform on them to the Germans. About what, I don't know." We visited other German/Russian friends as before. Spring had finally arrived. Again the trees that lined our street were breaking out in beautiful green. This year I was going to be six years old. My favorite place was sitting on our deep windowsill, or if it was warm enough, on our balcony, watching the traffic and people down below. Our yard was cleaned up. The holes had been filled in and Sister Erika and I were allowed to play outside unsupervised. Oma always reminded me to watch over my little sister.

One day, as soon as we arrived in the yard, I noticed by the outhouse someone had placed a rag, on which I saw as I came closer, five baby kittens. They were so little and so slimy-wet, absolutely awful looking. All of them were crying and kicking their little feet. I said to Sister Erika, "They were probably supposed to be thrown into the outhouse." So, I took each one and threw them in. They were screaming while Sister Erika and I watched them trying to stay on top of all the mess. A neighbor, who was hanging clothing on the line, came screaming across the yard. "What have you done? You no good German kids! Oh my God, they've thrown the kittens into the toilet."

I stood there not understanding why she was so upset. She was waving her hands in the air saying bad things about the German kids. Sister Erika got scared and ran to get Oma. Meanwhile the lady ran to her apartment and came back with a bucket full of water that sloshed against her skirt with each running step. She arrived at the same time Oma did. The two of them reached into the stinking mess and pulled out each baby kitten, washing them off in the bucket of water. The lady laid the kittens back on the rag, giving me a nasty look, saying, "Get away! Get away!"

Oma apologized, took my hand, never saying a word, and led me up two flights of stairs to our apartment. As soon as we entered she got her measuring stick from behind the kitchen cabinet and started to whip me with all her might. "Ella, the devil has to be beaten out of you. What made you do it? What were you thinking?" The strikes fell indiscriminately on my head and body. I tried to answer but could not come up with an explanation while running around the kitchen/dining room table. When her right hand got tired, she switched the stick to her left. I cried and ran around the room trying to avoid some of the blows. I finally made it into our bedroom and under the double bed, crawling to the farthest corner. She was on her knees trying to reach me with the stick, without success. "Ella, you had better come out from under the bed if you know what's good for you." I didn't.

Exhausted, Oma retreated to the kitchen, repeating herself as to what had made me do it. It had to be the devil himself. I stayed under the bed, falling asleep from sheer exhaustion. I woke when the squeaky door opened, then closed. Mama was home. I heard Oma relate what had happened. Mama came into the bedroom, imploring me to come out from under the bed. She was shocked at seeing my face and body swollen, turning red and purple. Oma was busying herself at the stove. Mama sat the kitchen table, put me on her lap, and said, "Promise me you will never do such a thing again." I promised.

1943

My seventh birthday had long come and gone. For days it seemed like explosions never stopped, and everywhere I looked the city was in flames fanned by a howling winter wind mixed with snowflakes. It had been snowing for weeks. No more trips to the river or to the park. Oma said, "This will be a long hard winter, mark my words. The snow started falling too early." I came home from visiting a German-speaking friend who lived up the street with the news that they were leaving for Germany this very night. In fact, this was the last train to Germany. My friend's mama told me to go home because they had to pack and be at the train station before midnight. The German army was going back to Germany. If my mama wanted to leave Russia with them, this was her last chance. If we stayed, there was no telling what the Russians would do to us as collaborators.

Arriving at home, I cried hysterically and begged Mama to pack so we could go to Germany also. Mama slipped into her coat and left for a while. When she returned, she was pale and nervous, telling Oma to pack. I was overjoyed because we were leaving this noisy place, blackened by fires, and going to the fairyland Oma was forever telling us about, a place called Germany, where everything was clean and orderly.

I stood at the end of our brass bed and watched in silence as Mama handed Oma our prized possessions to pack into our one and only suitcase. Everything went into that battered suitcase as before, when we were going to Tante Rosalia's, including the two metal coffee cups almost the size of little bowls. They were a mystery to me. If we were going to Germany, where everything was tidy, why did we need those old beat-up pots and cups?

I asked Oma this. Obviously dismayed with my question, her mouth drawn tight, she stopped long enough to say that the cups and pots would be used for coffee, tea, or soup on our occasional stops. We could use them to bathe and to eliminate waste.

Sister Erika and I were given a tablespoon of vodka each to keep warm. Mama and Oma had a good shot right out of the bottle. The rest of the bottle went into Oma's coat pocket. We were all bundled with only our eyes visible, trying to keep the wind-driven snowflakes from completely obliterating our sight. Silently, Mama and Oma took turns carrying the suitcase while Sister Erika and I, trying to keep up, were clutching for dear life onto Mama's hands. There seemed to be a lull in the fireworks as we made our way through the raging snowstorm.

At the train station, people were seated on their suitcases as far as my eyes could see. The explosions resumed, lighting up the night sky. I watched and felt as if the stars were coming down all at once right on me with a deafening sound. Some of the children were whining, crying, or arguing with their mamas. Mama encouraged Sister Erika and me, with other children nearby, to skip around the suitcases to keep warm, even sing a little song:

Alle meine Entchen, schwimmen auf dem See.
Köpfchen in das Wasser, Schwänzchen in die höh.

The verse was about little ducks swimming in the pond. When they put their heads in the water their tails stick straight up. The words barely penetrated the heavy shawl wrapped around my face and neck. They were almost lost in the general uproar anyway. Besides the noise of explosions, some women who had more than two children were continually scurrying around yelling out their names and trying to round up their broods. We could see and hear German soldiers running up and down the parked train while their commanders shouted all kinds of orders. During a lull in the bombardment, Oma shouted to Mama, "Elsa, when is our train coming?"

Mama's answer: "The train is not a passenger train. It's the freight train parked right in front of you."

This was not a train for people, but a train for cattle, I thought. There were no windows except for a tiny opening high up near the end of each car. I was saddened by the fact that I would not be able to see out of the opening. It was too high to reach. Mama did not care what kind of train it was, or whether it normally transported people or cattle. We had to get out of Russia. If the Russians should take us, we would be killed or, worse, sent to a Siberian labor camp. Since returning to Kiev I had been told every day: do not talk loud; do not speak Russian; do not ask questions; follow instructions; do not volunteer information about our family; always say, "I don't know." I was so eager, wanting to know all about our trip to Germany. I wanted to hear the stories (again and again) that Oma had to tell. I was so afraid to ask, afraid of saying or doing something that would land us in Siberia.

"Mama, would me and Sister Erika have to go Siberia too?"

"Of course. The Russians need slaves in Siberia. Children grow up and do the work of grown-ups someday, if they live that long."

While Mama and Oma stamped their feet in the snow to keep warm, they kept telling Sister Erika and me to hop and run in order to keep our feet from freezing. When we got tired, we took turns sitting on the suitcase just for a few minutes. Many children were hanging onto their mamas and omas and crying. Their noses were running—over their shawls, sometimes right into their mouths, down the fronts of their coats. Mothers took their time to wipe their noses, then wiped their own hands on their petticoats. The only men present were German soldiers.

Finally, after hours, the waiting ended. The loading started. A soldier with not so fancy a uniform counted forty people to a freight car. People went scrambling for the car doors trying not to get separated. Children were crying for their mamas while families tried to find little ones who had wandered off. There were no steps, so people helped each other up onto the straw-covered floor of the freight car. We were grateful to be out of the driving snowstorm. We waited for hours in the locked freight car, until the explosions subsided somewhat. Then, at last, the train inched out of the station. Lying on the straw in the darkness, I could hear women crying.

"Oma, why are they crying?" I whispered in her ear. "Aren't they happy to go to Germany?"

"Go to sleep, Ella, God will take care of their tears."

People lay huddled together on the floor, and after a few hours the gentle jostling of the train had lulled almost everybody to sleep. Even though I was tired, I listened intently to what Mama and Oma were discussing, "Elsa, do you think the Germans think of us as Russians, or do you think they think of us as Germans?"

Mama answered, "Since our forefathers come from Germany and we speak German and come from a German heritage, of course they will think of us as Germans. They will be happy to see us, and we will be happy to be there."

"Do you know if it is cold in Germany?" Oma asked. "Maybe it is another Siberia."

"I hope not," Mama replied.

The sun had broken through the darkness and was flashing its rays through the little corner window. Children and grown-ups relieved themselves in one corner of the car. Nobody was embarrassed or ashamed to do so in front of strangers. Mothers covered the mess with straw. Mama opened our suitcase and took out the loaf of bread. Carefully she broke off small pieces and handed them to us. The rest went back in the suitcase. Everyone had bread to eat. Then we spent the day lying in the straw.

"Mama, will you lift me up so that I can see outside, please?"

"There is nothing to see. I cannot even see for myself. I'm too short. All right, come here."

She lifted me up for a few seconds. I saw a blanket of snow racing by with all-white trees. Mama put me down. A little boy started to scream at the top of his lungs. His mother then gave him something to scream about. I was happy my mama did not beat me.

As the second night approached, we seemed to be moving away from the occasional sporadic explosions. Then, suddenly, a huge explosion came from up ahead. The screeching brakes brought the train to a dead stop with all of us being thrown first toward the front and then backward. Everybody screamed. After the screaming stopped, no wind, no snow, no sounds of a moving train, only an icy silence surrounded us. On her tiptoes, Mama looked out the opening. She said, "I cannot see a thing. It is pitch black out." The freight car doors were locked from the outside, so there was no way to learn more. Women speculated as to what was happening. Maybe the Germans had left us here to die; or the train had mechanical trouble; or we were going to get something to eat; or Russian partisans had blown up the train and God only knew what would happen to us. People brought bread and fatback out of their pockets and suitcases and shared with those who did not have any left. The metal coffee cups were now unpacked and used to collect water that dripped from icicles down the locked door. The sun came up and went down and came up again. It seemed like an eternity in the locked car. Finally, as darkness surrounded us once again, the train started to move. Oma passed around the almost empty vodka bottle for all four of us to get a good swallow.

We thought we had arrived in Germany because the next stop was very different. The door opened and a German soldier told us we could get out but to leave our things and remember our freight car number. It was late afternoon. Looking around, I saw very few people and even fewer houses. The train had stopped in a small station with outside toilet facilities. Tables were set up and now we could smell cabbage soup and hot tea steaming toward us. Mama, who was a beautiful woman with an infectious smile and great personality (this was during the time when plump women were considered beautiful), started a conversation with one of the soldiers. "Excuse me, is this Germany?"

"No, you still have a good distance to go. This is only a rest stop."

Mama asked, "Say, were you on this train all the way from Kiev?"

"Yes," he said.

"What happened back there?"

The soldier said, in a very thick accent that we could hardly understand, "Russian partisans placed explosives on the tracks, but there was no harm done. German troop trains always place two to three boxcars loaded with sand or wood in front of the locomotives in case of an explosion. Since repair crews and parts are carried on the train at all times, the tracks can be repaired within a reasonable time."

Mama asked, "Are you German?"

The soldier said, "Of course. I am from Bavaria. That is in southern Germany."

"Do all Germans speak such hard-to-understand German?"

He laughed as hard as he could. "No, not all Germans, only the Bavarians, maybe even the people from Schwaben."

Mama asked, "Katja, do you know anything about Bavarians or Schwaben?"

"No, I don't," Oma answered.

Turning back to the soldier, Mama asked, "Do you know where this train is taking us?"

"To Berlin," he said with a smile.

Germany

Joy, joy! We have arrived in the land that our forefathers left many years ago, the land of paradise. We are going to live in Berlin. When Oma was telling us about the Germany her parents left for a better life in Russia, it sounded like a fairy tale.

Now Oma was very happy, her eyes brimming with excitement. She was so eager to go into town to see things and meet people, she could hardly wait for the train to stop.

Finally it did stop. The doors opened. A booming voice from a loudspeaker instructed us to disembark and take our belongings with us. We were not coming back to this train. We were marched, families together, single file into a compound surrounded by barbed wire. Once inside we were registered and given a barrack number and bed assignment. The barracks were all similar wooden buildings, which made it easy to get lost. At the entrance of our assigned building, one long single room, a soldier counted the people as to how many beds were available.

"Leave your suitcases, remember the number of your barrack, and go to that big building."

When we arrived we were told to strip and then were directed, single file, into a small corridor, which opened into a large room. Following the instructions exactly, no one was afraid or in a panic.

I had never seen so many naked women and children. No boys! I thought, "What had happened to them?" I never saw a naked boy. I was really looking forward to the experience and was utterly disappointed.

"Where are the boys?" I asked Oma.

"They are in a separate room and will join their families later," she said.

The line moved very slowly. We went through a shower of warm water. Oh, how good it felt, not ever having had a shower before. There was soap in nice squares, not like the ones we used in Russia, where the pieces were misshapen and had a peculiar odor. It was hair-washing time. Oma made sure my hair was scrubbed briskly, with soap, repeatedly. The soap ran into my eyes and stung. I joined the choir of crying children. Mama worked first on her own hair, then on Sister Erika's. We finally came out of the shower clean, with red eyes, the result of a combination of soap and crying. We dried ourselves with already-wet towels. Our next stop was a room with showerheads overhead—but instead of water, we were sprayed with white powder that looked like flour.

"Oma, why do we have to take a bath in flour? Will it wash off? Do we have to do this every day?"

Much irritated by my barrage of questions, Oma showed her displeasure by squeezing my hand hard. "No," she replied. "This is not flour. This powder kills all kinds of bugs that we brought with us from Russia. The Germans don't want the bugs in Germany."

"What kind of bugs?"

"Fleas, head lice, and lice that live in your clothing, or other insects."

"Does it really kill all those bugs?"

"They say it does."

"Will it kill us too?"

Mama interjected, "I hope not."

The powder got into my nose and I started to cough, joining a cacophony of coughing already in progress. It tasted bad. Everyone was spitting that white stuff right on the floor. An old woman stepped in one of the white paste puddles, slipped, fell, and had to be helped up by other naked women.

Oma had me in her strong grip. She was tall and skinny, with deep crow's-feet embedded in her face. Her skin was sort of hanging down her body and looked all wrinkly and brown. Mama was short and plump, with white skin all over. Oma leaned over to Mama and whispered, "Elsa, you don't think this will kill us? What is this powder called anyway?"

"I think they call it 'disinfectant,' " Mama said.

Passing through yet another room, each person was given clean used clothing. People looked really funny in their new attire. Nothing fit. It was either too short or too long or too wide or too small. Some women wanted to know when they were to be given their old clothing back, only to be told that it would be burned. All of a sudden, these women, who had been so quiet and following orders up to now, became raving maniacs yelling, screaming, crying, and fainting.

"Mama, are they sick?"

"No. They just lost everything they had."

"They were only wearing old dirty bug-infested rags."

"When you get a little older you will understand things better."

"Mama, I want to know now."

"Do you remember when we left Poland, our home?"

"No, Mama, when we left Kiev."

"Ella, you are going to be the death of us. When we left Poland."

"Poland then. Tell me, tell me, please."

Mama explained. "Some of these people came from very wealthy families. They were rich, had a lot of money, which is no good here in Germany. They also had many priceless jewels that they sewed into their clothing and into their children's clothing. Now the old clothes are being burnt. I am sure somebody will go through them first to get the jewels out."

"What will they do with them?"

"They will keep them," Mama said.

Now fully dressed, the four of us were separated. We were told this was the Registration Department. The children were separated from their mothers, some kicking and screaming, and taken to an adjoining room. Close to my ear the whispered advice from my mama: "Ella, hold on to your sister. She is the only family you have in case we don't see each other anymore." I took Sister Erika's hand.

"Always stay with your sister so she won't be afraid and cry," Mama said.

"I will, Mama."

We followed the nurse into a small room. Oma was right. The nurse was all white, the room was all white, and the furniture was all white. Germany was really clean. A man sat behind a large desk. He was friendly and smiled. He motioned us to come and sit on his lap, which my sister and I dutifully obeyed.

"What is your name?" he asked.

"My name is Ella, and this is my sister, Erika."

"What are your parents' names?"

"My papa's name is Jakob Schneider. My mama's name is Elsa. My oma's name is Katherine. My mama calls her Katja."

"Where is your grandfather?"

"I don't know."

"Where is your father?"

"I don't know."

"Are you Christians?"

"I don't know what Christian is."

"Do you celebrate Christmas, with Christmas presents and a big Christmas dinner?"

"Oh, yes."

"I want you and your sister to sing a Christmas song," he said.

In my small soft voice, I started to sing "Silent Night" while Sister Erika played with her fingers.

Stille Nacht, Heilige Nacht,
Alles Schläft, einsam wacht
Nur—

It made the man smile. "That is enough. You did well. What kind of job did your mother have?"

"She worked for the German soldiers."

"You and your sister can go through that door and join your mother," the man said.

A soldier motioned us to sit on two chairs that were placed behind Mama and Oma.

We came in the middle of Mama telling about our family history. I wasn't too interested in what the grown-ups were talking about. However, every so often I caught partial sentences of Mama answering. One of the soldiers wrote down every answer. Sporadically, they would ask Oma a question. When the questioning stopped, one of the soldiers told all four of us to go to the next room.

Our pictures were taken. I told the friendly soldier that my papa made many pictures. Mama shook her index finger at me when his back was turned. Oh boy, will I get it again. I knew exactly what I had done wrong. How many more rooms are there? I wondered. A doctor and a nurse greeted us. The doctor was in a white coat and the nurse in a light blue uniform covered by a white apron, which crisscrossed in the back. The little cap with a red cross in the middle matched her outfit. In order not to give different answers, Mama and Oma decided that Mama would do all the answering, and if asked, Oma could always say, "I don't hear well" or "I cannot remember."

"What village did you come from, Frau Schneider?" Doctor asked Mama.

"Stariska."

"Where is that?"

"It is a German village near Kiev."

"Do you have brothers and sisters?"

"Yes. I have nine brothers and sisters."

"Are your brothers and sisters living and where?"

"I do not know. I think they are all dead."

"What did they die of?"

"They just died."

"Did a doctor establish the cause of death?"

"We didn't have doctors."

"Are your parents still living?"

"They died when I was about nine or ten. I was raised by my sister Rosalia."

"What is your husband's name?"

"Jakob."

"Where is he now?"

"When the war started, the Russians took him on the night of the 22nd of June, 1941. I looked for him the next day among the dead at the bazaar, but I could not identify his body."

The endless questions continued. My mind and eyes started to wander around the room. On a white sheet the size of a towel, some needles and cotton balls were laid out. The whole room had a peculiar smell. Finally, the doctor stopped asking questions. He motioned to the pretty nurse. She took me by my hand and led me over to the small table.

"Sit down, child," the nurse said. She picked up a needle. "Turn your head. It won't hurt." She pricked my earlobe. It really hurt. I cried out loud. I kept on screaming, hoping the nurse would not do anything else to me. Sister Erika started to cry. The nurse picked up my screaming sister and placed her on Mama's lap.

The nurse said to Mama, "You pin her hands down and put her feet between yours so she won't kick me." By the time they finished with poor Sister Erika, she had wet hair from perspiration and a puffy face from crying.

With Mama and Oma next, the bloodletting continued. Now we were told to take our clothes off. After undressing, Mama awkwardly climbed on a table and lay on her back. The doctor examined her from head to toe. Then it was Oma's turn. Mama didn't cry, so I won't cry. I was helped onto the table for my examination. The doctor pushed and probed all over my body. Then he ran his finger around my private parts, telling the nurse, "Alles in Ordnung" (Everything is OK). I wasn't hurt and didn't cry, and neither did Sister Erika.

This examination was followed by two shots, one in each arm. Now both my sister and I were back to crying again. The nurse was reassuring. "That is all." On the way out of the doctor's office Oma whispered under her breath, "Gott, sei Dank" (Thank you, Lord).

Only after we were showered, powdered with disinfectant, had our picture taken, doctor's examination, shots, and all our paperwork completed were we permitted to eat.

On the way to the dining facility, Mama and Oma were trying to brush the white powder out of their still-uncombed damp hair using their fingers. Then it was my turn. Since both my sister and I had cried, the white powder was now a cakelike substance. It stayed on our bodies and in our hair for days, no matter how many times we tried to clean ourselves. The amazing part was that we had no lice for a week.

The dining hall was built like our barrack except it had no beds, just benches and tables. We each received a bowl of turnip-potato soup with pieces of pork skin floating in it, and a slice of hard black bread. Sister Erika and I got a cup of warm milk. Mama and Oma had some steaming hot tea.

Back in our own barrack, we occupied two double-stacked bunk beds. Mama and Oma sat on the bottom beds facing each other while they talked. Sister Erika slept above Mama. My place was above Oma. I was trying to make sure I wouldn't miss too much of what was being said.

Hanging my head over the side of the bunk, I asked, "Mama, can I listen, please?" I asked.

"No! You cannot listen," Mama answered. "With all of your questions, your loud blabbermouth, and your unbridled tongue, you will be the death of us. From now on, you will not talk to anyone about our family. If you must, then only answer questions, but for goodness sake, Ella, do not volunteer any information! If you do and I find out about it, I will beat you half to death. Do you understand?"

"Yes, Mama, just don't kill me," I cried.

"With your big mouth," Mama went on, "I hope you didn't get us in trouble talking to the soldiers when I was not with you. Did you?"

"No, Mama. They only wanted me to sing 'Silent Night.' The man smiled when I sang and was happy. Mama, why did I have to sing 'Silent Night'?"

"Because the soldiers wanted to find out if we were Jewish. You see, they don't like Jews and don't want any of them in Germany. Jews don't celebrate Christmas. So they don't know how to sing 'Silent Night.'"

Ignoring me, Mama and Oma continued their whispered conversation. Now it centered on whether or not we had some Jewish blood in our families. I couldn't help butting in again.

"Oma, what is Jewish?" I asked.

"Jews are the people who hated and killed Jesus," was her short and irritated reply.

Oma reassured Mama that we could not have been Jews because "all of us were Lutherans, we didn't practice circumcision, the children were baptized in the Lutheran faith, and the men didn't wear yarmulkes."

I was struggling to understand. It didn't make sense to me. I had all kinds of pictures parading across my mind. I had never heard of Jesus being killed by Jews because they didn't like him. Must remember to ask Oma later what this "circumcision" and "yarmulke" were all about. I must not ask too many questions or Mama might beat me half to death as she promised. Finally, assembling my courage, I asked one more question, "Mama, what is a yarmulke?"

"That is a little cap the Jewish men wear on their heads," Mama answered.

Pushing my luck with one more question, "Mama, was Papa Jewish?"

With one voice they both answered, "No!"

"But, Mama," I said, "Papa wore a little cap on his head. We have a picture."

Oma got up, cupped my face into her long bony fingers, and in a loving tone said, "Ellachen, he was a carpenter and worked with all kinds of tools. He wore a cap only to keep his long hair out of his face. Now go to sleep and may the angels watch over you." I had many more questions to ask and much to ponder but sleep had mercy on me.

* * *

The following day the interrogation continued. Sister Erika and I were questioned anew while separated from Mama and Oma.

"Ella, where is your father?"

"He died in the war."

"Where are you from?"

"Poland."

"Do you know the name of the city?"

"No. Kiev, I think."

"Do you have tanten and onkels?"

"I think so, but I am not sure."

"Where are they?"

"I don't know."

"What do you speak at home?"

"German."

"Do you get Christmas presents?"

"Yes. Easter presents too."

"Ella, do you say your prayers at night."

"Oma and I always say our prayers."

"What do you say?"

Ich bin klein.	I am little.
Mein Herz ist rein.	My heart is pure.
Soll niemand drin wohnen	No one shall dwell in it
Als Jesus allein.	But Jesus alone.

As I looked around the room, everyone beamed.

Later, I asked Mama, "Why do I have to pray in front of all those people?"

"Because Jews do not pray to Jesus."

I wondered who were these Jews and who did they pray to when they got into trouble? I sure would like to see a Jew.

* * *

All that grilling by Mama and Oma seemed such a waste. Our official registration papers designated Kiev as our place of origin. Since the Germans were very meticulous and precise in record keeping, we could lie all we wanted and it would do us no good. The train we were on had originated in Russia, not Poland. The authorities paid no attention to what we said. We were registered as having come from Kiev, USSR.

Our papers said one thing, but to our neighbors and inquiring natives we said we came from Poland. They would never get to see our papers anyway (per Mama). She did not want anyone to know where we came from. Fleeing Kiev, Mama had forbidden us to speak German. Now, in Germany, she forbade us to speak Russian.

The difference in our German and that which the German soldiers spoke was very apparent. Some soldiers spoke an articulate and understandable German (Hoch Deutsch). However, this was different from what we spoke, which was another dialect, Volga Deutsch. We also encountered soldiers we could hardly understand. All of a sudden Mama realized and conveyed to Oma that no matter how good or pure and understandable our German was, we would always give ourselves away as soon as we opened our mouths. The natives would know that we were from somewhere else and not "echte Deutsche" (Real Germans).

* * *

A few days after we arrived in the processing camp on the outskirts of Berlin, we awoke to the piercing whine of sirens screaming in the night. There were no curtains on the windows. I ran and pressed my nose to the windowpane. The outside lights went out. In the dark, Mama and Oma dressed themselves, then us. The suitcase was already packed, needing only for the lid to be closed. A soldier with flashlight in hand appeared out of the darkness and said, "You will stay in your barrack. This is an air raid by the Americans. Not to fear, they are only flying over. Besides, we are too far from the center of town for bombs to hit us." I looked out of the window and saw searchlights illuminating the sky. Wrapped in darkness, I heard a loud rata-tata-tat. The sound was accompanied by a colorful display of shooting stars trying to hit airplanes, which were flying way up in the darkened sky. Mama, Oma, and Sister Erika joined me at the window. Fascinated, we stood in total silence listening to the sporadic rata-tata-tat and watching the illuminated sky on the horizon. When the noise finally died down and the "All Clear" sirens stopped their wailing, the lights came on. Looking around I noticed the sad, tear-stained, tired faces of us homeless people.

Almost every day Mama and Oma were summoned to the headquarters building to answer more questions. It was snowing, a beautiful snowfall, not the fierce wind-driven snow of Russia. The flakes danced very slowly down from the sky, some as big as my hand. I ran outside, turned my face to the sky, opened my mouth, and let the snowflakes fall on my face and into my mouth.

Quarantined from the outside world, days passed into weeks. Except for the soldiers barking orders, this was a manless society. The women in our crowded barrack were short on patience. They spanked their children for the most minor acts of childish mischief. There were many fights between women, refereed by the soldiers. The fights usually started over standing in line for food or in line for the toilet. Children called each other names and then the mothers got into it. Women pulled each other's hair and rolled around on the floor. Some women walked away bloody and had to be taken to the dispensary. Fighting always brought on a crowd of cheerleaders. They would take sides and root for a winner. These fights lasted only for a short time.

Nightly, the air raid sirens went off, followed by explosions in the distance. We had no bomb shelters or even basements to protect us. Oma dressed, dressed us, and closed the lid of our suitcase. Then we all sat on the lower bunk bed waiting in darkness. The excitement of watching the lights in the distance soon wore off. After a few nights of dressing and undressing, Mama just stayed dressed in bed. Her reasoning was, "If a bomb is going to hit us, it doesn't matter if we are dressed, undressed, or still in bed." We all followed Mama's example by going to bed fully dressed. All of us wore the same things day and night. I climbed into my top bunk and stared at the ceiling, just waiting for a bomb to hit us.

We acquired new passengers, lice. No matter how hard the authorities tried, we were never totally rid of the lice. The powder wore off. With nothing else to occupy our time, most hours of the day were taken up with delousing each other. Mama begged a soldier standing by a car or truck to give her a little gasoline in our cup. Some would. She washed our hair, rinsed it with gasoline, covered it with an old rag until right before lunch, then washed it again. This served only as temporary relief. When I objected to a delousing session, Mama said, "Do you want to look like Anna?" Anna was the girl in the next bunk.

"Definitely not! Mama, how do you know Anna has lice?"

"Her family doesn't delouse themselves as often as other people do," she replied. "If you get behind one of them, you can actually see the lice moving about on their heads."

One day I sat behind Anna, and sure enough, I could see little black or dark red specks crawling up and down her scratched neck.

Mama said, "Ella, you and Erika don't scratch your heads. I know when the lice bite it itches. See your friend Anna? Notice how her head is always broken out and bleeding? It is because she keeps scratching her head."

Indeed, Anna's hair, which once was a beautiful golden honey color, was now matted, partly with blood and partly with a yellow infected pus. She now had three hair colors: blonde, red from new blood, and black with dried blood.

Mama continued, "If her Mama doesn't cut her hair soon, I don't know what will become of her. I cannot imagine putting a comb through it."

I pondered, How in the world could her mama get a comb through that matted hair stuck to the scalp? My daily delousing session started with Oma sitting across from me in a straightback chair. With my head held between my knees and my hair hanging down almost reaching the floor, the hour-long procedure started. Using a rough motion, Oma dragged a fine-tooth comb from my scalp down to the end of my hair. Each stroke dumped a half dozen little black specks on a piece of newspaper placed on the floor. Oma stopped combing only long enough to reach down and squash the little bugs with her thumbnail. The lice being killed made a little popping sound. To the delight of my oma, I counted and counted. Sister Erika was next. Then it was Mama's turn. Last, Mama worked on Oma.

This delousing process went on daily for hours with minimal success. One day, in utter desperation after an unusually heavy crop of lice, Mama cut off her own hair. Then, over Oma's objection, she decided to cut Sister Erika's and mine. With scissors borrowed from the office, she cut Sister Erika's, followed by my fine, stringy-looking pigtails. Oma refused to have her hair cut. She continued to wear it coiled into a roll at the base of her neck.

The fine-tooth-comb method worked for the adult lice, but the babies had to be handled individually. The eggs (nits) attached themselves to the hair itself. Unless pulled off one by one, between the thumb and index finger, within hours they hatched a new batch. All home remedies were short-lived: soaking our hair in gasoline, covering it with lard for up to half a day, cutting it off, not associating with neighbors who Mama knew for sure had lice. Nothing helped for more than a few days.

"Oma," I asked, "how do I get lice? Do they fly from bed to bed through the air like flies?"

"No," she said. "You get them when you brush against a person who has lice, or you sleep in their bed, wear their clothing, or borrow their comb. Do not go near Anna again. Avoid her."

I did. However, the infestation of lice on my head continued.

* * *

We will be leaving this nameless place. Our venture into the unknown will start early tomorrow morning. There are no calendars, clocks, or watches to tell time. Time for meals is announced from loudspeakers. Other information is conveyed the same way. After a sleepless night, sitting on my bunk bed with my feet dangling over the edge, waiting for a bomb to hit us, breakfast comes early. On the way out of the dining facility, we are given provisions of bread and cheese for our journey, just in case we do not make it directly to our next destination.

We were marched to the train station, where a train with windows and regular doors waited. All were hoping to get a window seat. I did.

By now, there is an assorted gathering of women and their children on the train, all with different backgrounds. German is the common language. To pass the time, small assemblies of women speculate on our next stop. Children constantly interrupt. The mothers scream at them to behave or threaten them with a whipping. I positioned myself within earshot. The women did not care where they lived as long as it was in Germany. Perhaps they would be placed on a farm to help with the farming or in a big town to work in a factory. Their husbands were fighting for the German army somewhere on the eastern front. They have not heard from their men for a month or a year, but they were convincing each other that when the war was won they would find each other again. "Ja, ja!" was their unanimous reply.

All day long, we were confined to the train while it sat in the station. In late afternoon lunch was served in the same orderly fashion as breakfast, outside at the front of the train. Oma reached into the suitcase and brought out our beat-up aluminum cups. We ate bread and a thick cabbage-and-potato soup with pieces of fatback floating in it. The weather was cold, with snowflakes dancing down. Looking out of the window kept us occupied— watching the going and coming masses of people like us with suitcases or bundles in hand, moving up and down the platform. My window fogged over, and I wiped it clean with the sleeve of my coat. Women nursed crying babies until they fell asleep. Evening spread its blanket over our train. When we finally started rolling, it was into total darkness.

The train moved very slowly as it left the outskirts of Berlin. Once in the country it picked up speed, cutting though the night at a fast pace. From sheer exhaustion everyone had settled down to the sound of the metal wheels meeting track. Before long, with my head on Oma's lap, I was lulled into a deep sleep. Suddenly, I was torn out of my slumber by the screech of metal brakes. Some packages and suitcases, which had been stored above our seats, came flying through the air. People were thrown to the floor and children were screaming when the train came to an unscheduled stop. If Oma had not held on to me, I would have hit the floor as well.

We had stopped in a small village right on the outskirts of a larger city. I heard the heavy drone of planes overhead. Air raid sirens wailed in the distance. I was sure they had followed us from Berlin. As if that was not enough of a commotion, now the deafening thunder of the explosions started all around us. The doors were opened. German soldiers were running and yelling, "Raus! Raus!" (Out! Out!) Women were searching for their suitcases and at the same time trying to keep their children rounded up to exit the train. Some staggered out of the compartments. Others jumped, missing the stairs altogether and falling to the ground. Soldiers shouted orders, trying hard to be heard: "Take your belongings and change trains! Macht schnell!" (Immediately!) "Go across the track and board that train!"

We could hear bombs exploding all around us. Many families ignored the instructions to change trains and followed the sign to the nearest bomb shelter. Carrying the suitcase, Oma led us toward the other train. Mama was half-dragging Sister Erika and me by our hands, closing down on them with an iron grip. We reluctantly followed her through the screaming, panicked crowd. I was crying hysterically, begging, "Mama, please let's go to the bomb shelter, please," tugging her arm in the direction of the shelter. I finally wiggled loose and started to run with the crowd while Mama, Oma and Sister Erika boarded the other train. Suddenly, I realized Mama was not following me. I started back toward the train. It was now moving slowly in the opposite direction. Running beside it, I was shrieking, "Mama, where are you? Somebody, please help me!"

I kept reaching for the handrail of the moving train but my arms were too short. One passenger car after another was passing me. A woman's hand came down, grabbed my outstretched hand, and with one jerk pulled me into the car. The woman was a complete stranger to me. Sobbing, I walked from car to car until I found my family. After a tearful reunion, Mama punished me for my disobedience. With two pair of everything on, I could not feel the blows to my body but only to my head, which I covered with my arms. I was crying very hard, not because the thrashing hurt, but because of the fear of what might have happened if I had been left behind. I made a promise to myself. I would never leave Mama's side again. Oma cradled me in her arms to still my anxiety. As the train sped up, my crying, the noise of exploding bombs—which felt as if they were going off inside of my head—the commotion of people, the rata-tata-tat finally ended. The only thing I could hear was the noise from the tracks with an occasional whistle as the train approached a road crossing.

We had nice wooden seats to sit on. There was not much to see in the dark. A small village appeared, only to disappear just as quickly. Mama and

Oma were impressed with the comfortable ride. When I finally got over all the excitement, I lay my head on Oma's lap and fell asleep.

There were many jerky stops during the night, but none as violent as before. The following morning, at another stop, we were instructed through a loudspeaker to leave our packages and suitcases, stand in a line parallel to the train, and face the locomotive. Well-dressed soldiers were running around talking, laughing, and waving to each other. As I watched them, some came to a complete stop, clicked their heels, and saluted each other.

"Mama, why do they do that?"

"To show respect. Our leader is called 'der Führer.' He wants everybody in Germany to show respect to each other," she replied.

"Do we have to do it too?"

"No," she said, "only the men in uniform."

The slow-moving line led us to a group of women and soldiers who were serving breakfast. It consisted of bread, milk for Sister Erika and me, tea for Mama and Oma. Some of the bread was always saved for later, just in case. I was so excited I could hardly restrain myself, asking all kinds of questions.

"Mama, will I get pretty dresses now? Will I go to school? Will we have a nice place to live?"

All of my questions were answered with a very short, "Ja, ja."

Back on the moving train, the colorful and neatly painted houses, the barns, and the clean yards were going by much too fast for me.

At every opportunity Mama reminded us, "Now we are in Germany, none of you will speak Russian again."

Oma began to share her view on how our life in the "Fatherland" would be. "How different and good the land of our forefathers looks, and how happy we will be to be part of this cleanliness and orderliness. We have reached an orderly society. Not like the Russians, who have no breeding, who are stupid, never saw soap and water and can't even farm for profit. We should always be thankful that the Germans came to Russia to liberate us from the Communists. If it were not for the war by now we would be in Siberia doing slave labor or be dead."

* * *

The grapevine had it that our destination was Regensburg, a town in the southern part of Germany on the Danube River in the state of Bavaria. We knew towns ending in *berg* (mountain) or *burg* (castle) were old, castled cities. I could hardly wait to get there. I would be able to run through the meadows, pick flowers, see cows or visit the castle, finally attend school, go to a bakery, and visit a church. Hopefully, we could sleep at night.

We stopped on the track outside of a small village until the sun stood at noon in the sky (per Oma). People were moving about, going from one car to the other, standing in line for the toilet, and waiting for the train to move. The bathroom line was so long there were many accidents by the little ones. A sign on the bathroom door warned all of us that using the toilet while the train was in the station or stopped was forbidden by law. Only when the train was moving and had left the city or village was it permissible to use the toilet. No one paid attention to the sign. The toilet consisted of a very small room with a built-up seat that had a round hole in the middle. Since there was no catch basin, all the waste fell directly onto the track. No toilet paper. Our underwear served as a catchall. Now the train was moving again. We could see little villages, and farmers busying themselves in their fields. Mama and Oma were excited by everything they saw, pointing out the cows, horses, and even pigs. Oh, they kept saying to each other, we will really like it here.

The train slowed as it entered a city with large buildings, cars and bicycles everywhere. Mama read the sign out loud: "Regensburg." As we pulled into the train station, which was completely covered by a glass ceiling, I watched a flock of pigeons fly round and round trying to find a place to land. An unsmiling mass of people milled back and forth. The loudspeaker announced, "Stay together near the train until further notice!" Orderly, we complied. Suitcases in hand, families were led out of sight. Then our turn came. We followed a soldier outside the station to a line of army trucks filled with families and luggage. Just as soon as we were loaded, the truck moved slowly down the street, and within a short time we entered a compound surrounded by an iron fence and containing many three-story dirty white buildings topped by red roofs.

Our driver, a young soldier in a green uniform, said, "Get off the truck and go into the building to your right. Someone will be there to direct you." Inside, the building was spotlessly clean and had a marble staircase. The walls were adorned by beautiful paintings of maidens with golden braided hair and men with big muscles and sun-browned bodies. "Wow! Is that how naked men look?" I asked Sister Erika, who didn't mind some of my questions but who had no answers either. I continued, "I will like it here."

Mama and Oma approached a soldier seated behind a desk next to the entrance. They wanted to know when we would be able to leave the camp and begin to experience the real Germany, meet some Real Germans. He looked at us and said, "We must get you registered first. You know we cannot let a trainload of Flüchtlinge run around town. I'll let you know in a few days."

Mama and Oma talked to each other about us being Flüchtlinge. I wanted to know what that word meant. "It is a word for people who are fleeing, in our case from the Russians," Mama said. "We are now Refugees."

Registration time again. Our new official paperwork was initiated and completed as if we were coming from Poland because the old papers had been conveniently lost by Mama. She decided it would be better if we were from Poland. Mama and Oma had no problems with the geography. The Poles were almost the same as the Russians, only the language was somewhat different. Real Germans could not tell the difference anyway.

Families were assigned two to each room. There was a family of six in ours. Since some of the Refugees could not read or write German but only speak it, meetings were held once or twice a day on each floor so that instructions could be given orally as to what was permissible. "All the lights will go off before dark and be turned back on at dawn. You will be able to tell by the sound of the air raid sirens how fast you need to get into the bomb shelter. You'll learn how the All Clear sounds. You will not leave the camp. You will eat on the first floor when the bell rings. No food will be permitted in your room because of rats." All would say, "Ja, ja."

Days were filled by the grown-ups with gossip, delousing each other, walks around the inside perimeter of the camp, and basking in the warm sunshine while watching their children at play. People did what they wanted, including stealing and smuggling food from the food line back to the rooms. Who knew what tomorrow would bring? We should always have bread in our suitcase (per Oma).

Our nights were nightmares. Every night we were jolted awake by the maddening sound of the air raid siren, followed by the rata-tata-tat. The antiaircraft guns were on the roofs of our buildings. We jumped out of bed, put on our clothing to the light of the searchlights, closed our already-packed suitcase, and joined a mass of bodies running down three flights of stairs to the basement/bomb shelter. After a few weeks we didn't bother getting out of our clothing at night. On the way down to the shelter, I wondered if the bombs were intended for us. I hoped that they were for someone else in another city.

I am starting school, in walking distance from our camp, outside the iron fence. It has desks, books, teacher, and blackboard. Sister Erika is sick and cannot come to school. Boys and girls are separated. There are so many rooms I don't know which one to enter. A teacher, seeing a lost look on my face, asks what grade I am looking for. I don't know. I have never been to school. How old was I? Almost eight. Go on down to room number two. That is second grade.

When I entered, I was faced with a room full of beautifully dressed girls with clean aprons and long pigtails. The teacher introduced me and assigned me a seat. Just when she started to write on the blackboard, the air raid sirens went off. Scared and frantic, leaving everything behind—coats, pencils, paper and books—we all ran as fast as our feet could carry us down two flights into the basement. There were no mamas to comfort us. We all were crying and wanting to go home.

The teacher, an old lady, had a switch in her hand for emphasis, "If I hear one sound coming out of any of you I will give you a beating that you will always remember. Our Führer wants all of you to be brave, not a bunch of crybabies. Do not make a sound. Do not cry or pray. The Americans will hear you and will drop the bombs right on your head." Now, here in Regensburg, in school, we were forbidden to utter even one prayer. I must tell Oma. I squeezed my eyes shut, covered my ears with my hands, and waited.

After the first explosions, the reverberations of which penetrated through my hands, there followed a momentary silence. I opened my eyes to see a white fog. The ceiling had come down and settled on us. The bomb shelter became hot, dusty, and very quiet. It did not last. Once my hearing was restored, kids were screaming for their mamas, including me. The teacher was walking through the bomb shelter with a candle in her hand checking to see if anyone was hurt. No one was. One barrage of explosions followed another. It seemed to me an eternity before the bombing stopped. I could hear the All Clear sound. Children began to stand up and shake the heavy white ceiling dust off their clothing. The teacher led us outside. I looked up into the sky where a huge mushrooming cloud was reaching toward heaven. Our teacher said, "Go home now." I did not recognize our school that just a few hours ago was clean, happy, sunny, and warm. I could not remember which way was home. The air was thick with smoke. I could hardly breathe. I came out of the schoolyard and turned right. There was no street. It looked like a dump. I walked very slowly, climbing over all kinds of debris, not knowing in which direction our camp was located. Flames were jumping from one building to the other, sending gigantic smoke plumes into an already dirty sky. I had difficulty picking my way over bricks, chunks of cement, fallen trees, and other debris in the road, constantly looking for a landmark and seeing none. With tears streaming down my cheeks, I called out for Oma or Mama to come and get me. Old men were out in the street trying to douse the devouring flames. A few classmates now joined me. One of the older girls wanted to know where each one of us lived. I did not know. I described, as best as I could, our building as big, with a red roof. She knew where we lived because we were Refugees. She had me and the other kids follow her. Each time she came to a pile of rubble she said, "Look, Maria, is that your house?" or "Hans, do you recognize your house"

Mothers waited out in the street. Neighbors motioned to one of the children to follow them onto a mountain of rubble, where they disappeared into a hole in the ground. Some women and children were on other piles of rubble helping to save some poor soul who was pinned under a ton of broken bricks and bent metal.

When I finally found my way home to our beautiful brick three-story building, I breathed a sigh of relief. Mama was there to meet me. Since our building was located somewhat out from town, it had not been damaged. Even the windows were still in place.

A few days later a notice on our door stated that schoolchildren must report to school and it gave a different address, though still within walking distance. Mama was telling me, "No more going to school. If we get killed, it will be together."

If Mama did not send me to school soon, one of our neighbors would inform the authorities and Mama might get in trouble. She relented. I walked to the new school address.

At school, I often fell asleep at my desk from hunger and lack of sleep. We received a midmorning snack of one piece of bread spread with cod liver oil. Oh, how I hated that smell! I was heaving so hard, I knew it was just a matter of time before I threw up. Our teacher asked why was I not eating my bread. How dare I not eat it because of the smell! She sternly reprimanded me in front of the class, stating that "our soldiers, who are fighting for Germany's honor, would give anything for this piece of bread." From that day on I choked it down.

Each day that I spent in school I became increasingly withdrawn, frightened, and unhappy. I understood that we could not do anything about the bombings, but the teacher was hateful and mean. For the smallest infraction of any rule, corrections were administered with a smooth, well-used stick. The teacher called the offending individual up front and while the pupil leaned over her desk or chair the strikes were administered, whatever she thought was enough punishment for the crime. It took only a few times of witnessing this correction to instill in me a fearful respect. Most of the time I did what I was told because I knew if I misbehaved, I would get hit by the teacher. My classmates would then tell Mama, who would give her stamp of approval with another beating. If the teacher was within reach of your face, she smacked you openhanded across your cheek. The rest of the day, students who received her mark had a red four-finger imprint on their cheeks. Eventually, it was my turn to experience the teacher's scorn for answering back, "No, I don't know the answer because I did not hear the question." (My ears, still being stuffed with cotton to keep the yellow pus from running down my neck, caused me to miss a lot of what was said.) Every time the stick met my bottom, the pain was so intense that I cried out. For this, the strikes were increased. By the time I arrived home, my behind was streaked black and blue. I could hardly sit. Mama approved of the teacher's actions and proved it by contributing her fair share, with her hands, striking mostly about my head.

* * *

I did not have to go to school anymore. The air raids, most of which had come at night up until now, started happening day and night. Burned in my memory is the date of 12 February 1944, another daytime air raid. Sister Erika was still very sick with "die Grippe" (the flu). Mama and Oma had borrowed about a dozen drinking glasses, one candle, matches, and a teaspoon of lard from the first-floor meal supervisor. They were going to administer the grippe treatment to Sister Erika. She was burning up with a high fever. Her cheeks were bright red. Her eyes were shining like the stars, and periodically she made a little croupy coughing sound. She would not eat or drink. They laid her naked on her stomach on the bed, and Mama rubbed her with fat. The individual glasses were heated with the candle, then placed upside down on her back. It must not have hurt, because Sister Erika did not make a sound. When Oma removed the glasses, it left beautiful red rings on her skin. This treatment was just about completed when the air raid sirens went off, sounding a TAKE SHELTER IMMEDIATELY—THE PLANES ARE ALREADY OVERHEAD frequency. Mama grabbed naked Sister Erika and the blanket she was lying on. She was out of the door first, and then Oma quickly pushed me out to follow Mama.

Standing in the doorway Oma seemed to be right behind me yelling to Mama, "Elsa, I will go back to get something to wear for the little one." Mama reached the stairway and never acknowledged that she heard. Quickly, I ran after her. We were squeezed and pushed by a mob of people headed downstairs. As we reached the first floor a bomb hit close to the side of the building. I could not hear a thing for some time after that. The hall lights went out. I could not see Mama, Sister Erika, or Oma. I just kept moving with the flow.

Arriving in the basement/bomb shelter, I just sat down on the floor and prayed "Our Father in Heaven." When my hearing finally returned, I heard women calling out their loved ones' names. Eventually the families found each other. Then, in darkness, I heard Mama calling me. I made my way through all those people to where she and Sister Erika were sitting on a bench. Women were praying, crying, and trying to console their screaming children.

"Ella, did you come down with Oma?" Mama asked.

"No, Mama. She told you that she was going back to get something for Sister Erika to wear."

Mama began to weep, then to call out loudly and repeatedly, "Katja, we are over here."

Oma did not answer.

The explosions kept on coming. The ceiling was still holding, but masonry was dropping in chunks. Dust billowed everywhere. The small basement windows, which were even with the ground, came flying in pieces into the shelter, cutting many who were seated on the opposite wall. The flashes from the explosions let me see the people around me for a second. Some were bleeding profusely from embedded glass and shrapnel wounds. All of us were covered in white dust and could hardly recognize each other. People were crying and looked like ghosts. Some had blood caked on their faces. In between the explosions, my hearing temporarily returned to hysterical screams, and then a grateful silence fell. During one of the lulls, I heard Mama yell out Oma's name time and again, but there came no reply.

I started to scream hysterically, not because of the nonstop explosions, but because my oma was not answering Mama's call. Mama held me close.

Sister Erika was in her lap wrapped in a dust-covered blanket. She was gasping for air and whimpering.

With the next explosion, a gust of wind came through the window. Mama didn't cry or call for Oma anymore. She just lay quietly against the wall. Sister Erika had fallen on the concrete floor and was crying. I climbed on Mama. Her face and hair were all wet. In the next explosion that illuminated the room I looked at my hands and saw that they were covered with blood. I started to scream that my mama was dead, "Please, somebody help me." No one helped. I kept patting Mama's cheek. "Mama, please, say something. What am I supposed to do?" After a while she began to move.

"Ella, are you hurt?" she asked.

"No, Mama."

"Did Oma come?"

"No, Mama."

"Is your sister living?"

"I don't know. She fell on the floor when you got hurt."

Mama finally sat up, reached down, and picked up Sister Erika, still very hot and moaning. She used part of the dust-covered blanket to wipe the blood off her own face; mixed with the white powder, the smeared blood made her look funny. All around us, women with ghostlike faces held onto their ghostlike children.

Finally, the All Clear sounded. Bleeding figures made their way up the half-broken marble stairs that just a few hours before were beautifully polished. I could not believe my eyes. Was this the same floor that used to have the beautiful paintings on the walls? Leaving Mama and Sister Erika behind, I ran over bricks and half-broken stairs, elbowing my way through the ascending crowd of people in shock. After I got up the first flight of stairs, I could not remember what floor I was on. I just sat down and waited for Mama.

"Keep going, Ella. I will tell you when to stop."

Mama was slow in climbing the stairs. She not only had to carry Sister Erika but also had to watch where she was going so as to avoid being run over by the other people going upstairs.

"Ella, wait, I think this is our floor."

I turned from the hallway into a room that had no door. The wall opposite the door—the outside wall, where the windows had been—was completely gone. I was stunned. Mama kept yelling, "Ella, don't go any farther. You will fall out of the building. Do you hear me?" I could not answer. In my frozen position, I stared out on the horizon. The once-beautiful city, with its church spires, the cars, the beautifully dressed German ladies, was now a smoldering heap of rubble. Devastation was all around as far as I could see. All familiar landmarks had vanished. All gone, gone, gone. Our teacher was right. Americans were mean. They ruined everything that was pretty. Where do they come from? Do they have beautiful cities, children my age? How would they feel if our Führer bombed them? The whole town was in black ruins. Not a building was standing. There were no people in the streets, no cars, streetcars, horses, nothing. A heavy black fog hung in the air. I was standing on charred ruins. A gut-wrenching scream from Mama jolted me out of my astonishment. I turned around.

"Katja, Katja. My beloved Katja, please speak to me."

There was Oma on a big mountain of rubble. She lay on her back, motionless against the wall. Mama knelt beside her. The clothing was Oma's, dirty but hers. Her hands were lying limp by her side. The only thing that was hard to recognize was her head and face. The front of her dress was soaked in blood. Her head was cut open, exposing a gray mass mixed with red, blood pouring out of the wound and covering one side of her face. She was so still.

Mama screamed that the Americans had killed her. "They will someday have to answer to God for this!"

I was very quiet. No tears, no screaming, just staring. I wanted to ask Mama who the Americans were that were so evil, but I thought better of it.

I longed to climb over the mound of rubble to touch Oma, even kiss her. No, not kiss her. She was too dirty, and all that blood still running down her cheek. Maybe she would even wake up.

"Mama," I said. "Is Oma dead?"

Instead of an answer, I got an unbelievable shriek: "Jaaaa!"

Mama found our suitcase, somewhat smashed, dirty, covered by bricks, but still closed. She looked around and found a dirty dress and a pair of shoes that belonged to Sister Erika, who was still wrapped in the blood-soaked blanket, seated in the rubble and whimpering. Mama got Sister Erika dressed. I was still looking at Oma, wondering, Who will clean her up before they bury her, or will she get buried and go to heaven dirty? All the angels I ever heard about were dressed in white. Will God let her into heaven dirty?

Mama was ready to go. Refusing to leave Oma, I started to cry louder and louder. With a slap across my face, Mama stopped my hysterical outburst.

"Ella, come on before the building collapses on us."

Poor Mama had to carry the suitcase and hold onto Sister Erika with the other hand. All alone and feeling sorry for myself, I was thinking, I lost my papa and now I lost my oma, who always took up for me. No one loves me. I loved Mama and Sister Erika, but I was never very close to either.

Mama led us away from the rubble, heading out of town. I slowly tagged along behind Mama and Sister Erika.

We joined other people walking toward the outskirts of the city. The farther out we went, the fewer houses were damaged. Mama stopped at a small two-story house, no windowpanes, its broken shutters partially closed, and asked a lady who was feeding chickens if she could possibly put us up for a few days. The woman answered that we were welcome to sleep in the basement, where her potatoes were stored. She added that she had very little to eat, only potatoes and some sauerkraut she had made in the fall. It was February and very cold. There was no heat, but her feather comforter that she brought down to the basement kept the three of us warm. She shared a meal with us once a day. The old, hard, stored, dried-up bread in our suitcase was another welcome meal.

The three of us always went out together because Mama thought if we had another air raid, we would either live or die together. On a daily basis we accompanied her to check the notices pasted on the wall of our old building to find out where and when the funeral was to take place. Notices of all kinds were posted there. One said that Refugees were to come to a particular location to be given further instructions as to when and where the authorities would relocate us next.

One morning we found the notice of the funeral on the information wall among other papers. It was to take place a few days later. We hoped it would be between air raids. Many people had been killed during that particular air raid. The day before the funeral, Mama was very irritable and visibly upset because she did not have a black dress to wear. To her dismay, she had to wash and wear her blue one. She was very put out because she knew that the friends she had made in the camp, some of whom would come to the funeral to bury their own dead, would say something derogatory about her blue dress. One should always wear black to funerals. People to be buried should be dressed in black also. I should always remember. Whenever Mama's time came, I should make sure she was buried in a black dress.

We walked to the cemetery. It lay in ruins. The footpath wound itself around a big crater on the way to the four scorched, burned-out walls of the once-beautiful church. The steeple that had reached toward heaven before the bombing was no more. Bleached bones were strewn around craters in the ground. Most people were dressed in black, even the children. Like Mama, my sister and I had nothing black. We owned only two dresses each, counting our everyday dresses. We wore the other ones (flowers on a white background), freshly laundered. We wore the old and ill-fitting winter coats we had been issued in Berlin. There were many caskets to be buried by two old men. A few people gathered around.

All the caskets smelled like Christmas trees. They were not painted, made from a honey-colored wood, and all the patterns of knots and streaks made a pretty picture. The caskets were closed, with their lids nailed down. I just knew Oma went to heaven dirty. Maybe the good Lord had a reason to keep her out.

"Mama," I asked, "did Oma get a bath before she goes to heaven?"

"No, there were too many of them who died that day," Mama answered.

Mama was shocked to see that the caskets were placed into the ground feet first. The dead were standing up. She was telling a woman standing nearby that never in her life had she been to a funeral where people were buried standing up rather than lying down. This was a sure sign from the devil.

I wondered which casket Oma was in because all the nameless caskets looked alike. People were in constant motion, some coming and some going. We stood waiting for a while. Waiting for what? Some recited Hail Mary repeatedly. Some said the Our Father. No tears were shed, no prayers were heard from the three of us. After placing a long row of caskets into deep holes, one after another, the two old men shoveled dirt on them until they were covered. Then they started on the next row. Not even one flower was placed on or thrown into the graves. After many caskets were covered, one of which must have been Oma's, Mama took us by the hand and we began our long and silent walk through the debris to our temporary home. It was a cold, misty, dreary February afternoon. One day of no air raids to bury my beloved oma, Katja.

I was thinking, this was so sad. Oma had looked forward to living in Germany. In fact, that is all she talked about, the land of her forefathers. Sure, she made it to Germany, but she never met a Real German, only other Refugees. She never visited a bakery, a butcher shop, a Gasthaus (café/restaurant) and never heard German music or songs. The only Germans she met were the soldiers and the authorities in the camps.

* * *

Within a few days there appeared a notice tacked to the wall at our bombed-out building instructing us to report to a new walled-in compound. We walked a long time to reach it. It was an undamaged three-story building surrounded by a wall with only one entrance in and out. We reunited with our old friends, many of whom had lost mothers, children, and grandmothers. Air raids, again, continued around the clock. We were lucky to be assigned to a room with only three other people. Always, Mama kept Sister Erika and me close by. Our routine became pretty much the same every day. No sooner did we come up from the bomb shelter to our room to use the toilet than it was time to go back down. While the air raid sirens were wailing away and the antiaircraft guns on the roofs of the buildings were going rata-tata-tat, people were praying. I had never been to church or heard my mama pray, only my old oma had prayed with me every night. Whenever the air raid sirens went off and everyone made it down to the bomb shelter, seated and waiting, the chants, prayers, singing, and reciting of psalms started, and this became a ritual.

Looking around the bomb shelter, I saw some women and children crossing themselves and praying Hail Mary. The same prayer over and over again. I soon learned to cross myself and recite the Hail Mary as well, joining in the chorus. To change the monotony I recited Our Father followed by Hail Mary. I figured that it would not hurt to pray something different. God must get tired of listening to the same thing everyday from our basement packed with people begging for all kind of things. Maybe He wasn't even listening. Maybe God was too busy and so Mary, Jesus' mother, helped Him. Wonder what Jesus was doing all this time? I could not understand just how He fit into this picture. Somehow, I did work Jesus' name into my prayers. God forbid they were made-up prayers and someone heard me. Prayers were prescribed by the church. Old women would start a hymn, and some of the same faith joined in. I learned hymns. Some recited the psalms. Others corrected the verses.

By now I could tell who was Catholic and who was Lutheran. Mama's explanation of the difference was that Catholics did not know the Bible because it was in Latin, which could only be read and interpreted by a priest, whereas Lutherans could read the Bible because it was written in German, and they were encouraged to read what God had to say to them directly. Some old people seemed to have put the whole Bible to memory. I wanted to be able to do that too. I wanted to ask Mama so many things about God, the Bible, Jesus and Mary. Mama always said, "You have no business to ask questions. A child's place is to listen and learn, not to blabber. What does a child know to add to a conversation?" Nevertheless, I continued to pester Mama with questions.

"How could God understand all that jabber in all those different languages? Did He have an interpreter?"

The answer was a stern look from Mama's dark brown eyes. It was not a good time for me to be asking such questions.

In my heart, I was afraid that a bomb would hit me any day. I just knew our turn would come. But with so many women and children praying, maybe God would have mercy on us to let us see another day. I wanted to find an old priest who had a friendly face and ask him why God was having the American planes come over and drop bombs on us. Why so many women called on Mary and she never answered? Why some called on God all the time, and where was Jesus?

I couldn't wait to go into a church and see God. Maybe the Americans would not destroy all the churches, and I would get a chance to visit just one. I overheard someone talking about nuns. Their whole lives were spent in a cloister, in individual small cells, which were bricked up to the waist. All they had to do was pray every day. The other nuns brought them food and water. Maybe there were no bombs where the priest and nuns lived. Maybe I could become a nun and join an order of Sisters. By being a nun and reciting a million Hail Marys, I just knew I would be spared by the bombs.

The basement shelter was always heavily laden with dust and permeated with the smell of urine and dirty diapers. The filth and body odors were overwhelming. "Your nose is oversensitive," was Mama's response to my complaining. It made me sick to my stomach. To Mama's consternation, I would throw up then and there. Kids were begging for something to drink, rubbing their yellow-running noses on faces already caked with day-old snot. Their mothers ignored their cries and kept on reciting Hail Mary and Our Father. Whenever my nose started to run, Mama pulled up the inside of her skirt. I blew into it, and then she rubbed it together until everything was absorbed by the material.

The only relief from the sound of crying, begging, and praying was after a near-miss bomb explosion. Such moments were always followed by a total silence.

At last, after what seemed like hours, the piercing whine of the air raid sirens sounded the All Clear. We climbed out of the basement looking like dirty street people.

At the end of our street someone had erected a wooden board where people put notices. The notices, some with pictures, said things like "My dear daughter, Ilse Braun, I am now with your oma on the farm. If you are still living, please come." Mama read the notes aloud and repeatedly to me. "Remember the person's name," she told me, "just in case." I should commit these names to memory because someday, somewhere, someone might ask me if I ever knew such and such person.

"I am Inge Ötz. I lived at 25 Regensburger Street, my children are dead. I have gone to live with my relatives in Oberalteich."

"Otto Zug, if you ever come home from the war, I can be found in Dingelfing."

New notes were added to the old every day. Neighbors read them and remembered, so when Otto did come home and was asking around town about his family, someone could tell him where his wife might be found.

Within a few days, Mama found a notice addressed to the Refugees. It ordered us to report to an assembly point. On the way, we passed a church. It was not gutted or in ruins. Surprisingly enough, all the damage that it had sustained was a few holes on the outside walls, some windows blown out, and part of the steeple missing.

"Mama, please let's go into this church. I must see where God lives."

She gave in to my pleading and begging. Inside, sitting in the back pew, I decided that if I prayed more Hail Marys, went to church at least twice a day, crossed myself more often, I would become a nun. I walked around in the aisles while Mama and Sister Erika sat close to the door. The church looked very bare. The paintings on the walls had many pieces missing. The pedestals were empty of their figurines. Some of the stained-glass windows were broken or completely missing. In their dust-covered brown cassocks, the old priests were busy cleaning, polishing, and sweeping. Some nuns in black habits girded by what used to be shiny white aprons joined them. I could just see myself in a big black hood with white trim, covering my dirty, lifeless, brown, white-streaked, lice-infested hair. When a little bell rang, they all stopped, got on their knees, crossed themselves, and prayed for a while. How I longed to be one of them and be near God. Priests and nuns didn't have to get a job or worry about where their next meal came from. They just had to pray and clean up after themselves.

I walked up to the magnificent altar that was hardly touched by the explosions and asked a nun, "How can I become a nun?"

"My child, you have to be worthy."

"What do I need to do to become worthy?"

"Are you a Catholic?"

"What is a Catholic?"

"Does your mother pray Hail Mary?"

"No, just Our Father."

"You have to be a Catholic first of all. Speak to a priest and he will decide if you can become a nun."

I saw Mama standing up in the back pew. Reluctantly, I ran to join her. A nun's voice echoed through the sanctuary, "In God's house you do not run, you always walk."

As we left the church I said to Mama, "I want to become a nun."

"Have you lost your mind completely?" Mama stopped in the middle of the street. Shaking her index finger in my face she said, "Your forefathers are going to turn over in their graves knowing you have forsaken the only true faith. We don't have to give our money to the pope, who is evil, nor have Mary, the mother of Jesus, to intercede for us. When we need anything, we go directly to Jesus and He will take care of us."

I was stunned to hear Mama go off in such a tirade. My dream to become a nun, which I had thought was a great survival strategy, vanished.

* * *

Mama, with suitcase in one hand, Sister Erika in the other, and me tagging along behind, made our way to the given address. Here we encountered many faces we knew from a year ago, when we lived in Berlin. Our room on the second floor was large. We shared it with three other families. There was a community kitchen on the first floor run by a loudmouthed lady with a thick Bavarian accent. Once a day we were given bread and well-seasoned but watered-down cabbage soup. More families joined us every day.

The nightly air raid sirens continued. People were irritable with their children and with their neighbors from the lack of sleep. In our basement/ bomb shelter, families were now staking out their places with chairs, blankets, German army canteens, books, candles, and toys. We would not dare sit in someone else's area. That would definitely cause a fight. Since Mama had made no provisions to secure a place for us, we had to make do with the space that was left.

This particular night the only seat available was a corner bench. Reaching under the bench, I located an open can, which contained an orange powder. Somehow I touched the powder, then rubbed my tired eyes before falling asleep. When Mama awakened me, I could not see. I opened my eyes but still could not see. The following day, leaving Sister Erika with a friend, Mama walked me to the nearest hospital. Everyone was so nice. The doctor examined me. He told Mama to go home and bring the can. Meanwhile, I stayed in the hospital. I had a much younger roommate who whimpered for her mother whenever she was awake. Just after Mama left, the air raid sirens went off. A nurse came, took me by my hand, and led me down a flight of stairs to the basement/bomb shelter. My cries for Mama were unanswered. Other children cried even harder than I did. The nurses kept saying, "In a little while we all can go back to our rooms." I could hear the bombs going off in the distance, accompanied by the rata-tata-tat of the antiaircraft fire. The nurse reassured me that the hospital had a big red cross painted on the roof. The Americans promised not to bomb any hospitals. My prayers were now just a string of Hail Marys and Our Fathers followed by all kinds of promises. I promised to be good, go to church, pray more, obey more, on and on.

Many nights passed before Mama came. I just knew she had been killed, and my imagination went rampant. Where would I go? Who would take care of me? Where was Sister Erika? Lying in my bed, I was too scared to breathe. The nurse pleaded with me, "Don't cry, Ellachen, because your eyes have to stay dry." The nurse changed my bandages daily. No matter how hard I tried, I still couldn't see through the wall of black. Then Mama came. Her loving hand held mine. I did not want to let go. After her short visit, I worried and invented more worries until I was mentally and physically exhausted, and then surrendered myself to a short sleep until the sirens went off again. A few days into my hospitalization I was moved into a private room. No one to talk to, just lie there and listen to footsteps going up and down the hall. Mama hadn't been to see me for days now. I must know about Mama. I said to the nurse, "Is my mama dead?"

"Oh, no, child. She cannot come to visit because you have the measles and we don't want it spread all over the city."

"How long will it be before she can come to visit me?"

"Probably another week," she said.

That was the longest week I spent in my entire life. Then one day while the nurse was changing my bandages, I saw the light hanging from the ceiling and screamed, "I can see, I can see!" The nurse put all her tools down and hugged me. Mama came. She and the doctor had a long conversation in the hallway. She had brought a freshly washed dress and clean underwear

Family portrait: Elsa and Jakob Schneider, Erika, and Ella, 1938

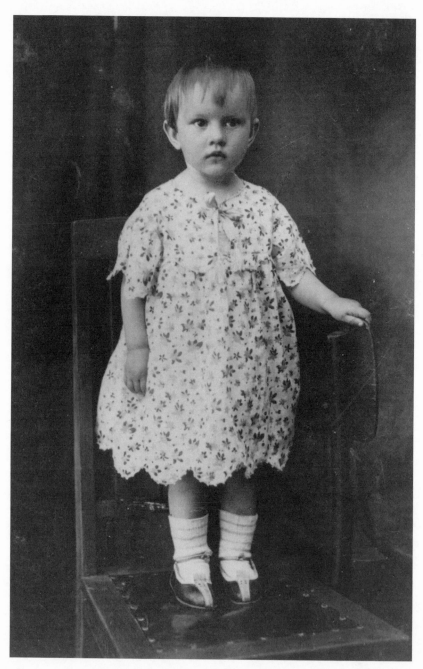

Ella in Kiev, USSR, about 1938–39

Ella, Mama, Sister Erika, Kiev, 1940

Opa and Papa in Papa's workshop in the basement apartment in Kiev, 1940

Oma Katherine in Kiev, 1940

Camp Hofstetten in a 1963 photo; Ella and her family lived here from 1945 to 1952

On the Danube about two miles from Camp Hofstetten: Papa Theodor Puder, Sister Lida at his feet, Sister Erika, Brother Otto, Mama, 1947

Ella's confirmation picture, 1950

Friends Herta, Ella, Giesela, and Gerda, confirmation, 1950

School outing to the mountains, 1950; Ella is in the top row, fourth from left.

Ella's Kennkarte, or Identity Card, 1950

Ruins of the shack in which Ella and her family lived
as indentured servants in Mississippi

Gerda, Herta, and Ella; Hansi sitting in front of Ella with unidentified friend; 1951

Theodor and Elsa at house on Salem Street, Holly Springs, Mississippi, 1953

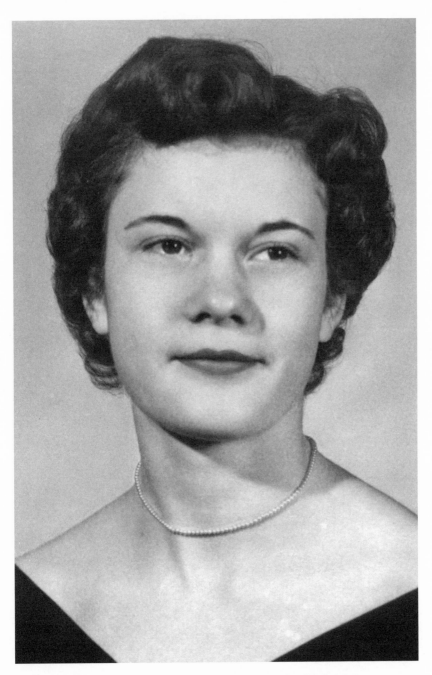

Ella's graduation picture, Holly Springs High School, 1955

Ella with Tom Hilton at a Belhaven College formal in Jackson, Mississippi, 1956

and socks. Let the bombs fall, I was with my mama again. I skipped and jumped ahead of her all the way home. Even Sister Erika was happy to see me, wanting to know everything I had seen or heard, but most of all, the food I ate. That evening, sitting on the bed and getting ready to say my prayers I asked, "Mama, did you take the can the doctor asked you about?"

"Yes, I did."

"Did he tell you what caused me to lose my sight?"

"He said it was some sort of a chemical that the German army used. By mistake they left it behind in the bomb shelter when they relocated."

On one of our daily visits to the information wall, Mama found another notice: Refugees from Russia, Poland, and other countries were to be at the train station the following day. We were to board a train for Passau. Maybe Passau was not as burned-out as Regensburg. Making our way to the station I saw close-up just how burned out all the buildings were. Old women with brooms were in the streets cleaning up debris from the night before. There were no smiles or hellos, only sad, wrinkled, dirty faces. The streets were cleared of all the debris. A clean street snaked itself around ruins. People were pulling little four-wheel wooden wagons filled with all kinds of things, including feather beds, small children, or old people. These wagons looked almost like play wagons. Where were they going? Maybe they knew a place where bombs were not falling out of the sky.

"Mama, where are all these people going?"

"I don't know, but I think they are probably going to their relatives in the country. At least they could stay in their barn."

It was cold and rainy when we arrived at the train station. People with suitcases and children were milling around everywhere. After making inquiries, Mama found the right platform. We joined a crowd pushing and jostling to get in line for a piece of black bread and the kettle that dispensed hot tea. After taking out our two tin cups, Sister Erika and I sat on the suitcase while Mama joined the herd. It seemed like hours before she returned with four pieces of bread stuffed into the front of her coat and carrying steaming hot tea in both hands. Mama still kept Oma's papers and collected her portion of food.

Mama smiled now and then. Miraculously, we had survived the bombardments. She got reacquainted with some people who had traveled with us on the train from Kiev. Mama had to show the conductor our Kennkarte or Ausweis (Identification Card), the new one we had received in Regensburg. He checked his list and told us the car number in which we were to travel. This was a train just for Refugees.

At long last it came—a passenger train, not a freight train. We just got on and grabbed seats. I kept praying that the train would start and take us out of there before the next air raid. Finally we moved out of the station at a snail's pace. Soon we were in the countryside. I had made sure I was seated next to a window. As woods, lakes, and small villages came into view and then quickly disappeared, I wished I could live in one of those beautifully whitewashed houses. Each windowsill had flower boxes already prepared to receive new plants. How I longed to be out there with all those people working in the fields. Children riding bicycles waved at us as we went by. I bet they didn't have air raids. It seemed as if the train came to a complete stop at each road crossing. I rolled down my window and listened to church bells chime in the distance. Sometimes I could hear people singing. This was altogether a different world. What did one have to do to live in that little hamlet? "Mama, will I ever have a bicycle?"

"If we live long enough."

Darkness fell like a curtain on us. Very few streetlights were on as we exited the train. We had finally arrived at another new home.

* * *

Passau, southeast of Regensburg on the German-Austrian border, sits on a spit of land at the confluence of three rivers: the Danube and two small tributaries, the Ilz and the Inn. The Danube is wide and dark brown, the Inn has a milky color, and the Ilz is a smoky topaz. A huge fortress overlooks one side of the river. Oh, what I wouldn't give to live in that castle! On the other side of the river is a big monastery. Majestically, cherry orchards surround its cathedral.

Within a few minutes, it became obvious that we were not going to live in the castle. Trucks transported us to the monastery, which had been transformed into a refugee camp. Sitting on the back of a big army truck, among a convoy of many trucks, I couldn't see much because the following truck's headlights shone directly into my face. After we arrived we were each given room numbers and provided with a piece of black bread and a small piece of cheese. I crawled onto the top of the bunk bed completely dressed, with Mama reminding me not to drop crumbs on the bunk bed below, where she and Sister Erika would sleep, or urinate on the already smelly mattress.

The monks made sure the parents knew to enroll us in school. A dozen or so of us made the long walk down the mountain each morning to a little village by the Ilz. Mama would not let Sister Erika go because she was too little. I was truly happy to be in school. It lasted only until noon. I did not participate in classroom discussions because I could not read or write very much and all I knew was the name of the last bombed-out city we had come from. I learned to sing German soldiers' marching songs, to march and salute, "Heil Hitler!" I did not have one piece of writing paper or even a pencil. The lady teacher provided me with what I needed with a condescending smile. I smiled back at her with a curtsy and "Dankeschön" (Thank you). Within a few days, I received some cast-off clothing, including a white short-sleeved blouse and a short brown skirt. I treasured the outfit because, wearing it, I looked like everyone else. I looked like I belonged.

Everyone at school treated me like a second-class citizen. It did not matter that I spoke perfect German. It was not the local Bavarian dialect. As soon as I said anything, they knew I was not one of them. Not a day passed without someone at school telling me to go back to Poland where I came from. It hurt, but it didn't matter. As long as the bombs were not falling, I could endure almost anything or any treatment by the natives.

The monks were in charge of the Refugees. I now attended mandatory Catholic religious classes that the old monks taught, with the emphasis being that you had to be a Catholic in order to be able to go to heaven. I wished I could talk to Mama about it. Approaching Mama on that subject was not easy. Usually she said, "Go make yourself useful." (Useful doing what? She never specified.) She had no time for such foolishness as discussing or explaining religion to me. My spare hours were spent sitting in the grass overlooking the city of Passau and worrying over the fact that I was Lutheran—how I would get into heaven?

"Mama, how do I know what is a Catholic Church and what is a Lutheran Church?"

"Very simply, Catholic churches have a cross at the very top of the steeple, Lutheran churches do not."

I looked everywhere but could not find one church without a cross on its steeple.

Weekends, I'd walk for hours in the countryside, inhaling the tantalizing aroma of flowers, shrubs, and trees in full bloom. When there was no school I'd visit churches and cloisters and talk to women working in the fields. There were no air raids, so we could sleep through the night. No planes were coming over. There was no war in Passau.

Mama spent her time with Sister Erika and talking to her friends about the good old days. I was left pretty much to my own devices.

One day while I was exploring fields and forests I discovered a camp with a high barbed-wire fence, almost like ours in Berlin. But this camp was different. There were German soldiers with guns walking around the fence. As I approached, one soldier yelled, "Halt!" I froze in my tracks. I was scared to death thinking he was going to shoot me. As he drew closer, he asked, "What are you doing here?"

"I am taking a walk," I said.

"Does your mother know you are running around the countryside? If not, you should be getting a spanking. Now go home immediately and don't come back here again."

Crying all the way, I hurried home, stopping to catch my breath whenever my side ached. I sat in silence on my bed. My tears dried up, leaving behind the telltale sign of red and puffy eyes. Mama chatted about trivia for a while, then she wanted to know about my day. At first, I didn't want to tell her, figuring what the consequence would be. Nevertheless, I told her what I had been up to. She was enraged. I received a good old-fashioned beating. Mama demanded my promise that I would not wander off again. I promised.

Cherry-picking time had come. During the time the monks were having their prayers, I climbed their cherry trees, stole as many cherries as I could reach, and carried them home in my apron. I enjoyed eating the sap that seeped from the bark more than the cherries themselves.

Going out on my own, I discovered many interesting places and things. If I brought a friend along, she would probably blab it all to Mama. I discovered a place not too far from our encampment that had a free-standing six-foot high brick wall covered in green moss. This was the place where the monks raised snails. These slimy creatures with their houses attached to their bodies fascinated me. Getting up early, just as the sun came up, I watched those little oozy creatures making their way up the moist, moss-covered wall. Some kids collected them in metal water buckets. Someone had built a stove out of two big rocks with a metal grate across it in the backyard over the objection of the monks. They covered the snails with water, then cooked, cracked, and ate them. Mama did not want anything to do with anything that was slimy. Many women cooked whatever their children stole and brought home to supplement the daily rations dispensed by the monks, our keepers. I stole potatoes right out of the fields, cherries and apples off the trees, and other edible unattended fruits or vegetables in season. Never snails.

1945

One night we all awoke to a heavy drone even before the air raid sirens went off. We knew the sound. Heavy-laden bombers were approaching. Little did we know they were intended for us. We always hoped that the bombs were intended for someone else. Now we heard the air raid sirens going off in the valley below. Dressing as we went, we made haste to the basement/bomb shelter. Some people were already there. There were three or four light bulbs hanging from the ceiling along the long basement corridor—not enough to give much light. It didn't matter, because once the bombings started, the lights went out. It became pitch black in the basement, except for the flashes of exploding bombs through the small windows, which were just above ground level. Once the terrified confusion of grown-ups and children settled down, everyone sat either on the wooden benches that lined the walls or on the hard cement floor, children stopped crying and went to sleep, and grown-ups prayed.

I could hear the bombs exploding. They seemed close, but none hit our mountaintop camp. The next morning, emerging from our bomb shelter and looking down on what used to be the pretty town of Passau, we saw a smoldering black mass in some parts. The grown-ups were angry with the Americans, who had no respect for beautiful things. Voicing their rage, they assured one another that "Adolph will take care of them."

Mama forbade my outings as the air raids became increasingly numerous. But occasionally, during the daytime bombings, I sat in the grass overlooking the city and just counted the planes that droned by on their way to God knows where. I watched the planes drop their loads on the city below. I sat intrigued, trying to count the plummeting bombs that came out of each airplane. I was fascinated by this spectacle. Mama would be furious and administer a beating after the air raid. We spent more and more time in the bomb shelter. During lulls in the bombings we had time to relieve ourselves and get a drink of water from the well. I was extremely tired from lack of sleep and always hungry. Black bread and cooked oatmeal were handed out daily. There was no playtime outside or inside anymore. Someone's child was always getting trounced, most of the time not even by their own kin. Children crying, old people praying, all using different languages, the nauseating smell of body odor and dirty diapers wafted throughout the whole building.

"Mama," I said, "Will this ever end? Will we be killed?"

"Only God knows."

After the All Clear reached us on top of the mountain, it became very quiet. Children stopped crying. Women stopped praying. The air itself, heavy with smoke, seemed to be holding its breath.

Days passed into weeks and then months. After a fly-over but before the All Clear had sounded, a woman who was nearest the stairway went out to check what was going on. We could hear her screams all the way back down the stairs. When she came into view she was wringing her hands and tearing at her hair, screaming all the while, "Mein Gott! Mein Gott! Die Russen sind da!" (Dear God! Dear God! The Russians are here!) She looked wildly around the basement. "The Russians! There is no place to run to now! What are we going to do? Somebody answer me! What are we going to do? Where are we going to run to now? This is the end! Before I let the Russians take me and my children, I will kill my children and myself. Where are you, my children? Come here to me and hug your mama."

I was completely mesmerized by her terror. Her children came to her one by one, three in all. I was hoping she would not kill them and herself in front of us.

As if on cue, all the people in the basement started screaming. The women were screaming because we would be under the Russian occupational forces. The children were screaming because their mothers were screaming.

Mama climbed over people to get to the woman. When she spoke to her, the woman stopped screaming and so did her kids. They stood there in the dim light from the open basement door, in a fog of dust from fallen plaster.

I heard Mama say, "These Russians, what did they look like? I am from Kiev and can identify a Russian. Where are you from?"

"We are from Poland."

"Have you ever seen a Russian?" Mama asked.

"No."

"Please describe what they looked like."

With her kids clamoring onto her skirt, the woman said, "When I went out into the yard, there were a bunch of trucks and a little car with a long antenna sticking straight up. One soldier approached me yelling something and brandishing his rifle that had a knife on the front of it. He motioned me to put my hands up. I looked around and there were half a dozen men with their rifles pointed at me yelling something I couldn't understand. Some had black skin, big white teeth, red lips, and their mouths were moving even when they were not yelling at each other or me. At first I thought they were painted. Can you believe, except for the red lips and their pink palms, even their hands were black. I turned and ran straight back down here."

Mama burst out laughing. She laughed until tears came streaming down her face. The harder she tried to maintain her composure the more she laughed. The bomb shelter became so quiet you could hear a pin drop. She was laughing and laughing, unable to stop herself. Everyone watched this unfolding scene. Finally, she said, "I came from Russia, from the Volga. I am a Volga Deutsche. I have never seen a Russian who was black or looked anything like what you described. Dear lady, you made a mistake."

"I saw what I saw," the woman replied. "You tell me then. Who are these soldiers? Hopefully, they are German soldiers who are painted black."

"I don't know," Mama said, "but I know one thing for sure. They are not Russians."

Within a few minutes, loud shouts came from the top of the stairs. All I could make out was a uniform, and a rifle pointing into the basement. "Raus! Raus!"

I was scared, clinging to Mama's hand. No one wanted to go first. Women didn't know what fate was awaiting them. They were talking about being raped (a new word for me to ask Mama about when she was in a talking mood). After some hesitation, a single file of women and children snaked itself up the stairs. In the sunshine, we all looked like ghosts from the plaster dust. Most of us were coughing and spitting white saliva on the ground. Some had gotten sick at their stomachs while going up the stairs, so the people following were stepping into it all, slipping and falling down into the mess.

Once outside, we were all lined up against the building. We stared at the group of soldiers in front of us. The terrified woman had been right. Some of the soldiers were white, but some were as black as if they had been painted. One of the white ones yelled in broken but understandable German, "Are there any German soldiers in the building? Who are you and where do you come from?"

Before answering his question, one of the women nearest to the inquiring soldier asked, "Are you Russians?"

The soldier turned to his buddies, said something, and they all laughed as hard as they could. I couldn't get over how shabby these soldiers looked, black or white. They didn't even look like soldiers. They looked like hired farm hands coming home from a long day in the field, wearing baggy pants that were covered in dried mud. I had never seen such dirty boots. The white soldier needed a shave. The black soldiers were constantly chewing something. They were very different from the German soldiers I had seen over the years. I remembered the first German officers who came into our home in Kiev. Our German soldiers always looked sparkling clean and highly polished.

"No," he said. "We are American soldiers."

At this point all the women fell on their knees with upraised hands and prayed, thanking God for delivering us into the hands of the Americans.

The white soldier who was in charge was taken aback. He said, "No, no we are not going to shoot you. We are here to liberate you."

The children were all clinging to their mamas. All of us looked with astonishment and fascination, scared to death, at the black soldiers who were standing near or sitting on the trucks. I had never seen a black person before and couldn't even imagine that there were such people on this earth.

At first, it looked as if we would have to leave our mountain camp. But the longer the white soldier asked questions, the longer we stayed.

"Where are your men?"

The standard answer, "Fighting on the eastern front."

"Where are you from?"

A barrage of answers greeted him: Russia, Poland, Czechoslovakia, Hungary, Yugoslavia, and so on and on. He shook his head and went into a huddle with his buddies, then informed us that the trucks were to transport us into the city of Passau proper, to a holding area with other Refugees. We were to be registered, accorded medical attention, and given something to eat. We must stay here until a decision is made as to what to do with us next.

The spokeswoman, the one who had first asked if they were Russians, kept repeating the question to the German-speaking soldier: "Are you sure you are Americans and not Russians?" Mama kept reassuring her. Whatever they were, they were not Russian. If they spoke Russian, she would understand them. This language she couldn't understand at all.

The lady's other question was "Are there different colors of Americans?"

"Most Americans are white," the soldier explained. "Some are black, some are red or even yellow."

Wow, maybe I would get to see red and yellow people!

While we were being questioned, four soldiers came back from the main building and said, "It's OK." His order to us, "Go and get your belongings." Single file we accompanied a soldier, rifle in hand, upstairs.

Mama found our suitcase. One corner was bent. The lock was bent as well. Someone had tried to force it open. Nothing was missing except Papa's leather belt, which had held the suitcase together. Mama took the rope we used as a clothesline, wrapped it around the suitcase, and tied it in a knot.

As we were slowly gathering in the yard, a black soldier came toward us and handed me a long yellow thing. I didn't know what it was and had never seen anything like it before. His smile revealed the most beautiful set of white teeth. I took it, not smiling, with no "Dankeschön," and hid it behind my back. All the kids received one. Lessons from school echoed through my head. When you find something never pick it up. It may explode and tear your hand off. Americans will do anything to kill Germans. Did that apply to the long yellow thing? After smelling the yellow thing, some kids started to eat it, peel and all. This brought a big smile to the soldier's face. He was laughing, waving his hands in the air, saying, "Nein, nein." Still smiling and shaking his head, he took another long yellow object from the back of the truck, peeled it, and ate it. I followed suit, giving half of it to Mama. We took a bite and could not figure out what the taste was. Mama didn't know either. It was food. After observing this display, the white soldier said, "Banana." An uneven chorus of children's voices answered, "Banana."

While we waited apprehensively, women were saying among themselves, "Let's hope these soldiers are not lying to us." Now everyone was assembled in the yard, excluding the old priests. The German-speaking soldier was talking into some kind of telephone connected to a box. After a lengthy conversation, he came back and announced in a loud voice, "Since the building didn't take a direct hit, you are to stay here until further notice." So we moved back upstairs to the same beds with the same flea-infested and urine-smelling mattresses.

Up to now I could understand what was being said in Russian or in German, even in some varied German dialects some words were understandable. Now I could not understand one word. Our spokeswoman thought by really explaining everything in detail to some of the Americans, on a first-grade level, she would be understood. Sign language with many words were used, not only by the Americans but also by the Refugees. One word everybody got right off the bat was "OK." It didn't matter what cluster of words or sentences were thrown at me if it ended in "OK," or somewhere in the sentence "OK" was used, then it was all in order.

We spent at least two months in that monastery camp after the war ended. Food was given to the priests, who doled it out to us. Most of it was dry rations in small cans. We had no books to keep us busy, no radio, and the grown-ups had no patience or inclination to answer the persistent questions of the children. I wanted answers to so many questions. There was no one to ask. I could not summon up the courage to approach Mama. A natural solitude was my salvation. I escaped my present environment by taking long investigative walks. I stopped and tried to talk to farmers turning hay in the fields. Wrinkly-skinned, suntanned old farmers who had been friendly before the Americans' arrival now ignored or hollered at me, sometimes with an upraised fist, to get out of their way or off their land. Puzzled and afraid, I ran.

One day I decided to go back to the camp that I had found once before and see what had become of all those people. There were still men and boys walking around inside the camp. The only difference I could see was that the German guards had been replaced by American soldiers. The barbed wire was still in place. When I returned home I asked Mama what would become of all those people in the other camp. Mama's explanation was that all of them would be gone in a few weeks. Who is taking them and where are they going? And will that happen to us? She assured me that it would not happen to us.

"Those are people who the Americans promised the Russians would be taken back to the Russian side after the war."

It didn't matter if they wanted to go or not. The Americans didn't understand or care because they had made a deal with the Russians to return those people (repatriation). At night a convoy of American trucks loaded the people, against their will, and transported them across the border to be handed over to the Russians (it was less than forty miles to Czechoslovakia). They didn't want to go back to Russian-occupied lands, from which they had fled days, months, or years before. That became obvious when, the following morning, the road was littered with the bodies of men, women, and children who had committed suicide. The hand-over of people and the pickup of dead bodies continued every morning for days. Mama told me not to go down the mountain into Passau for a few days because she didn't want me to see the carnage.

Women began to bring home materials—jewelry and paintings and the like. I watched and saw that they left early in the morning. I followed a few of them. Lo and behold, my journey led me to the castle across the river from our mountain camp. I met women and a few men heading down the road, their arms filled with all kinds of things. Some even had little wagons piled so high that someone had to walk next to the wagon and hold the stuff in place. The castle walls were blackened with tongues of soot. The beautiful stained-glass windows were gone, with only shards remaining in the frames. People were taking everything they could carry, even doors. We Refugees didn't have a place to call our own, so what good were doors? They must have been taken by the Real Germans who had houses, damaged perhaps. Or maybe the doors would end up for sale.

I walked from one room to the other trying not to fall over broken furniture. All of a sudden an air raid siren went off. I could not imagine where it came from. People started to scream and drop things while running out of the castle. At the entrance American soldiers with rifles shouted, "Raus! Raus!" Not until I got to the gate of the castle did I realize the siren was attached to an American car. Having taken nothing, never looking back, I ran with the crowd all the way down the mountain, across the bridge, then up the mountain and home.

For us the war was over; no more bombings, no more explosions, no more crying, nor yelling, nor cursing, nor praying, nor running. Everything stopped.

Mama and her friends became afraid of being repatriated by force to Russian-occupied lands. As she so often said, she would rather die. "Ella, I will never, never go back to Russia and live under Communism, and neither will you or your sister Erika." I was too scared to ask her if that meant that Sister Erika and I would have to die as well.

Mama had a plan. One evening she tied the rope around our suitcase. As it started to get dark, the three of us made our way down the mountain by moonlight. We crossed two bridges and arrived in the dimly lit city of Passau proper. Mama asked the first person who we met, "Where is the homeless shelter?" The lady said it was in an undamaged hotel on the Danube River side of town.

We found a big hotel that had been converted into a shelter for homeless people. The ballroom was missing windows, but the roof was still holding.

The ceiling was painted with beautiful floating women and half-dressed muscular men looking down on us. German army bunk beds were set up side by side with only enough room to get in and out. The people in authority pointed us toward a bunk bed for the three of us. I slept on top and Sister Erika and Mama slept on the lower bunk. Here, to my amazement, we were surrounded by Real Germans whose homes had been damaged or destroyed. They were now fed by American soldiers. They had been reduced to our level.

Mama strung the suitcase rope between our beds. On it she hung the extra blanket she had received using Oma's papers. It served as a makeshift divider and gave us some privacy. Other people did the same thing.

We had contended with lice and fleas for years; now we had to fight bedbugs as well. These creatures were flat, about a quarter inch long, and would fill with blood. During the day they hid in the joints of the bed. Short of taking the wooden bed apart and dipping the ends in boiling water, there was no way of eliminating these pests (per Mama). The next best thing was to run a piece of paper between the joints and kill the bedbugs that came out with a thumbnail. Feeding time was always at night. In the morning Sister Erika and I woke covered in big red spots that itched all the time; the more we scratched, the bigger the bites became and the more they itched. Scratched bites often became infected. Mama begged our lunch providers for a hot cup of tea, washed all the bitten places very well, and covered the sores with washed green leaves from the sidewalk. She also laid down a new law: "Ella, do not scratch or I am going to give you something to scratch about." Since we had no scissors, Mama bit off our fingernails to prevent us from scratching.

The mattresses we slept on were old burlap bags filled with matted straw. I tried to avoid the spots that were moist. The smell was almost unendurable. Mama always told me my nose was too sensitive and if I dared to throw up I would really get a whipping. That would be terribly humiliating before all these strangers. I was not allowed to cry regardless of how hard the beatings were to endure. Nightly, I could hear some child or other getting walloped because he or she hadn't made it to the bathroom and the urine had seeped through the straw mattress and wet whoever was sleeping below.

American soldiers (now known as "Amis," pronounced *ah-meez*) provided us with our daily bread for months. The meals were cooked somewhere and then brought to our shelter by truck. Amazingly, the food was always steaming hot. We were told most of it was cooked from powder. All we had to do was show up with our cups or bowls to receive a good portion of whatever. We weren't sure what some of the foods were. One thing was definite: after the first try, no one ate turnip greens. Turnips yes, greens no. We didn't know what to make of the cornbread. There was always a lot of it left on the truck until someone explained to the Amis that Germans didn't eat cornbread. Corn was grown only for animal feed. After trying a piece, Mama pronounced it tasty. She encouraged me and Sister Erika to eat some. It tasted like cake, good and sweet. So we ate cornbread with our meals. We ate as if we were rich because now we also had white bread. I got used to the smell of powdered milk and powdered eggs and was very happy and grateful to have something good to eat. Cold powdered milk? No! We didn't drink cold milk. We drank warm milk. Someone brought to the Amis' attention that the milk was to be warm or hot. They aimed to please. Except, when boiled, the powdered milk invariably scorched and tasted terrible. But it was food. It was hot. We even developed a taste for it. The oatmeal was not much better burned. Burned powdered scrambled eggs smelled to high heaven, and try as I might, I could not develop a taste for them. Cans with small portions of everything were handed out periodically: peaches, pudding, beans, milk, eggs, soups, and small cakes. Come to think of it, the eggs tasted better as a powder.

To our delight, we children often got a chocolate bar, an orange, or a banana. I had never seen a chocolate bar or chocolate candy filled with nuts before. Maybe these people called Amis were not so bad after all. It was hard for me to understand how complete strangers, who didn't even speak our language, were so good as to share their food with us. That was more than the local farmers were willing to do.

My introduction to chewing gum was a most painful experience. It was right after mealtime. An Ami was standing around waiting to drive the truck back. As I was leaving the line with stew in my bowl, he handed me a pack of candy. I thanked him and ran back to our bunk, hoping not to spill the contents of my cup. I unwrapped the candy from its silver paper. It smelled good, like the peppermint tea that we sometimes drank during the war. I put it in my mouth and, after a couple of chews, swallowed it. I finished off the complete pack. The following few days became a problem for me. I could not have a bowel movement. I had such a stomach ache that I doubled over into a ball. Mama told an Ami. He took us to a doctor, who asked me through an interpreter, "What did you eat the last two days?" I told him what I ate, including the candy an Ami had given me, some peppermint candy. I had to describe it, how long, how thin, and what it tasted like. "Whatever he gave me was wrapped in green and silver paper. I ate it."

Nurse and doctor laughed and laughed. The interpreter told Mama, "That candy is called chewing gum." All I was supposed to do was to chew it. When it loses its taste you can patch holes in shoes, hang pictures on the wall, and do other things with it.

"What do Amis do with their tasteless gum?" I asked.

"They stick it under tabletops and under chairs."

On the way out, I looked under a tabletop and saw all kinds of used-up gum glued to the wood. Revolting habit, I thought. The medication I had to take was nasty, but within a few hours I went to the bathroom and felt better.

* * *

I was nine years of age when I noticed the noises coming from the bed next to ours. We used a strung-up blanket for privacy again. Others did likewise. The only light came from a few bulbs way up in the ceiling. Men trickled in from the war. In fact, there were very few men who had returned from the war. They had spent weeks trying to find their wives and were extremely happy to be reunited. Invariably, once united, a fight would break out between husband and wife that could be heard throughout the ballroom. At night, I could hear the muffled sounds of filthy words coming from the men. Men talked or grunted during this nightly activity accompanied by a bed-squeaking sound. I could hear the heavy breathing and the rocking of the bed next to ours. At times, I thought it would come apart. I never heard the women say anything—only heavy breathing or whimpering.

I could not imagine what was going on. I heard few short sentences: "Move over, you fat cow." I tried to imagine how two big people could sleep in the same single bed. "You smell like a pig. When will you take a bath?" That man must be stupid, I thought. How is she going to take a bath when there are no facilities? "Don't get pregnant. You know what to do if you should get pregnant. We don't need another mouth to feed. Don't just lie there like a piece of wood." I must ask Mama what a woman was expected to do. The next morning women avoided going out or even leaving their beds. When one did come out from behind the partition, her face was all red and puffy with her eyes black and almost swollen shut. I asked Mama, "Is this what is going to happen to you when my Papa comes back from Siberia?" I received no answer, only a halting glance from Mama. Sex was a forbidden subject. There was no one to ask.

Kids had to get their fathers something to eat from the truck. The men were too proud to stand in line. They always wore a cool mask of bravado. Being up all night, they usually stayed behind the partitions and slept half the day. Later, they took walks and gathered cigarette butts that the Amis discarded. After a few days, the women's red faces turned to blue and purple. The nightly moaning and groaning throughout the huge ballroom continued.

"Mama, do you hear the noises at night?"

"Sure I do."

"What are they? Are people sick?"

"No."

"Is he beating her?"

"No, no. There is nothing wrong with the people. Besides, you are too young to know. A few years from now, when you get married, you will find out everything you need to know. Don't go around asking questions of other people or I will have to give you a spanking."

Right then and there I made up my mind that I would never marry. I never got a straight answer as to what happens between a man and a woman in bed. Sure wished I was older and knew all these things instead of being put off by Mama all the time.

Each day I awoke with great anticipation and much joy in my heart. I couldn't wait to begin exploring the city. Mama didn't care where I went as long as I was home for meals. Strolling along the Danube, I saw an old lady sitting on a bench sunning her face. I joined her and we started a conversation. She was a Real German. Her husband was dead. She had no children. She lived on the other side of the Danube. Where was I from? Well, I really couldn't say. (I must ask Mama where I was from now that the war had ended.) Her name was Frau Fuchs. Did I think Mama would let me come for lunch at her house every Monday? I thought she would. Frau Fuchs gave me her address with directions on how to get there. When I related all that to Mama, no, she didn't mind. Try to bring some leftovers back to her and Sister Erika. This is the first time in my life that I experienced pain and pleasure at the same time. The pain was from not being able to take my family. The pleasure was from sitting at a tablecloth-covered table, being served on good china, eating my first Bavarian dumplings, as big as a fist, with a prune in the center and served with sauerkraut. I lived for Mondays. Frau Fuchs showed me her doll collection. It was beautiful. I told her I only once had a toy in Kiev, a stuffed rabbit my oma had made.

"Would you like a doll?"

"Yes, thank you."

She rummaged through an old wooden box and came up with a doll. It was plastic, wore a dress, and had no hair.

"Ella, you can take a doll carriage as well. I have an extra one."

Going home that afternoon, I pushed the doll carriage with pride all the way home.

"Sister Erika," I said, "you can play with the doll and carriage when you want to, as long as you like."

Just a couple of nights later my doll and carriage, which had been standing next to Mama's bed, were missing. I searched and searched the whole ballroom until I found the doll carriage. I just rolled it back to our bed. I never found the doll.

I visited Frau Fuchs for weeks. There was never much food to bring home to Mama and Sister Erika except for a few homemade cookies.

My Monday lunches ended when Mama decided to take a trip.

* * *

Mama spoke very softly to our next-bunk-bed neighbor lady. Would she mind looking after Sister Erika and me for a few days? She was going to Straubing by train. The following morning after breakfast, a Monday morning, she told us she was leaving but would be back in a few days.

My heart sank. I was terrified. I just knew she was abandoning us. It was not uncommon that a mother simply left her kids and disappeared. My imagination worked overtime. I was very quiet and didn't cry. Sister Erika was screaming, clamoring onto Mama's skirt, and would not let go. Once the lady loosened Sister Erika's grip, Mama was gone. Now Sister Erika held onto me for dear life. I couldn't even go to the bathroom without her.

Mama never discussed anything with us. She always did what was best for us and I never questioned any decisions she made. I figured Mama knew best. Still, those were the longest five days I'd spent since my hospitalization for the measles in Regensburg. I was too worried to go to sleep, imagining all sort of things. Someone will come and steal us before Mama gets back. Maybe she sold us to someone. What happens to us if she doesn't come back? Will we be sent back to Russia without her? The lady who was commissioned to look after us made sure we didn't miss any meals and were in bed before dark. The noises at night, moaning, groaning, and bed-squeaking, took on monstrous proportions. I slept with Sister Erika in the lower bunk bed. Thinking about Mama made me shake so hard that Sister Erika asked, "Are you cold? Can't you stop shaking? I can't go to sleep." None of Mama's friends knew she was missing. No one ever asked, "Where is your mama?" Our days were spent sitting by the main entrance of the shelter, on the cold marble steps, waiting for her.

At last the day arrived and was almost gone when Mama showed up, to my relief and Sister Erika's great jubilation. She was carrying a small canvas shopping bag. I had to see what was in this new acquisition. It contained a dress, a comb, and a pair of underpants. I questioned her at every step to our bunk beds: Where had she been? What did she do? Her reply, "All in good time." After we had our handout evening meal, she took us for a short walk and told us that the next morning we would catch a train to Straubing. She mentioned something about a man she'd met. He had a daughter, and his mother was with them as well. It didn't make any sense. By the time we returned back to our beds, I was too mentally and physically exhausted to ask why we were going to Straubing. My last thought before going to sleep: Where is Straubing?

* * *

From the window of the train, everything looked nice, clean and green. It was the middle of October. Farmers were out plowing up their crops, with women and children following behind picking up potatoes or sugar beets. They carried small baskets that, when filled, were emptied onto the back of a horse-drawn wagon. But these people were not friendly anymore. They did not wave as they used to. There were no smiles or laughter on the train either.

"Mama, why are we going to Straubing?"

"We are going to Straubing so that you and your sister can have a new papa. You see, Ella, I don't think your papa is coming back. Now that the war is over, no one can come back from Russia. Most people were sent to Siberia, even whole families. The Russians need all the workers they can get. In order to have a normal life, since I am not trained to do any kind of work here in Germany, I need a man to take care of us. I heard from a friend that there was a man who is from almost the same place we are from, a place called Wolinien in Russia. He is living in Straubing. His name is Theodor Puder."

I did not believe it because everybody I had met so far in my life lied about where they came from and what they did, whether they had family, and even whether they were married.

"He is a stern and strict man," she continued. "You and your sister better do what he wants you to do because he will not stand for any back talk, questions, lying, or foolishness."

"Tell me more about this new family," I said.

"He has a daughter, Lida, younger than Sister Erika. His mother, Theresa, lives with them and takes care of Lida, whose mother died while giving birth on a horse-drawn cart coming to Germany during the winter with the German army retreating from Russia."

My first thought was, how did Theodor manage to come out of Russia with the retreating Germans, with his wife, daughter, and mother? All other men were in the army and separated from their families, some even in prison camps. I did not dare ask Mama.

We received permission to use a train going to Straubing free of charge by the ticket-counter man because the people in Passau were happy to get rid of any Refugees. We were a drain on the economy (per Mama). The train stopped at every little village. Finally, in the late afternoon, we arrived in Straubing.

* * *

The city of Straubing, on the Danube between Regensburg and Passau, was pretty much intact. There were but a few houses burned or demolished. It looked like the main war had passed it by.

We were met by Theodor, a very thin, medium-height, serious-looking man. Mama introduced us. With a little curtsy, I shook hands with my new papa-to-be. He took the beat-up suitcase, and slowly our bedraggled family of four headed toward our new home as a few streetlights came on. Looking at the people who came toward us, it occurred to me how the proud, clean, happy Real German people had changed from just a few months ago. Now they looked like us Refugees. Most were dirty, glum, and not talkative at all, looking at us with suspicion. They spoke in the Bavarian dialect I found challenging to understand. We walked at a slow pace with the narrow cobblestone streets echoing our every step.

Finally, we arrived at the Karmelitenkloster (Carmelite monastery). The monks looked very unhappy to see another bunch of Refugees standing at their door. The monastery had acquired only a few nicks during the war.

Meanwhile, it got dark. Entering the monastery, we could see that some Priest had lit oil lanterns at short intervals. We walked up two flights of squeaking stairs and along a long dark corridor. We were a noisy bunch, with each step on the old worn-out wooden floor announcing our presence. People came out from behind closed doors and just stood there staring at us, not saying a word.

We stopped at a door and Theodor went in first, followed by Mama. There were three beds in the room. I fell from sheer exhaustion onto one bed with Sister Erika beside me. I thought how good God was for creating sleep. If death were like sleeping, it really wouldn't be that bad to die. After a few whispered words with Mama, Theodor said, "Gute Nacht" (Goodnight) and closed the door. We slept in what we wore.

The next morning we awoke early to the smells and noises of women cooking, children laughing, and men walking with their heavy boots up and down the wooden stairs and hallway. Theodor brought in his mother, followed by our sister-to-be, Lida (short for Lydia). Oma was short, skinny, and slightly bent, mousy faced, with a long aristocratic nose, hair twisted into a single knot at the back of her neck. She wore all black and covered her head with a black kerchief. We were as much of a surprise to her as she was to us. It was an awkward situation. Lida was short and stout with a round face, rosy cheeks and big brown eyes. I tried to give her my hand and say, "Guten Morgen" (Good morning), but she moved out of sight, peeking out from behind her oma's skirt. Breakfast consisted of black bread and a strong tea that Oma had brewed.

Mama and Theodor left for a few hours. When they returned they announced they were married. It was 23 October 1945. The state marriage certificate read Elsa Ludwigowna Jeske-Schneider and Theodor Puder. Mama told me later she cut five years off her age in order to be the same age as Theodor, otherwise he would not have married her. He'd never know.

After the whole family was assembled, Papa sat down on a bed and said, "We are a family now. Mama will be called Mama. Oma will be called Mutter"—("Mother" in German)—"and if you and Sister Erika want to, you can call me Papa. Do you and your sister want to change your last name to mine, Puder?"

"Yes, we will call you Papa," I answered.

I thought for a few minutes, remembering my real papa, and said no to the name change. Sister Erika and I had to stay with our old papa's name.

My reasoning was simple. If we took our new papa's name, then whenever our old papa came back from Siberia he would not be able to find us.

When Mama was alone I said, "Mama, why did you get married? My papa will have no family when he returns from Siberia."

Mama replied, "Ella, your papa will never come back. We will not have much of a life here in Germany, being Volga Deutsche and Refugees. If we ever get a chance to emigrate to America, Australia, or Canada, we must have a family. I must have a husband with an occupation. Theodor is skilled."

I was astonished to hear Mama saying the word America.

* * *

After a few days being cooped up in the monastery, I told Mama I needed to go out and look around. Our new home was about a block from the Danube River bridge, adjacent to a small castle that was completely filled with Refugees. The monastery was enclosed by a high brick wall. Attached to our monastery on one side was a beautiful gothic church. On the other side there was a brewery (Karmelitenbrauerei) where the monks made their own beer from hops donated by the faithful. The monks didn't care for us at all. Walking around in their brown hooded robes, looking at us children with mean eyes, forever telling us to get away from whatever and not touch this or that, they were like policemen. The apples that the farmers brought them were given to kids who were Catholic. We were not Catholic and had no intentions of becoming Catholic. No apple. There was a very old priest who carried a batch of apples in deep pockets under his robe. He motioned to us girls to come and hug and let him kiss us, then we would get an apple. Desperate for an apple, I let him kiss me. It was nasty and wet. First I spit, then I wiped my mouth on the hem of my dress. It was disgusting. I resolved, no more kissing a priest, but I did get my apple.

The Carmelites busied themselves to find a place for us Refugees so that they could clear their monastery of all the riffraff. Early one morning, a few horse-drawn wagons that the monks borrowed from their Catholic faithful were parked in the street in front of the monastery. A monk knocked on each door and in a somewhat loud voice said, "Pack and get out." Some women questioned him: "Why are we being evicted?" In short sentences he answered, "We need our monastery. You are going to be taken to a new place three miles outside of Straubing."

I was excited that I would get to ride on a wagon to a place I was sure would be heaven. I looked happily into the future. All I could think about was that this would be a start-all-over-again camp. Our friends and neighbors didn't know much about the camp or its location. All they knew was that it was three miles out of town traveling on the Ittlinger Strasse, then the Schlesische Strasse parallel to the Danube River. We were assigned an apartment. A policeman (a Real German) pedaled into the camp, stopped at each apartment entrance, and announced that within three days all families had to register at the police station in Straubing. *Flüchtlinge* was stamped across our official papers. There was no running away from the label. Papa inquired at the police station about our camp. The explanation was that "Hofstetten" used to be a German army training camp. But then, we never believed anything we were told by anybody.

The camp was built like a horseshoe, with one entrance. There were fourteen single-story wooden army barracks and two outhouses. The outhouses were partitioned, with separate entrances for men and women, and could seat six people on each side. We had to take our own paper, if there was any: paper from the butcher or the fish man, or an old magazine that we picked up in the trash in town, read, then tore the pages out of to use in the outhouse.

The barracks were built out of single boards with a crawl space underneath from one end to the other. No insulation whatsoever. Families with children were allocated a three-room apartment, which was furnished with German army wooden beds with smelly straw mattresses.

Each barrack had three entrances. The first entrance led to two apartments, one with two rooms and one with three. We were lucky enough to get the apartment with three rooms. The Riemer family, with three children, lived on the other side of our entrance. One bedroom was for Sister Erika and me. It was the size of a walk-in closet. We slept in a single army bed. One room was my parents,' and one was the kitchen/living room. In the next entrance, the middle entrance, Sister Lida and Mutter had one room of a three-room apartment. They had two army cots and a potbellied stove. Frau Dinter, a woman with two children who was waiting for her husband to come home from the war, occupied a second room of the apartment. In the third room lived an old man called Herr Lux. He was digging a bomb shelter underneath his room for years, throwing shovelfuls of dirt out his window. Mama said, "Mark my word, one day the whole barrack will disappear into that hole." Both three-room apartments off the third entrance were occupied by the Schneiker family, with seven children and her parents.

Mama and Papa went out daily, like the rest of the Refugees, and scrounged whatever the Real Germans discarded. The dump was visited regularly. We acquired a beat-up woodburning stove, and Mama and Papa brought home a metal-frame double bed for their bedroom. Papa's bike was scrounged, piece by piece, from the local dump. It was a man's bike with the bar running from seat to handlebars.

At night the bedbugs were waiting for us. There was no hiding from our head lice and fleas. They were our constant companions. Nothing, but nothing, worked to eliminate them completely. Even if Mama missed just one louse or one nit during our daily delousing session, it took only a few hours for the creatures to multiply and feed on my scalp.

It was my chore to take out the Fass, the half-barrel chamberpot, which, unlike the one we used in Kiev, did not have a lid. We used it only at night in the summertime, but both day and night during the winter. In the daytime Mama also deposited all kitchen scraps in it. The accumulation of human waste, food scraps, and dishwater kept in a warm room for twelve to eighteen hours smelled unbelievably bad. Windows were frozen shut and our trips in and out of the house were limited because we could not let the warm air out, even if it smelled nasty.

I carried the contents to the outhouse about forty-five yards away. It was heavy and I had to walk very slowly so as not to spill a drop. God forbid it splashed on my clothing. Sometimes the snowdrifts were so high that the emptying was delayed until midday or even until evening. After emptying, the chamberpot had to be washed or it would smell even worse. There was no other way than to use ice water from the well and a little brush to remove the half-inch-thick paste coating before bringing the pot back into the kitchen. Neighbors who happened to come to borrow something, never to be paid back, didn't complain about the horrible odor because their kitchens were in the same situation.

The well, a short distance from our barrack, was just a hole in the ground with a bucket tied to a long rope. It was dangerous to draw water from it while standing in wooden clogs on two feet of accumulated ice around the opening. My hands were almost frozen by the time I returned to the warm kitchen.

Besides the stove, our kitchen was furnished with an army cot, a rickety table, and two chairs. Sister Erika and I sat on the cot when we ate. In one corner was the Fass. Papa built a bench the length of the room right under the window. It held his tools and served as a workbench, as well as a place to wash dishes. Its bottom shelf provided a storage area.

Begging for bread or milk became my occupation. I would walk into the nearest village, knock on a door, and say, "Could you give me a piece of bread and maybe some milk?" Most of the time a piece of bread was grudgingly given; milk almost never. If they didn't give me anything, I stole whatever I could find to eat. We had been forced to steal whatever we could that was unattended, edible, or useable. Then we started to receive food stamps. Mama was happy that I didn't have to beg or steal anymore.

* * *

When Papa went out for a walk, a neighbor lady came over and asked Mama to read the cards (Karten legen) for her. Mama used a regular deck of cards. I was there to listen and learn. I watched her telling fortunes to strangers, neighbors, or friends, and more than once, over time, the predictions came true. Some people came back to tell Mama that this or that had really happened. So I took a special interest in her trade. As I grew older, I told her I wanted to learn to tell fortunes. She showed me what each card meant and how to read it. Most of the readings were the same:

Your husband is a prisoner of war in Russia.
He is dead.
Your kids are giving you trouble.
You are going on a trip (by foot to the next village).
You will have a tooth pulled.
You will have a fight with your husband (if she had one).

Most of her predictions had a very general time frame: they would happen sometime in the person's life, not at a specific time. The pretty girls would always marry an American and go to America. The old people would have an illness. A married woman whose husband was missing in action was encouraged by Mama to find someone else because the likelihood of him coming back from the Russian front or a Russian prison camp after all these years was nil.

Mama's predictions gave me pause to wonder if God knew what would happen to us. If He was the only one who decided whether I lived or died. Maybe Mama was close to God, like a messenger, the go-between, she could relate the future to the people. Surely there was nothing wrong with that?

People paid Mama with food or sometimes a few yards of material. Other times she even got some money. All this came to a screeching halt one day when Papa came home early and caught Mama. He waited until the lady left then threw a fit. He did not want the devil living in his house. He considered fortune telling the devil's work. She stopped telling fortunes after that. I often wondered if Mama had a real gift to foretell the future. I don't know. But Papa put an end to the practice, and my dream of becoming a fortune-telling lady vanished.

* * *

Living in different camps, being bombed out and having to move on, I never really started or finished any kind of grade or learned much of anything in school. I had gone to school briefly in Regensburg and in Passau only from January 1944 to May 1945. The thing I most enjoyed was singing marching songs, while wearing a white blouse and mustard-colored skirt. It didn't matter what the words were. All that mattered to me was that I was accepted. Someday I would look like the girls and boys on the posters. I wouldn't have to worry or lie about where I came from anymore. Mama wouldn't have to tell fortunes to make money. We would have pretty dresses to wear and a nice house like Real Germans. I felt wonderful sitting in class with all those Real German children. Whatever it took, I would be one of them. That had been all wishful thinking during the war. Now, after the war, I was determined to fit in.

Ittling was a small village about three miles east of Camp Hofstetten. The school was located next to a medium-sized gothic church surrounded by a large cemetery. The little village did not take any direct bomb hits during the war, and the Ami soldiers hadn't found anything of interest in Ittling to shoot at as they drove their vehicles through it on their way to Straubing, where they encountered pockets of resistance.

I was surprised the school had separate rooms for each grade. It was also divided by gender, girls in one room and boys in another. It soon became apparent that those of us from the camp were far behind the Real Germans in every subject. Little did they realize just how far we had come and how much we had lost. The Real German kids also looked much better than we ever did. Girls wore clean aprons daily. I had to make do with only one apron for school for the whole week, and the same went for my dress.

During our midmorning break, I walked into the church cemetery and ate my dried piece of bread while seated on someone's grave. Everyone was scared to go into the cemetery because of all the dead people. That never frightened me.

The cemetery looked like a beautiful flower garden. Family members tended it religiously every week. They planted fresh flowers with the seasons. In the wintertime they made decorations from dried flowers, straw, pine cones, and chips of bark. Mulling things over, I sat there and wondered: Where did these Real Germans get the money to spend so much on flowers? We didn't have enough for a good lunch. It was obvious the Real Germans didn't like us at all and had no use for us. We were labeled "failures" no matter how hard we tried, "awkward" in how we did things, and "stupid" for not understanding their dialect. Of course, we were homely-looking because we could not afford store-bought or professionally tailored dresses. Oh, how I wanted to be like them!

We stole whatever we could from the farmers: early potatoes right out of the ground, cabbages covered with straw and dirt and stored in the fields from the previous fall, and whatever else we might pass on the way home from school. After about three months the village people got together and decided they didn't want us to be in their school anymore. Their children were good children. We were a bad influence.

A barrack was converted into a school at Camp Hofstetten in the spring of 1946. It was furnished with old benches, one bench for each grade, eight in all, with a blackboard and a desk for the teacher. At the grand opening of our school our new teacher, Herr Lehrer Mohr (Mister Teacher Mohr, the formal title by which we addressed him), told us how grateful we should be to the people of Ittling. They cared for us so much that they had furnished our school. In reality, they wanted us to have our own school so we wouldn't come into their village.

Herr Lehrer Mohr was one of us, a Refugee. He had served in the German army, but by his accent we knew he was not a Real German. We never learned where he came from. He was crazy. He always screamed at us and applied severe physical punishment for the most minor infractions of his rules. Speaking was not permitted. Speak only when spoken to. He had a big stick and if he couldn't catch you (boys tried to outrun him), he threw whatever he had in his hand. He always managed to hit his intended victim. One day I talked back to him and he threw a key ring with a dozen keys at me. It hit the side of my head. By the time I arrived home, the swelling was obvious.

"What happened to you?"

"Nothing, Mama."

Mama to Sister Erika: "What happened to your sister?"

"She talked back to the teacher."

Mama called upon Papa to support the teacher. He promptly complied. The next morning I left for school with a big knot on the side of my head and a swollen face. Herr Lehrer Mohr ordered me to come up front so he could use me as an example: "This is what happens to you when you talk back to your teacher."

Herr Lehrer Mohr didn't have a family in camp. If he'd ever had one, we never knew about it. In a way, he was handsome. All the married women whose husbands had not come back from the war and most of the girls eighteen and older were enamored with him. He never dated. I thought he was old, half-bald, at least forty.

We had no books. All books used during the war years had disappeared. We had to write down everything Herr Lehrer Mohr said on lined paper that we bought from him for a penny per sheet. Our homework was to transcribe our class notes, every page, into intelligible German. We were graded on handwriting, sentence structure, punctuation, spelling, and drawing. Every day he dictated a long poem for us to recite from memory. The hardest memory work was "Das Lied der Glocke" (The Song of the Bell) by Friedrich von Schiller, two pages at a time until all fourteen pages were memorized.

Some of the boys didn't take Herr Lehrer Mohr very seriously—until they felt the stick on their backs or behinds. The stick was a constant reminder of who was in charge. It took only a couple of "corrections" and everybody made sure to memorize the lessons. The sheets were to be handed in for grading. We created a book for each subject: German, math, history, science, and Bavarian cooking. Never once was the war or Hitler mentioned. Once the newspapers and the magazines started coming out again, we had to cut out pictures to add to the different subjects. Some of my friends whose sisters were running around with Amis thought they had it made. Only once did they come to school with ballpoint pens. Our teacher told us that picking up whatever the Amis dropped or gave us would blow us up one day (ballpoint pens were filled with explosives and would take off most of our fingers). Herr Lehrer Mohr insisted that using ballpoint pens in his classroom was strictly forbidden. Besides, they ruined your handwriting. With a bad script who would hire you? Yes, he had seen Ami handwriting. It was so bad he could not read it. I kept thinking, where did he see an Ami write?

Ironclad rules: no ballpoint pens, no chewing gum, and a constant admonition to "remember you are Germans and don't take handouts from the Amis." He would go on a tirade, saying, "Don't we Germans have any pride left?" He never smiled. He always had a red and sour face.

I had suppressed feelings of anger and disappointment in my life so far. Here I became happy because now I made friends and could go anywhere I wanted. One of my new friends was Giesela Schwarzer, who lived in an adjacent barrack and came from a family with eighteen children. I asked Giesela, who was my age, why her parents had so many children. "Because they were singled out by Hitler himself and received a special recognition medal called the Mutterkreuz" (Mother's Cross). It was true. Good German mothers received a bronze Mutterkreuz for having four children, a silver one for having six, and a gold one for having eight. Giesela's parents received the highest award with pride. "My parents never had to work, and my papa didn't have to go to war," she said. When I asked Mama about these "breeding" families, she said, "They were always given the best of everything: housing, food, clothing, and schooling for their children. Old people even had to give up their seats on the bus or streetcar. They were treated like royalty with the greatest respect. No standing in line for them. At the butcher shop the best cuts of meat would go into their baskets. A helper or nurse was assigned by the government to help them take care of the brood and arrived first thing in the morning."

Now they were reduced to our status of collecting food stamps and whatever else they could steal, struggling for their very existence. Now even Hitler's medal didn't help.

* * *

With no shoes available, old or new, Papa made Pantoffeln (wooden clogs) for the family. He carved a piece of wood to shape for the sole and nailed a piece of soft leather across the top. The leather came from old shoes scrounged at the dump. Our toes stuck out.

When the river began to melt, Mutter and I walked on its banks and collected the branches that washed ashore or were tangled up with the shrubs that grew there. The banks of the river were reinforced with big granite boulders. It was almost impossible to walk, much less jump, in our homemade shoes from rock to rock to reach the water's edge, where the driftwood was. In order to avoid skinned or broken knees, we had to be careful. Papa nailed strips of bicycle inner tube to the bottoms of our clogs to keep us from sliding. The driftwood was wet and very heavy. Mutter carried some rope in the pocket of her long black skirt. We busied ourselves by following the raging river until we collected a good pile each. She tied the branches together in two bundles and we each carried one on our backs. There was no stopping on the way home because it was too difficult to load the bundles on our backs again.

In the back of each barrack was a grassy lawn that each family used as a vegetable garden. The contents of our nightly chamberpot were used as fertilizer. In the winter, if I could not make it to the outhouse with the filled chamberpot, I just dumped the contents in the garden. Since all the neighbors did the same thing, you could see these big brown frozen spots on the white snow in the back of each barrack until the spring thaw. Then the garden would be turned over and the spring planting begun. When the spring thaw came and the windows were opened, the air was horribly polluted with the stench of human waste. It permeated everything. It seemed to me that Mama and Papa never noticed or talked about it, and neither did anyone else in the camp except me.

After the Lindenbaum (lime tree) bloomed, we plucked off the blossoms. Mama dried them in the sun on an old yellow newspaper then saved them in a burlap bag. We used them for tea for months, but it was always a race with the mice and the rats. Tea was brewed in the soup pot.

Mama cooked the best meals ever on the old rusty stove. We lived on a limited menu. Mama always started with a pot of water. She only had to cook for herself, Papa, Sister Erika, and me. For breakfast we had bread and tea. Lunch was a piece of bread spread with nasty-smelling cod liver oil. Dinner consisted of soup and bread. No leftovers. We gathered sorrel in the spring, at least three times a week. Its skinny, dark green leaves tasted slightly sour (Sauerampfer). It grew on the side of the road. After the leaves were washed many times and chopped, they were added to the boiling water with a few potatoes. This was my favorite soup.

Papa built a small wooden shed from scrounged boards right outside the bedroom window. We raised two rabbits in it. In no time, they multiplied to twelve. It was my job every day after school to cut succulent dandelions for their meals. Burlap bag and small knife in hand, I headed to the Danube, sometimes with my girlfriends Herta Schlolaut and/or Gerda Schwarzer (no relation to Giesela Schwarzer and her family of eighteen kids). Before long we filled the bag, talking and joking and discussing our lives and all the "what ifs." If there was no horse meat to be bought, a rabbit would be slaughtered.

The outhouse was cleaned out twice a year. Early in the spring Herr Beckmann's handyman loaded a metal drum attached to the back of his horse-drawn wagon. With a coffee can fastened to a long sturdy stick, he dipped into the toilet, then emptied the can into the barrel. When the barrel was full he led the horse and wagon to a nearby field. Invariably, he left a trail of feces and maggots after each wagonload. Mama closed the windows for the day. At the field he opened a small hole in the bottom of the barrel and the manure oozed out as the horse walked down each row. The hired hand whose unpleasant job it was walked very slowly up and down the field, not missing a spot, until it was all well saturated. Manure was not wasted. After the soil was turned I couldn't smell the human waste anymore.

I feared my new papa. He was a medium-size man, skinny and gaunt. No matter how much he ate, his cheeks always sunk into his face. He had deep-set brown eyes with dark circles underneath, thin sandy brown hair, and a good tan even in the winter. When he laughed, he always sucked the air in through his teeth. His laughter was inhaling rather than exhaling, which gave it a hissing sound. His beatings started right away. He looked like a madman with his long hair flying in his eyes, spewing nasty words with foul-smelling breath and spit flying everywhere. Even for a minor delay in obeying his command "Go and buy beer," meaning right this minute, brought a beating with his belt or his fists, which felt to me like they were made from steel.

He hated everybody. He blamed the Jews for starting the war. The Russians for killing his first wife. The Germans for losing the war. The Americans for getting into the war and bombing Germany. Most of all, the Communists who would continue to pursue him to the end of the world.

Mama did her wifely duty, never, God forbid, disagreeing. She never complained even when he beat her. She wouldn't even cry out: couldn't have the neighbors or we children hear her. The following day, the only telltale sign was her distorted face, red and swollen, but not a sound or complaint. The women all around us fared no better. Men, those who came home from the war, were in control and letting out their frustrations on their families. Occasionally I found Mama crying, with bruises on her chest and around her neck.

"Mama ," I asked, "how did you get the red spots?"

No answer. A few days later they turned blue and black.

Same question, "Mama, what happened to you?"

"Now that I made my bed I will sleep in it," she finally answered. To change the subject she said, "You are too little to understand. We must get out of Germany because we have no future here as Refugees. You children have no future here. The Germans want us to go back to Russia. But who wants to go back to Russia, to Communism? We hate the Russians worse than death." She never explained her bruises.

Mama was a saint. She accepted his abuse physically and mentally, never complaining.

1946

In Germany the saying goes, "Women are created for three things, the three K's: Kirche, Kinder, und Küche" (meaning church, children, and kitchen). In my child's mind I thought surely I was created for more than these three things. Seeing how brutally the men treated their women, I never wanted to get married. I promised myself that I would not be beaten or abused by a man. But that meant no children and no cooking. The only thing left was the church.

Papa had to have cigarettes. It was my job to supply him with cigarette butts (Kippen sammeln). With much apprehension and shame, I made my way into Straubing to scavenge them after school and on weekends. Sometimes, when I was lucky, I found a whole cigarette or one cigarette overlooked in a pack that was crushed and thrown in the gutter. I spent the daylight hours walking around town picking up cigarette butts and window-shopping.

Women were out in the street each day sweeping in front of their damaged homes. Since all the rubble had been removed in some cases, they swept only dust. The rubble was transported to the outskirts of town and eventually formed a mountain. The mountain was then covered with dirt, and in some areas trees were planted. The little wagons that during the war years were used to transport old people, children, and their belongings now carried bricks, wood, groceries, milk cans, and all kinds of other things.

It was fun to be downtown. The outdoor restaurants did a brisk business with beer, coffee, and cake. Some Gasthauses had small bands playing outside. I'd stop to listen and admire ladies chatting over drinks, wearing old-fashioned hats and pretty dresses. Where did they get the money to buy those pretty things? Were they carried over from the war? Sometimes we did not have enough money to buy bread. We were fighting for our mere existence while the Real Germans were having beer, wine, coffee with cake, smoking cigars or cigarettes, and generally having a good time. How could the Real Germans lose the war and yet live so well? During times like these I wondered just where I belonged. What would happen to me? Where would I find direction for my life? Would I always be an outsider? Talking to my girlfriends was no help. They had no answers, and furthermore, they were not concerned with the future. They didn't come from Russia. The future would take care of itself. It seemed to me that the pattern of my life was set to be a Refugee forever. Whenever someone asked me where I was from, I answered "Poland." Knowing full well how the Germans hated the Russians, just saying I was born in Russia would give them another reason to hate me.

When I returned home from gathering cigarette butts, Mama had saved me something to eat. Papa was pleased. He sat at the rickety table, opened all the butts, and placed the loose tobacco in a little pile until he had enough to make a whole cigarette. The rest was stuffed into a very small pouch. Then he rolled the tobacco, using a piece of paper that we brought from the butcher or an old newspaper I found in town, and smoked it with such a contented look on his face. Smoking made him happy. After the first few inhales he'd start coughing uncontrollably, while insisting that this was the best cigarette he'd had in a long time. Yes, the Amis knew how to make cigarettes. He had to give them that.

For my tenth birthday Mama made a cake out of lumpy mashed potatoes decorated with raw and boiled carrots, slices of cucumber, and red beets cut so that they resembled roses. Since the beets were boiled, they were placed on the cake right before serving. If left too long on the mashed potatoes they would have bled and turned the whole cake pink. We licked our plates so clean sometimes it was hard to tell if they were ever used.

On laundry day everyone had to get up with the sun. Mama was already boiling water outside in a huge pot. I could not understand why Mama was so secretive when doing some of the laundry. The stench coming from one of the rusty cans underneath the counter did not escape my sensitive nose. One day I took the lid off the can, only to find a few rags and old, dark, bloody water.

"Mama, what is this?"

"Children who want all the answers will get old too fast. Is that what you want?"

"No."

"Whenever you get old enough, in a year or two, I will explain it to you."

Every month she spent a lot of time washing those rags, rubbing them for a long time on the washboard and then boiling them in the big pot outdoors. When the rags were white as snow, she hung them on the nearest shrub to dry. All the neighbor women would admire her white wash. When stains or spots were visible, the neighbors always talked about one another, saying things like, "What a dirty kitchen she must keep if she can't even have white laundry."

Mama's face was round as the full moon and she was getting fatter every day until her dresses almost didn't fit. The rusty can of foul-smelling water disappeared. She smiled a lot. No more bruises on her face and chest. She and Papa spent many Saturday evenings in the local Gasthaus. The last day in July she became very ill. She was so pale and complained her stomach cramped. She needed a doctor. Papa took her on his bike. She sat on the crossbar in front of him. It was about three miles to the hospital. They were gone for hours. When Papa returned he was by himself. He carried a bottle of vodka on the back of the bike.

"Where's Mama?" I asked.

"She's in the hospital. She's fine. I have a son now." Papa beamed with pride. In the warm July evening, he went outside, gathering our male neighbors to share the good news and pass the bottle around. Mutter and Sister Lida came over to join Sister Erika and me. The four of us sat on the cot and the two chairs talking about this big surprise, a brother.

For the next two weeks Mutter cooked for all of us. Sometimes we had brown soup. The flour was browned, added to water, brought to a boil and some lard added, with salt and pepper to taste. It looked and tasted like thin gravy. Papa pedaled his bike to the hospital daily. Our new addition was named Edward Otto after Papa's brother. Papa paid one of the farmers to bring Mama and Brother Otto from the hospital with his horse and wagon. Mama arrived with a bottle of alcohol and some cotton that had been given to her at the hospital for the baby. She didn't know what to do with the alcohol. Papa did. He made vodka (like my real papa had done back in Russia) and consumed it almost in one sitting. The cotton I used for my runny ears.

Brother Otto was a little pink beautiful baby boy. When he was nursing on Mama's big breast, I could hardly see his little face. Would I ever get big breasts like Mama to nurse a baby? I took care of him as if he was my own.

I was thinking back to the hotel ballroom in Passau. I had a doll. She was plastic, wore a dress, and had no hair. Within a few days she was stolen from my bed. Little Brother Otto became my doll. Mama was ecstatic and very proud of her boy.

His diapers were not changed very often. Dirty diapers were placed in an old can outside the front door until Mama ran out and it was an absolute necessity to wash them. Washdays became more numerous. First, Mama had me fill the chamberpot. She rinsed the diapers in it and poured the water out of her bedroom window into the vegetable garden. After I watched Mama a couple of times, it became my job to wash, boil, and rinse diapers. I tried to pinch my nose in order not to smell them. It didn't work because I had to have two hands to wash and diaper the baby. When I complained that I could not handle the smell and sight of a full diaper, Mama said, "Ella, this is only milk, breast milk. How can it be all that bad?" I was amazed how affectionate Mama could be, how she kissed, loved, and cradled her precious son. Papa was starting to talk about teaching Brother Otto all these different occupations—carpentry, weaving, making shoes. Since we couldn't afford a baby carriage, Papa made one out of willow branches. He fashioned them into a big oval basket and attached four small wheels scrounged from the dump. Sister Erika and I could take Brother Otto anywhere for a walk, even all the way to the Danube. On special occasions when Mama and Papa were seated outside, Sister Lida walked him around the camp. Papa busied himself weaving all kinds of baskets that Mama could use in the kitchen. Mama became the envy of the camp. I was happy we had a baby buggy because I didn't have to carry Brother Otto. I could take him everywhere. On my long walks to steal apples or potatoes from the fields, the stolen goods were hidden underneath the straw mattress. Nobody ever thought about checking a baby carriage.

Since Herta, Gerda, and I had chores to do, we had few opportunities for playing games. Whenever time permitted, we did play ball. Using two balls, which were the size of tennis balls, we'd take turns throwing them against a barrack wall. Both balls were moving at the same time, like a juggling act. It took a lot of practice and coordination to do it well. If you dropped one ball, the next person took over. This game could be played alone or with friends. Mama hated it.

"Ella, when will you grow up and do something productive?"

My reply: "I don't want to knit socks anymore."

The threats became actions. "You come in and knit or you'll get it."

I did.

Most of the time we hid and played ball at the other end of the camp. "Ella, Ella," Mama yelled, and everyone in camp knew she was looking for me. If I didn't come in right away she sent Sister Erika to look for me. Sister Erika also played ball and she knew exactly where to find me. Once I arrived home, I got it from Mama across the face. I was always thankful to God that Papa wasn't home.

Other games that we liked to play were hopscotch and jump rope. I kept thinking there had to be more to life than this existence. But what? There was no one to ask.

Fall arrived too soon for me. I asked, "Mutter, can I go with you today?"

"If you bring Theodor's bike and a burlap bag, you can come along," she said to my delight.

The sun had not come up yet when a knock on the window awakened me. Mutter, who was hard of hearing yelled, "Are you ready?"

I jumped out of bed, put on my old everyday dress, and slipped into my Pantoffeln. Taking a piece of bread from the cold oven—the only place safe from the mice—quietly, in the dark, I left the barrack. When we hit the main road I started off with, "Mutter, tell me about life in Russia," a land bigger than my mind could comprehend. Mutter was as old as my oma, but shorter and skinny. I loved to hear Mutter talk about when she was a girl growing up in Russia. How she courted and when she got married and about her seven children. Only one lived now, Theodor.

In her sad monotone voice she began, "I never thought that I would end up in a place like Germany, where we are reduced to begging, lying, cheating, and stealing. I tell you, Ella, we will never be accepted here in Germany. Never." She continued, "Since we speak a pure German, without a specific dialect, they know right away we are not natives. These people here live a pampered life, always have enough money and never have to work as hard as we did in Russia. I lived in a place called Wolinien. It was a place where not many Russians could be found. We had German schools, German Gasthauses, and German churches. We were all landowners and had many acres of land and livestock. Once a week our oldest son took the butter, fruits, vegetables, and boots for sale to the local bazaar. August, my husband, was a cobbler. For miles around he was known for making the softest shoes and boots. He used pigskin soaked in human urine to make it soft and flexible, then dyed them black or red. We used the money to buy things from a list that I prepared, like salt, sugar, and yards of material."

Silence followed the last statement, then she would wipe away a few tears, blow her nose on the inside hem of her skirt, and say, "Those were the good days."

We had been walking for a couple of miles before the sun came up. Mutter commented, "It is going to be a hot day."

My feet were beginning to hurt, as well as my arms and hands. Holding onto the handlebars of the bike gave me blisters. I said, "Mutter, where are we going and how long will it be before we get there?"

"See that farmhouse in the distance? That is where we are going. Today we are going to get straw."

When fall came and the farmers were harvesting their wheat, we would go and beg for straw. Mutter headed to the nearest hamlet. If allowed, we filled our burlap bags, placed them on the bicycle, and then pushed it home. It took many trips, begging at different farms all over the area, in order to replace the contents of four mattresses. I did not like the new straw even though it smelled good. It poked through the mattress cover and pricked my body. There was no sheet to separate my skin from the new straw, only the burlap mattress cover. It took months before the straw flattened itself out and was good to sleep on.

* * *

My dream all these years was finally to come to fruition: to get to know Jesus and His mother, to whom I had prayed millions of Hail Marys in the bomb shelters. One of the empty barracks was converted into a church on Sunday mornings. All the partitions were taken out and two rooms were made into one. I was very excited to go and hear of all these people about whom Mutter told me children's Bible stories.

The Catholic service was at 8:00 A.M. on Sunday and the Lutheran service at 10:00 A.M. A pastor from Straubing came on his bike, put on his black robe, and led all the women, children, and very few men in our Lutheran service. The first time I attended, I was very disappointed. Our pastor didn't wear beautiful robes like the Catholic priests. Our cross was bare. Likewise, the altar was a plain wooden table with the Bible. It was a very simple, solemn, and joyless service. No one made the sign of the cross. There was no Communion. No one prayed Hail Mary. I had watched the Catholic service, standing by the open door. The Catholic priests, dressed in elegant regalia, brought apples and pears for their kids. Our Lutheran pastor brought nothing. They had lighted candles, Jesus on the cross, prayed Hail Mary, and crossed themselves over and over. It was such a contrast. Now more than ever, I wanted to be a Catholic.

A few days before Christmas, Papa helped himself to a fir tree from Herr Beckman's nearby woods. He nailed it to the bench. After Brother Otto went to bed, Sister Erika and I decorated the tree with small apples, pecans, and cookies that Mama had baked. We added cotton for snow puffs and cut out paper snowflakes. Six small candles were placed between the branches without holders. The tree was topped with a homemade paper star. After we went to bed, Mama placed our presents under the tree. Knitted hats, scarves, mittens, and socks had no names on them. We just picked out what we liked. We also received a store-bought orange wrapped in tinfoil paper. Sister Lida and Mutter came over the following morning to share in the festivities and the lighting of the candles. Holidays were celebrated with a "Himmel und Erde" (heaven and earth) dish. It consisted of mashed potatoes and applesauce.

I looked forward to Christmas and going to the Catholic cathedral midnight mass in town. I gathered with my girlfriends and a few boys and walked to St. Jakob Kirche in Straubing. Churches were not heated except for the first ten pews. A small electric wire ran the length of each pew. It was turned on while the church service was in progress, then turned off. By the time we arrived, the church was filled with people. The midnight Christmas mass was beautiful with the glow of hundreds of candles, dried flower arrangements, and the smell of incense. I felt that God lived in this particular church. (Always wondering, What about all the other churches in the world?) I did not understand the Catholic service, and neither did my Lutheran friends. It was conducted in Latin. The Bibles were in Latin as well. I was sure the Real Germans understood. Why would people come to church and not understand anything the priest said?

After the service, which lasted at least an hour and a half, and by the time we wandered through the cemetery adjoining the church enjoying the scenery, it was close to 3:00 A.M. I loved the cemetery tour. Most of the graves were decorated with very small Christmas trees, with miniature ornaments and little bitty candles flickering in the wind. The whole cemetery was transformed into a winter wonderland. As far as my eyes could see, candles were glowing through the falling snow. Families assembled around the grave of a loved one. Staring back from the gravestones were embedded pictures of men in army uniforms. At times like these, I always mourned my poor oma. Did anyone put a tiny Christmas tree on her grave?

On the walk back home we sang Christmas songs at the top of our lungs. The boys wanted to sing German army marching songs. To appease them we ended up with Hitler songs. We joked and talked about our dreams and our wishful futures. Our camp was three miles from town, no woods, just flat farmland. There were no streetlights and only five houses along the way. We got caught in a blinding snowstorm. Holding onto each other, we battled against the howling wind-driven snowflakes. We were grateful when one of the five houses left a light on, our only marker. I arrived home half frozen and soaking wet. Mama said the midnight mass would be the death of me.

1947

Our camp school had two new teachers, Herr Lehrer Bahle and Fräulein Dimmelmeier. They were both Real Germans, living in town in their own houses, whereas Herr Lehrer Mohr lived with us in barrack number one.

Students were divided by age. After a few months, we were separated again by how much we knew. Separated again, then again, all depending on how you progressed in your studies. When elevated to the next grade you moved back on the benches, in most cases from the first row to the second or third row.

The war had not been kind to Herr Lehrer Bahle. His left eye was glass and watered constantly. He had been shot through the palm of his right hand. He held his crayon or pencil between his thumb and middle finger. He came to school on his bike wearing short leather pants held in place by leather suspenders, a white short-sleeved shirt, and a dark green felt hat, the Bavarian national dress for men and boys. The pants were never washed, and unless you gained a lot of weight, you never had to buy a new pair in your lifetime. This was a status symbol. Years of accumulation of dirt, water, and grease made the leather very soft and pliable. In the winter he wore three-quarter-length pants made out of deerskin. They reached right below his knees and were in the same condition as the shorts. A pair of hand-knitted wool knee socks reached up to meet the pants. He wore regular shoes. When the snow got too deep, he walked from Straubing rather than use his bike. He never talked about the war or about his family. When we asked any of the returned men, "Where did you fight?" or "Did you fight the Amis?" the answer was almost always, "No, I fought the Russians on the eastern front," and that was the answer given by Herr Lehrer Bahle. He was very likable and soft-spoken, with some meat on his bones. He was my favorite teacher, no comparison to Herr Lehrer Mohr, who was a yeller with a big mouth. Up to now I knew only a few songs, German army marching songs and Christmas songs. Herr Lehrer Bahle, who played the flute and liked to sing, taught us German children's songs and Bavarian folk songs.

Mama found a peppermint plant in the market place one day. She started to grow her own mint for tea. What a pleasant change from the Lindenblü-tentee. Mama was also blessed with four chickens, bantams, with a beautiful little rooster in charge, that she bought one Friday at the Farmers Market. The little rooster got up too early to wish everybody a good morning. The neighbors complained. His life was short. One of the brownish speckled hens found a good place to lay eggs. She would fly in Mama's open bedroom window, lay her egg, and not leave one spot on the white linen bedspread. Once she gave her cackling announcement that she had laid an egg, she'd fly back out of the window.

My second most unpleasant job, next to emptying the chamberpot into our vegetable garden, was to catch a hen, stick my finger in her behind, and check by feel if she carried an egg. Until they laid their eggs, they were confined inside the small compound right outside Mama's window.

Occasionally Mama gave me a raw egg to suck. She said it was good for me, since I was tall for my age, skinny and always sick. ("sickly" is how Mama described me to our neighbors.) It took some time to get used to sucking eggs. I gagged on the first mouthful. But then I developed a taste for it and liked it.

Sucking eggs did not put weight on me or cure me of whatever ailed me. My ears still ran yellow; seldom did I go without cotton in them. Then came something new: My mouth was broken out and hurt. Inspecting it, I could see round red places with blisterlike centers on the sides of my tongue, the insides of my cheeks, and the opening of my throat. They came and went. Whenever I was afflicted with them, they lasted for weeks until they healed again. I could hardly eat anything except for soup, and bread dipped in hot water. Mama made me rinse my mouth with saltwater and drink hot chamomile tea.

One day in school, one of my friends, Roswitta Bauman, said, "Ella, why don't you let my tante pray over you." Even though they were staunch Catholics, I convinced myself it wouldn't hurt, in fact it might help. The following day I visited Frau Bauman and told her about my problem. She said she could help me. I followed her to the back of her barn and knelt with her at the nasty-looking and putrid-smelling compost heap, an accumulation of animal manure. She picked up a piece of straw that was covered with manure, held it to my lips, not touching, and prayed Hail Mary. I closed my eyes, not wanting to see the compost heap. I listened closely when she started to pray for God to heal my affliction. After a while she said, "Amen." Then she said, "Now run along, Ella, you are healed." When I arrived at home and told Mama about this healing, she only shook her head and said nothing. It took a while before my mouth healed, but in no time the blisters came back. I continued to suck raw eggs.

* * *

Two or three weeks before Easter, Mama started collecting eggs and onion skins. The three of us, Sister Erika, Sister Lida, and I, looked forward to participating in the egg-dyeing ceremony and listening to Mama explain the traditional Easter celebration of her small village of Stariska in Russia. She boiled some eggs, then boiled the onion skins and drained them. The eggs were submerged for about fifteen minutes. They turned a beautiful golden/brown/yellow.

"Ella, run out in the yard and cut whatever is green—grass or weeds."

Boiled and drained, another batch of eggs turned a beautiful green color. For red she boiled a beet or two, and for blue she used a few drops of blue ink. All the eggs were laid in a grass-filled basket that Papa had woven from weeping willow branches he had gathered on a special trip to the banks of the Danube River. He peeled the bark from the thin branches, split them, and then wove them into a large basket. Mama never hid our eggs as other families did. We were given four eggs, one of each color. The morning of Easter Sunday was spent attending church in Straubing. Everyone who was confirmed went to Communion. When we came home, Mama prepared a nice lunch for us. She made little bullets out of flour and lard and dropped them into boiling water. In a smaller pot, she browned a chunk of lard and wild onions before adding it to the bullet soup. Salt and pepper flavored this tasty dish. It was called Rübelsuppe.

Easter afternoon I went on a long walk with my girlfriends along the Danube. The high point of our day was when the boys joined us. One of the games we played was to hit our eggs together. The one whose egg cracked first had to hand it over to the winner. One of the boys collected quite a few eggs before we realized that he was using a wooden egg.

At the opposite end of our camp lived a Russian Orthodox family, the Kharakashes. They celebrated Easter a week or two later than the Lutheran Easter. I always made it a point to go to their barrack and give them a Russian Easter-morning greeting, "Khristos Voskrece" (Christ is risen). They answered, "Voistinu Voskres" (He is risen indeed). They rewarded me with money for my special blessing. Since they had two small daughters, I would always give them two of my colorful Easter eggs.

Papa celebrated Easter with a bottle. When Papa got drunk, he invariably started to brag about his contribution to the war.

"Theodor, shut your mouth. Don't tell the children about the past."

"But Mama, I want to know," I said.

"No, you don't want to know. You wouldn't understand. Besides it will only get us all into trouble."

Sporadically he told us a partial story, out of earshot of Mama. It was always a different beginning without an ending, or an ending with no beginning.

"Papa, what did you do in the war?"

"Oh, I was in the Russian army."

"Really," I said.

"Then I escaped and went over to the German side. They were happy to have me because I could speak Russian and German. They needed me. With all those different people in all those different camps, the—"

Mama interrupted, "Theodor, shut up. Take another drink and go to bed."

At another drinking session I asked, "Papa, how did you get to Germany?"

"Well, I put Lida's mother and Mutter on a horse-drawn wagon and headed west. It was wintertime and snowing. When I came across Russian partisans, I told them, 'I'm going to the next town to deliver my family. I'll be back.' My wife was pregnant, and before we came to the German front she lost the baby and died."

"Papa, what happened then?"

"Theodor, shut up!" Mama said.

So there was this big void of time, from the German army's arrival in Russia to the end of the war. Another drinking bout:

"Papa, tell me how you got to Germany."

"Well, we got to Germany in the wintertime. I had my wife and my mother in the back of a horse-drawn carriage. It was very cold. She was pregnant, had the baby in the back of the wagon. The baby was fine, but she bled to death. When I got a job in the camp as a carpenter, I was always a good worker and I always got the job done."

"What job?"

Mama, "Theodor, shut up!"

In fact, in all the years that he was married to Mama, he never once told a story of his youth and his arrival in Germany or what he did during the war that matched a previous version.

Papa did not make friends. Like the rest of the men who returned from the war, he isolated himself within his family because he always feared the Communists. One never knew who was a Communist—or a Nazi. The motto after the war was, "Don't trust anyone." One had to be very careful. Nobody in camp had found any relatives, and very few men had returned home from the war to their families. The men who did come home were sick in mind and body, pretty much stayed to themselves, and became loners. The government gave them money every month for services rendered during the war. No one revealed the past.

All the Refugees who lived at Camp Hofstetten and came from the east swore that they would never fall into the hands of the Communists. Worse than death would be deportation to a slave labor camp in the coal mines of Siberia. In fact, even after the war, women made plans to kill themselves and their families rather than go back to the Communists.

Men seldom spoke to each other. There was nothing to talk about. They all came from different backgrounds—teachers, cobblers, farmers, the only thing they had in common was the dream to get to Germany, the land of their forefathers, the land of promise. The German people would embrace them and they would be treated like citizens. Wrong, wrong, wrong! Maybe if Germany had won the war a man would have been respected and given a nice home, a job, a future for the family. But that wasn't what happened. There was no future. Once a Refugee, always a Refugee. It might as well have been branded on our foreheads (per Papa).

Friday was market day. Mama came home from the market carrying a small paper bag. We couldn't wait to open it to see what made that little pecking noise.

"I couldn't help myself. I just had to have it," she said.

She put the bag on the dining room table, and the whole family assembled in great anticipation. Mama reached into the bag and lifted out a little furry chick.

"Elsa, do we really need another chicken?" Papa asked. "I can imagine the messy floor every day until it gets big enough to go out."

"Theodor, this is not a chicken. This is a gosling."

"That's even worse," Papa pronounced. "Whenever it grows up it will be noisy, louder than a watchdog. What will the neighbors say? It's bad enough with the chickens."

"I'll endure it."

"Will the neighbors?"

"They'll just have to get used to it," Mama said.

In early summer the cycle of collecting continued, usually early potatoes. The days I did not spend in school, I went with Mutter. I encouraged her to tell me about her life when she was young, which she related enthusiastically with a twinkle in her eyes. I had an insatiable curiosity about where we came from and life back in Russia. Going with Mutter pleased Mama because I was making myself useful and not hanging out so much with my friends. Of course, the family also benefitted from the things we collected.

Mutter talked about the time her mother and father and her seven brothers and sisters were sent to Siberia. Whole villages were taken to Siberia by train. There they built crude one-room log cabins attached to one-room barns. The life of hardship started anew.

Most of the old and frail people died the first winter they were there. A baby had a chance to live if it was born in the springtime. By the time winter came, if it had its first teeth, it could eat on its own. A baby born in the winter lived only as long as the mother's milk lasted. If the mother didn't get much to eat, her milk supply dried up and the baby didn't have a chance.

Mutter and her family's one-room log cabin had a hardened shiny dirt floor. A stove in one corner of the room served for cooking, bread baking, and heating. It was made out of bricks of dried mud mixed with straw. In the winter, as soon as the stove cooled down, the children slept on top of it.

"Mutter," I said, "how did you get the dirt floor clean?"

"In the summertime you sweep the floor real good. All the sand and dirt has to be removed. Then you take some fresh, warm cow manure, spread it on the floor, starting in one corner, and work yourself to the front door. It takes a few hours to dry. It had the most beautiful shine. I did it every summer."

"Didn't it smell?"

"No, not at all," she said with a laugh.

"Mutter, did you know my oma when she was a little girl?"

"No, I did not. Why?"

"I just remember she told me the same story when we were in Russia. Go on and tell me more, please."

"In Siberia we suffered a lot. Women worked as well as men, like slaves, in the coal mines. We had gardens and eventually acquired some livestock. All of us had to work together, and it was very hard to survive."

"Did you have babies in Siberia?"

"Yes, but that was very hard too. If a woman died in childbirth, some other woman who was nursing a child would automatically take and nurse the baby. She raised it until it had a good set of teeth, then the child would be returned to its own family."

There was a silence while I thought about that, then she said, "We prayed daily that the good Lord would return us safely to our old homes. After about five years we did return, but not to our old homes. During our absence the Russian farmers had moved in and taken over. We lost everything: our land, our homes, and our way of life. Upon our return, the government gave us a small plot of land where we raised vegetables and pigs. We built a house that accommodated our family and a newly acquired cow and horse. We were slaves again, just as we were in Siberia."

Mutter spent Sundays doing nothing, not even cooking. She cooked enough on Saturday for Sister Lida and herself to eat the same meal on Sunday. Sister Lida sat quietly and listened to Mutter recite verses from the Bible and sing. When Mutter did go to church, which was not too often, she never included Sister Lida. Sister Lida never decorated a Christmas tree or went to church, never went into town to window-shop, and only rarely participated in our family activities. She didn't play with children her own age very much, not until she started school, but stayed close to Mutter. She was so loved by Mutter that I was somewhat jealous and always wished I had someone to love and care for me as much.

*　*　*

Mama awoke me ever so gently. "Ella, it's time for you to get dressed." The reason I had to get dressed was to go and stand in line to buy some meat. The meat we could afford to buy was horse meat. Time to get up was five o'clock in the morning. I climbed out of bed, combed my hair and braided my pigtails, put on my dress without the apron, and walked in the dark to Straubing. It was Saturday. I walked into town and stood in line at the butcher's. The butcher's shop was located on Heerstrasse. Half of the building was a Gasthaus. The other half, two rooms, was a butcher shop. The owners lived upstairs. When I arrived, there was already a line, mostly of old people. Mama should have gotten me up earlier. Maybe if I came at midnight I would make it closer to the door.

As I stood in line, I was met with solemn faces. Not like the people in our camp, who smiled, laughed, sang and danced on the lawn on Saturday nights, and were happy to be alive. I stood there for four hours. The butcher opened his door about eight. The line moved slowly. Even so, I was afraid my turn would come before Mama arrived. Mama timed it pretty well. She relieved me about ten o'clock. She took my place in line and I walked back home, hungry and tired. I cut off a piece of bread, drank tea, and went back to bed. Mama came home around noon with all kinds of good red meat and some bones.

"Theodor," I heard when Mama came in, "you would not believe the favoritism that goes on in the butcher shop. The Real Germans are still getting the prime cuts from underneath the table. Whenever I ask for the same cut, it's sold out. I just open my mouth and everybody knows I'm a Refugee. And why shouldn't we get the same good cut of meat that the Real Germans get? We have lost everything. They still have their farms, cars, bicycles, and their kids have nice dresses and go to a nice school. We need to get out of this country!" Mama was fuming about the discrimination.

"Just where do you think we would be welcome and give our children a better life? Just where?"

Mama: "I don't care. America, Canada, Australia, any of those places would be better than this place. Besides, we are too close to Russia and the Communists. If they don't know where we are, then they cannot get us back. You know these Real Germans will sell us out to the Communists just to be rid of us. If we emigrate to America, Canada, or Australia, it would be harder for the Communists to find us."

This became a subject dear to Mama's heart, and she talked about it for hours. I made my way into the kitchen.

"Why are the Real Germans always acting so sour?" I asked while sitting on the cot.

"Because they lost the war," Papa said.

Mutter came to see what Mama had bought. She shook her head and said, "Horse meat! Mark my words! Horse meat will be the death of you. I don't care how you camouflage it. Horse meat is horse meat! They may have even got it off a horse that dropped dead of disease. Just remember when you get sick, even with a cold, it's the horse meat."

I really didn't care where the meat came from as long as I could have just a small piece. Mama prepared the meat as usual. It was always boiled in a pot of water with bay leaves.

"Mama, why are you always boiling the meat?"

"It stretches," she said.

She removed the meat and added a few potatoes to the broth. She cut the meat in small pieces and put them back in the pot, then tossed in wild onions and old crusty black bread. This was an absolutely delicious soup. The soup pot was a permanent fixture on the stove until every drop was gone.

Mama said, "I don't understand why Mutter doesn't want to eat horse meat. It is the cleanest meat there is. The pig, by contrast, is the dirtiest. It eats anything, whereas a horse only eats grass or hay."

"Mutter doesn't trust the Real Germans," Papa responded. "She may be right. For all we know they may be selling meat from unhealthy horses, and we really could get sick from that, even die."

That made sense to me, but it didn't matter. For a few days, it felt like we were celebrating a birthday or holiday. Sister Lida came over very rarely, but when Mama cooked horse meat she'd slip by and eat some without letting Mutter know.

We heard through the grapevine that a fish store was opening next to the Danube Bridge in Straubing. I followed the same procedure as with the horse meat. Getting up early, standing in line to get a few pounds of neatly cut white squares of fish without bones. It was cooked in the soup pot with carrots, bay leaves, and potatoes.

On one occasion, Mama was cooking sauerkraut with a few bones in it for flavor. She was going to pour in a little oil to make it taste better. Instead, she grabbed the liquid soap bottle. There went our appetizing dinner of sauerkraut, bones, potatoes, and all.

Papa was angry. His verbal abuse came fast and furious. "All women are stupid cows. All you are good for is having children. In fact, you can't even have sex without getting pregnant." According to Papa, men had to assert themselves daily to show who really was the head of the house.

Papa and Mama settled into a loveless marriage. Because they wanted a sense of security, they tolerated each other. Papa had to go to work because the Germans got tired doling out money each month. He was an accomplished carpenter. The Job Placement Office found him a job at a building site with a prestigious firm called Bayer. It was at the start of summer, and school was out. My job was to carry his lunch to the work site, about an hour's walk. Mama started cooking right after he left. By eleven o'clock I had to be on my way to the construction site. I waited patiently while, sitting on a pile of bricks, he ate. Then I gathered all the dirty dishes and made my way back home.

One day he came home and announced he was not going back to work. He wasn't going to take any more harassment from the Real Germans. And he didn't. To be truthful, Papa didn't like to work. The only money we received from the government was Kindergeld (child support), so much for each child per month. His main occupation from now on was to read the Bible. That consumed most of his day. No one was to disturb him. The conclusion he drew after many readings was that all the evil in this world was the Jews' fault. "Look at the Old Testament," noting one battle after another. "Mark my word, Jews will start the next world war. Because the Jewish nation did not convert to Christianity, they will suffer from God's anger forever. Whatever it takes, God will bring the Jewish nation to its knees."

The Bible also reinforced his belief in corporal punishment. "Wer seine Rute schont, der hasst seinen Sohn; wer ihn aber lieb hat, der züchtigt ihn beizeiten" (die Sprüche Salomos 13:24). Spare the rod, spoil the child. It was written in the Bible, how to beat a child into submission. Papa did just what the Bible said. He was the enforcer of God's Ten Commandments. It was the law written in stone. Papa's word was a command.

He would go off on a tirade to whoever would listen. Neighbors avoided him, but strangers with time on their hands might listen and argue. He was a very angry and emotional man. The Old Testament was his Bible. No, he did not have to have a pastor tell him about God. He knew much more than any of them ever did. Mama sat by silently with hands in her lap, or sometimes crocheting. "Elsa, what do you think?" he asked. Mama nodded her approval. Papa continued, "The Jewish propaganda that the Americans put out is all a lie. I never heard or ever saw any Jewish concentration camps or Jews being killed."

Lighting up another cigarette, inhaling it deeply, then removing it with his thumb and forefinger, which were permanently stained yellow from years of accumulated nicotine, Papa kept our rooms under a constant cloud of smoke. Mama opened the windows, only to have to shut them because Papa couldn't stand a draft.

Disciplining children in our camp always involved corporal punishment. One method Mama employed for infractions of rules was a slap across my face. Her four fingers left a red, swollen mark on my cheek and a sting that lasted for hours. I didn't mind the pain, but I suffered from embarrassment if I had to go out and my neighbors and friends saw me with the mark. I felt humiliated. I was forever trying to hide my shame until the swelling and redness disappeared. The boys made fun of me until they got it themselves from their fathers or mothers.

The walls were so thin that I could hear people snoring on the other side. The fights neighbors had with each other, husband and wife, a woman shacked up with someone else's husband, grown children fighting with parents, were very vocal. The reason they were loud was so that those who listened could take sides. The neighbors knew who was getting a thrashing, and it would be the main subject of gossip when women gathered at the well or out in the street. Because I was the oldest, I was to set the example. I was forbidden to cry when I was disciplined. It was practically impossible not to cry out when I was hurt, sometimes badly. Mama protected Sister Erika and Mutter protected Sister Lida.

I was punished for every little offense: don't talk back; get this or that, meaning immediately; respect your elders; don't lie; do well in school; give back change when returning from the bread or milk store; take care of the chickens or rabbits; weed the garden; speak only when spoken to and don't interrupt when grown-ups are talking. The list never ended. If I failed to adhere to these rules, I received a chastisement with the "Korbatsch." This was an eighteen-inch hand-carved stick to which were nailed seven thin leather strings. Sometimes I hid it. Mama usually kept it within arm's reach. If she couldn't find it, I knew what I had to do. I would go out to the nearest willow bush, break off about three branches, and bring them in. Mama used those mainly around my legs. If I didn't get the branches, ran away or hid outside, and waited until Papa came home, his belt hurt much worse. It was better to endure Mama's wrath.

One day Papa told me to get a bucket of beer. On the way back from the Gasthaus, a flock of geese refused to let me pass. A gander started to bite my legs, and in order to get away from the pain I ran. In the process, I spilled half of the bucket of beer.

On seeing the bucket half empty, Papa asked, "What did you do with the rest of the beer? Did you drink it?"

"No, I didn't."

"Did you give it to your friends to drink—or to the boys?"

"No, I spilled it."

Now came a barrage of blows to my head. "I'll teach you to lie. Do you know that beer costs money?"

"Please, don't hit me anymore. A gander came after me and I ran so he couldn't bite me. While I was running the beer spilled."

"How many times did I tell you to be careful and avoid the geese? Do you ever listen?"

I cried, covering my head with my arms.

"You thickheaded child, I'll teach you to lie."

His fists felt like big stones falling on my head.

"Next time you go and get your own beer," I screamed.

"I'll teach you respect," he yelled, red-faced, his long stringy hair falling into his eyes making him look like a wild man. He took off his belt and pummeled me. The strikes fell, not on any particular spot, but from my head to my feet.

Now on my knees, I begged, "Papa, please stop. Mama, please help me!"

Mama sat there with her hands in her lap and said nothing.

Papa threatened, "If you cry, you'll get double the beating."

It was so hard for me not to cry when the belt hit across the small of my back. I tried to remember that the neighbors were listening. Now the belt buckle got me across the kidney area. I could not hold it any longer and I urinated. He hit me even more because I had wet the kitchen floor. On my knees with my hands folded in a praying gesture, I begged him to stop. Sweat pouring from his face, his hair wet, he didn't stop until he was completely exhausted.

Sister Erika was watching from the corner of the room. Mama sat unmoving. No help for me from anyone.

I was thinking, how many times will my body be able to stand such pain? One of these days he'll probably kill me. "Dear God," I prayed, "I'm so young, can't you help me? I don't want to die yet."

Finally, with his hands shaking, he put on his belt.

"Get up, you no-good pig, and clean the kitchen floor. I want it shiny by the time I get back."

That meant the floorboards had to be scrubbed with a scrub brush, washed and rinsed, to remove the urine stain. The floor consisted of boards that years of washing had bleached white. It was almost impossible to get the yellow urine stain out. I went to the well to get buckets of clean water. On my hands and knees with a scrub brush in my hand, hardly able to see the stain through the tears still streaming down my face, I kept scrubbing, on and on. My hands turned red and blue, my fingers looking like sausages. After what seemed like an eternity, Mama told me to stop scrubbing.

My face was swollen, my hair wet, and my body ached. I stood up, reached for the empty bucket, and headed back to the well for more water. Praying silently, "Please, dear God, please don't let any of the neighbors see me."

Most of the time I tried to avoid Papa as much as I could. For that matter, I avoided Mama too. My life was with my girlfriends and my church. As least I could talk to God, not that He changed anything in my daily life. What kind of God was He when He let Papa beat me like that? Mama had to go along with this cruel behavior to keep peace. I was afraid of Papa. I was sure that eventually he would beat me to death and that Mama would let him. From then on, I started to lie to my parents.

Lying had been an integral part of my way of life ever since the NKVD knocked on our door so many years ago. We all lied about where we came from. We lied wherever we went. In most instances, the lies were for self-preservation. We had been living in fear that the Communists would find us. The locals knew as soon as I spoke that I was not a native German, but they had no idea just where I came from. They didn't like Refugees, and they made no bones about it. They wanted all foreigners to go back to wherever they came from.

Other than returning my Easter greeting, the Russian family, the Kharakashes, never had anything to do with anyone in the camp, not even us. People from Soviet countries especially never talked to anyone about their pasts because they did not want the Communists to know where they were. Papa lived in constant fear the Communists would somehow find and kill us, or even worse, drag us back to Russia.

Our identification papers were full of lies. Every time we moved, we re-invented our family and ourselves. Whenever we registered in a new city, we Refugees invariably had lost, misplaced or thrown away our original papers and could make up any story we felt like. Many people did just that. Where would the authorities check? The identification cards the Nazis had given us in Berlin were worthless and disposed of long ago. The heavy bombings we had endured in Regensburg took care of any questions about the loss of identification papers. No one could prove anything. Everyone made things up as time went by.

Since most people had lost their papers during the evacuation and bombings and new official papers were made, you could be anybody, with any name, any believable age, from anywhere, with whatever occupation you wanted. Most Refugees took advantage of this by changing names, citizenship, birthplaces, even marital status. If you said you were not married, and in fact you were married but your husband had not yet come home from the war, it didn't matter. When he did come home, you had your papers changed again. If you owned land and a house, and even if you didn't, but said you did, later on the German government reimbursed you. Some of the families in our camp really made money from that scam. Papa never collected a penny from the German government for losing his farm in Wolinien.

Like most women in the camp, Mama was always afraid that we children would tell the truth about our past. It was an absolute dictum never to discuss our family with anybody, ever. Even after the war, we never knew who was our friend or our foe.

All of us children were drilled in what we should say. We always claimed we came from Poland. We avoided Polish people because we didn't know the language and that would be a dead giveaway. Russian was hardly ever spoken anymore in our home, except when Mama and Papa wanted to tell me or Mutter something others should not know.

* * *

Almost daily, my girlfriend Herta and I took Brother Otto down to the Danube to pick blackberries. One day as we were beginning to pick, we heard these funny noises. We walked toward the sounds. Puzzled, we stopped to witness a surprising scene. A motorcycle was parked nearby. On a blanket, a stark naked couple was cavorting around in all kinds of contorted positions. Herta and I looked at each other for only a split second and then back to the blanket. Our eyes locked on them in order not to miss any of the action-filled wrestling match. We tried hard to keep little Brother Otto from making noises so that we could watch this spectacle. He would not cooperate. The couple looked in our direction but never told us to leave, so we just stood and watched. We were completely hypnotized by the calisthenics going on in front of us. After what seemed like hours to us, forgetting to pick the blackberries, we beat a hasty retreat. Once back home, we laughed until we cried. This scene was our secret and a topic of conversation for years to come.

Amis were visiting different girls in our camp. It was a constant flow day and night. Some of the soldiers were black. All looked clean-shaven, wore clean uniforms and clean boots. Still, they were a far cry from the German soldiers I compared them to, the perfectly dressed German soldiers and officers who I had seen in our different camps when we arrived in Germany, with medals on their chests. The girls in our camp who ran with Amis talked openly about how to pick up a soldier and taught anyone who wanted to learn just what American catch words or phrases to use. Of course, my girlfriends and I were in our early teens and eager listeners. We wanted to learn American, just in case.

Amis yelled at pretty girls. Their favorite saying, "Fräulein, Kommen sie hier" (Miss, come over here). Sometimes, "Do you want a Yankee dime?" What was a Yankee dime? My, how I wished I was old enough to get a pair of stockings, dark stockings with black seams running all the way down the back of the leg; or whiskey and cigarettes for Papa; or food for Mama; or chocolates for us kids.

I added a new word to my vocabulary that I hadn't heard or known before: "Whore."

"Mama, what is a whore and what do they have to do to get money and all these things from the Amis?"

"Ella, you are too young to know about such things. When you get older I will tell you all about it. For right now, stay away from girls who run around with Amis. You don't want to get a disease or get pregnant and then have to have an abortion." I better wait to ask Mama about the word "abortion."

"Absolutely not," I agreed.

This was the end of the discussion with Mama about whores. Just like sex, it was put on the back burner to be discussed in a few years. Right now, I was too young. I couldn't wait for Mama's explanation in a few years. I had to have an answer now. In a few years I would be too old, and the Amis might have left by then.

Our next-door neighbor's daughter had Amis going in and out of their two-room apartment day and night. She only had a mother, brother, and older sister. Her father never came back from the war.

I was determined to find out how one could become a whore. One evening I found the nerve and asked her, standing right outside our front door, what I had to do to go out with an Ami. She explained to me in great detail how she did it, from beginning to end. She stood at the corner of the street (in white high heels) after dark, waited until an Ami car came by and stopped. "Schokolade" (chocolate) was the key word, then hold up fingers for each bar. Usually they drove to a hotel for the night. In the summertime, they went to the Danube. There they ate, drank, and had sex in the grass. Sometimes, in the wintertime, her mother agreed for her to bring the soldier home and they would use her mother's army cot. Her sister, mother, and brother slept behind a bed-sheet partition. "Sex is easy," she said. "You just do what the man wants you to do."

"Are you afraid of getting pregnant?"

"Oh no. I'll just get an abortion. Sometimes it's good to get pregnant because then the soldier will marry you and you go to live in a big house in America."

Must ask Mama about "abortion."

One or two black Amis came to the camp, not as many as white ones. I never saw a yellow or red one. The black Amis did not or could not marry, just have sex. The explanation was that it had something to do with the American government.

I now began to watch the whores every day. They were never called by their first names by our neighbors, only by their last name and whore. For example, die Schmidt Hure (the Smith whore). The whores always seemed to have fun. They laughed, wore makeup, had money for movies and beautiful clothing and good food for their families. Surprise, surprise! One of our neighbors' daughters married an Ami and went to America.

Long hours were spent discussing sex with Herta and Gerda. We decided that love is sex. When you say to a boy that you love him then you are telling him you are ready to have sex with him. It could be done somewhere in the bushes in warm weather or, in the wintertime, in a rundown burned-out building on a dirty floor or in a farmer's haystack.

One thing we knew, sex with the boys we grew up with was a no-no. They always talked about the girls who had sex with them for nothing. They did it just for the fun of it. Gerda was two years older than Herta and me and more knowledgeable about such things, having learned much from her sisters, and was very happy to share all kinds of information. She said, "When you go to bed with a boy, he could use a Gummi [condom] to keep from getting you pregnant." Showing us one she said, "This is a Gummi. You can it put on your finger or blow it up as a balloon." Whenever a German girl running with Amis wanted to marry one, she would not let him use anything and would get pregnant. Then he had to marry her and she was allowed to go to America. That is, if he wasn't married already.

If he was married, he lived with the girl on weekends and paid her with dollars, chocolates, stockings, high heels, canned goods, lipsticks, cigarettes, and all kinds of fresh fruit. Some of these things they sold to neighbors and friends, then used the money for whatever they wanted. They always had money for hairdressers, nice clothing, and good things to eat. When they found out he was married, usually from his buddies, he would always say he was going to write and take care of the baby (if there was a baby). Most never wrote. The girls picked up another Ami to continue their lifestyle and to learn more American until they found someone, maybe after a couple of children, who was willing to marry them. Actually, some made out rather well. The Ami contributed and the German government paid Kindergeld. The government also paid Unterstützung, money for stay-at-home mothers. When it came time for a married couple to go to America, the children were left with grandparents or relatives. Then the payments, in dollars, to raise the children came in monthly installments from America; along with the child-support money from the German government, that meant the children were well taken care of and lacked for nothing. It really didn't matter whether he was white or black. Black Amis had their fun but could not always get permission to marry.

"Sex with a Neger [Negro] is different than with a white one," one of the whores said. I wanted to know what the difference was, never having had sex. The girls who slept with them wouldn't tell. But then we asked one who bragged about her boyfriend being black. "What's the difference between having sex with a German or a Neger?"

Her answer was that the difference between them was that the German men had their penises covered with skin, but the Amis, white and black, didn't. Then she added smugly, "But once you have sex with a Neger, you'll never want to be with a white man again." We pressed her to tell us more but she wouldn't.

Not ever having seen or felt a German penis, how could I compare that with an Ami penis, white or black? That was always a puzzle to me. I was often tempted to ask one of the boys I grew up with to show me his, but I never had enough nerve.

Since we had no pictures, I often wondered what a man's private parts looked like. One day I saw a man heading for the outhouse. I went into the women's side a few minutes later, not to use the toilet but to peep through a hole to the other side and have a look. I saw all this flesh hanging down. For the life of me I couldn't figure how all of that fit into a pair of pants, and what did the men do with all of it? I couldn't ask my mama. She probably would have killed me. Herta and Gerda didn't know either. I couldn't see any difference between men or boys other than size. They all had the same thing.

After an Ami left Straubing, the girl who ran around with him couldn't find anyone to marry. No German man would even look at her. She would be the talk and gossip of the whole camp and all around to the nearest village. Most of them were not bothered. They lived well and their families always had good things to eat. Their fathers, some of whom came home after the war, didn't mind that their daughters were running around with the enemy as long she brought home cigarettes, whiskey, and American beer. The whores I knew who lived in our camp were all Refugees.

After all those revelations, different penises, how to compare them, what to do and not to do about getting pregnant, I decided not to have sex or children with an Ami. I would stay in Germany even if I had to clean houses for a living and hopefully find a German boy who would want to marry me. It was all too complicated.

★ ★ ★

Nothing would do but Mama had to have a pig. She did not want to waste our table scraps. Papa built an additional shed at the end of our garden about fifty feet from Mama's bedroom window. This pig was raised first-class. It had its own swimming pool, an indentation in the earth with a small cement covering. It was my job to change the water daily, clean the 16-by-12-foot fenced-in living area, and delouse the pig. After changing the water in the pool and washing all the mud off the pig's body, the delousing process started. The "pig's lice," as called by Papa, looked like moles on human skin, flat and dark, easily seen on the pig's clean pink skin. I scraped them off with my fingernail and then smashed them between my thumbnails. After smashing many, my fingers took on a bloody appearance.

Besides our own table scraps—potato peelings and so on—all the neighbors contributed to the fattening of our pig. Papa spent many hours sitting outside chain smoking, staring into the pen, and daydreaming.

Whenever Papa felt like it, he collected the waste. Most of the time I was assigned this nasty job. It was shoveled into a bucket and buried in the vegetable garden between the rows of carrots, potatoes, cabbages, and strawberries. Mama said, "Bury the waste in the vegetable garden and you will always have a good crop." When the first strawberries ripened, they were very tasty and as big as plums. The carrots were as thick as a man's wrist and as long as from wrist to elbow. Mama was right.

It was a Friday evening, "Ella," Mutter said, "do you want to go gleaning with me tomorrow?"

"Yes, I want to go."

"Then you must get up early."

The next morning on the road I asked, "Mutter, why is gleaning not considered stealing?"

"The Bible does not lie," she said. "If Ruth did it and God didn't punish her, He will not punish us. It goes back to biblical accounts in the book of Ruth, when Ruth and her mother-in-law were gleaning in Bethlehem. Gleaning is a term that means that anybody can go into a field once the farmer is finished with harvesting the crops. It doesn't matter if it is wheat, potatoes, or sugar beets. Once the farmer leaves the field after the harvest, anyone can go into the fields and pick up whatever is left." I marveled at her explanation. She added some technical advice: "The best place to glean will be the end of the row where the horses turned around and missed the row they needed to be in."

Gleaning wheat had to be done while the weather was still warm and it hadn't rained. Once it rained you could not glean because the wheat, lying on the bare ground, would get wet, sandy, and unusable.

We arrived at the wheat field shortly after the sun had burned off the dew. I eagerly started to pick up the wheat heads, separating them from the stem and placing each head in my burlap bag. It was hard to talk with both of us forever bent over. After a while my back started to hurt every time I straightened up. I knew for sure that I did not want to be a farm maid or a farmer's wife. Since my toes were exposed, my big toe slipped out the front of the clog and hit a straw stubble. It hurt and started to bleed. Mutter put a broad green leaf on it, which she picked from the side of the field. That put a temporary stop to the bleeding until I hit the same toe again. Reinjuring the same toe continued all day long. By the time I arrived home it was twice normal size and very painful.

Mutter consoled me. "Don't worry child, time heals wounds. After a while your toes will get used to it and develop a thick skin. The straw stubble will not hurt anymore." Sure enough, she was right. By the time wheat season was over and potato season began, all my toes were healed.

Mutter looked up into the sun and said, "It is noon. Time for us to rest and have something to eat and drink."

I was amazed how she could tell time without having a watch.

"Mutter, how do you know it's noon?"

"By the sun," she said. "When it is directly overhead it is the middle of the day." She added, "Also, whenever your shadow is the shortest it is noon and when your shadow is longest it is evening and time to start back home."

Mutter looked all bent even when she was standing straight. I looked at her and wondered if I would look like her in twenty years. I hoped not. Looking like that I would never get a husband.

Lunch consisted of a hunk of black rye bread and a few sips of water. The water holder was a canteen that a German soldier had used to carry his water. We drank very little water because it had to last the rest of the afternoon. After a couple of good swigs each, Mutter put it back into a small black bag that hung on the bicycle handlebars.

We relieved ourselves on the edge of the field since the broad-leafed plants grew there. We used them to clean our private parts as best as we could. I lived by example. My role models were my family and friends. Since there was no water or paper, I did as best as I could under these conditions. If a little bit of feces got on my hand, I wiped it with the inside hem of my dress or skirt.

The procedure for a runny nose was almost the same. I closed one nostril with a finger and blew out the other. When done with both nostrils, turn up the hem and wipe whatever was left onto my skirt, then rub the material together until all the foreign matter was absorbed. On washday, the hem of the skirt or dress received extra long rubs on the washboard until every bit of evidence was removed.

If we were lucky enough to be gleaning next to a running brook, we took time to wash our private parts, hands, face, and feet then dry them with the inside of our skirt or dress.

"Cleanliness is next to Godliness," Mutter would always say.

If the Real Germans knew how unclean we Refugees had become while living in their clean Germany they would kick us out.

When the sun began to cast a long shadow, Mutter looked up and said, "I think it is time to go home." I felt like my back was going to break. Mutter never complained of hurting at all. Between the two of us, we fastened our huge burlap bag of wheat to the bike. On an extra good day, we were blessed with two full bags. Then one bag was put over the main bike frame and the other was placed on the back seat. Taking turns, Mutter and I pushed the bike the three or four miles back to our camp. A bag of wheat was not heavy in comparison to potatoes or sugar beets.

The following day we placed the wheat on a blanket outside our front door in the sunshine before going off to glean again. Wheat had to be very dry in order to separate the kernel from the chaff.

Whenever we collected enough and it was dried out we beat it with a long stick, which was attached, by a foot-long leather strap, to a much smaller stick. The wheat was stored in the same burlap bag until a windy day. Then Mutter would spread a sheet on the ground, fill a small bowl with wheat, and throw the wheat up in the air. The wind took the lighter chaff away while the heavy grain fell back on the sheet. This procedure was repeated all day long until the wheat was nice and clean and no chaff could be found. The chaffless grain was collected until we had enough to take to the miller to grind into flour.

Mutter and I loaded the cleaned wheat—about half a large burlap bag of it—on Papa's bike. The mill was about an hour's walk away. There we waited our turn to get our grain ground into flour. Mutter paid the miller in food stamps.

The flour she divided into equal parts. For Mutter and Sister Lida, their share lasted all winter. For our family of five, it lasted about a month.

Mutter was a very devout Christian. I heard her singing in her room during the day, out gathering food or wood, and all day on Sundays. She read her old beat-up Bible and sang what religious songs she knew. One story that impressed me immensely was about an angel. One of Mutter's old neighbors in her German village in Russia, a widow lady, was very old and ill. Everyone in the village took turns taking care of her, from taking her milk every morning to meals at night. She was bed-bound and had no children to help her. Mutter was an apprentice in a dressmaker's house next door to the old woman.

"Do you know what an apprentice is?"

"No," I replied.

"It is a slave who learns to sew on the side. The family I lived with had about a half dozen children whom I had to take care of before the first stitch was made. In order to learn to sew, I had to clean, cook, and do whatever the mistress needed. I was about fifteen or sixteen years old. I tended the livestock, milked two cows, and worked the garden. I was determined to learn to sew, and I did. Today I do not even have a sewing machine. I have to sew by hand. One day in the summertime, the windows and doors were wide open to air out the house. I heard this great commotion of women out in the street praying aloud. I ran to the door and out into the front yard. A neighbor woman ran up to me and pointed to the house next door, where the poor sick widow lived. I raised my eyes to the roof of her house and I saw an angel hovering over the house, wings spread, all in white with long yellowish hair, the feet not touching the roof. I fell on my knees and made the sign of the cross. I didn't know what else to do. My eyes fixed on the roof of the house, I prayed for God's blessing, not only on my neighbor but on me as well. I thought the end of the world had come. Women and children were in the street, all kneeling, staring at the top of the roof watching this angel. It seemed that time stood still. It was quite a while before the figure faded into thin air. Needless to say, that was the talk of the whole village and for miles around. We who saw the angel at that very instant were bonded together by reverence, awe, and wonderment. After the men came home from working in the fields and were told what happened, they didn't believe a word. We knew what we saw. We may have lost our land, in many cases whole families were killed, but we had God and our faith."

* * *

Six weeks before Christmas, Papa wanted to know when were we going to eat the noisy, skinny, penned-up goose.

"We will have this goose for Christmas dinner after I fatten it up," Mama said. "Ella, put two handfuls of flour into a bowl and add just a tiny amount of water. Mix it well then shape little bullets out of the dough as long as your little finger."

After I did what Mama had instructed me to do, she said, "Now watch. This is how to fatten up a goose."

She caught the frightened goose in her pen, sat herself on a three-legged stool, and placed the fighting goose between her legs while holding tightly onto her beak to keep it closed. Now she was ready for me.

"Hand me one at a time."

Mama straightened out the goose's long neck.

"Take the bullet, stuff it down the throat, keep going, push it with one hand, between your thumb and forefinger, down to her breast or until it disappears."

It worked. This was a daily chore until a day before Christmas when Mama cut the goose's throat. She scalded the body in hot water, then pulled out all the feathers. The rest of the down was singed off and the body cut into pieces and salted down until the next day. What a happy Merry Christmas feast we were going to have.

1948

We lived about a mile from the Danube. It was never too cold for me and my friends to go to the river. Our second winter at Camp Hofstetten was so cold the big, swift river froze solid. My friends and I watched the Amis drive their jeeps and trucks across. The Real German kids skated on the frozen river. We slid around in our open-toed clogs.

One day I said to Papa, "Why don't you make me a pair of skis? You are such a good carpenter, you can do it."

He went into town and came back with two boards about four feet in length. Papa worked on those boards every day. He tied up the tip ends and left them in the soup pot filled with hot water overnight. The next morning I could not believe my eyes. The tips were bent. Papa added strips of leather, cut from old shoes, to brace my feet and used a candle to wax the bottoms of the boards. When he finally decided that his job was perfect and completed he said, "Ella, take good care of these skis. These are the only ones I will make."

I was the only one in the whole camp who had skis. The following morning I was up early trying them out on the newly fallen show. After many ups and downs, with two good-sized sticks to support me, I was finally able to overcome my fear of falling. I was out for hours skiing down the earthen dam that kept the Danube from overflowing. My pride and joy were short-lived—two weeks. Papa reminded me daily, "When you come in from skiing, always put the skis in hot water and bend them." He showed me how. One day Herta, my dearest girlfriend, dearer and closer to me than my parents or my siblings, called me outside. I forgot about my skis. When I returned there was no water in the pot and the skis were flat boards again. Papa could not be persuaded to make me another pair.

Papa was always a heavy smoker. Some fathers fared better in getting cigarettes because they had daughters old enough who slept with Amis, and for that they got packs of cigarettes. You could buy cigarettes from one of those whores. Some German men would not take an American cigarette, even when it was offered to them, because they still considered the Amis the enemy. Some who had tobacco shared half of a cigarette with their neighbors or friends.

Eventually Papa bought his own tobacco seeds and planted them, in early spring of 1948, in Mama's garden. He tended them faithfully. Since seeds take time to germinate and grow, I continued my routine of picking up cigarette butts.

I was busy every day after school and on weekends doing different chores and uprooting dandelions for our rabbits, which had to last for two daily feedings. I was to clean the pigsty, clean the chicken coop, collect wood, haul water, help with the laundry once a week, glean, work in the garden under Mama's supervision, and keep our apartment clean. A priority was picking up cigarette butts, which some days was more important than everything else. When school was in session all the work was left for after lunch. School lasted only until noon. There was no idleness in the wintertime. There were always sweaters or socks to be knitted or darned. Some of these jobs lasted for a short time while others, like washing the kitchen floor, took an hour or more with hot, sudsy water, which had to be heated first. When it rained and we came into the kitchen (our main living area), it was instantly turned into a mud puddle. It was a daily chore to keep the kitchen clean. We didn't have any rugs.

I always loved summertime in Camp Hofstetten. I took long walks alone or with Herta and Gerda. Usually we went to the river and watched the boats go by. We stripped down to our underwear (no bras) and jumped in. I learned how to swim in the rapidly flowing river, almost drowning. I swallowed river water almost every time. We were on a constant lookout for floating trees, boxes, and all kind of debris. All three of us had jumped in one day and were swimming with the swift current when we were overtaken by the huge bloated carcass of a dead cow on its way downstream. We yelled to each other to get out of the water. The dead carcass scared us a little. Just as soon as she floated by, taking with her the smell and the dark brown water that swirled around her body, we went back in the river. On hot Sundays entire families joined us. Men and boys kept on their underpants. Women came into the water just in their slips. After a dip I could see the complete outline of their fat bodies. Children swam naked until they started to develop, then they wore an undershirt and underpants. The German songs that praised the Blue Danube were wrong. I never saw it blue. It was a polluted, dark body of water. This was a golden opportunity for washing myself, no soap, just water and air dry my long fine hair.

Endless hours were spent daydreaming and talking about our lives, facing the "what ifs" of an uncertain future. I had beautiful dreams, whereas my parents looked toward the future with much trepidation.

When the Danube was at flood stage, my girlfriends and I walked around barefooted in the fields, which had standing water up to my knees in some places. After a couple of days the muddy waters settled and became as clear as glass. The holes that the mice had dug for homes were under water and hundreds of poor mice were now dead and floating on top. A few days after the water receded, the most beautiful flowers grew. I made a crown for my hair, a bracelet and ring to match, and took a bunch home to Mama, who loved flowers.

One morning I started early and headed for the fields to pick bunches of wild daisies. Placing them in our beer bucket, I walked to Straubing and tried to sell them in the middle of town where the Stadt Turm (city center tower) was located. It was a very disappointing endeavor. I didn't sell even one bunch.

Our rabbits lived outside of Mama's bedroom window and the pig only fifty feet away. Since pigs were only butchered in the late fall, the stench was overpowering from January until November, and especially potent in the summer with open windows and doors. When our neighbors started to add chickens and geese to their minifarms behind the barracks, the odor and noise were overwhelming.

"Why are you not eating?" Mama inquired.

"I can't. The stench makes me sick to my stomach."

"No wonder you are so sickly and skinny. You are too sensitive for your own good. If you don't eat, Papa will give you something that will make you eat" (meaning, a good belting would give me an appetite).

And he did, and it did.

Mama's rather small vegetable garden, well fertilized by the pig, chickens, and rabbits, provided plenty of beautiful vegetables in the summer and carrots in the fall. Mama never fixed turnip greens. She did fix turnips, sometimes in soup, raw, or mashed like mashed potatoes. Other times she boiled them whole or quartered with salt and pepper. They were a main meal with bread. I didn't eat much because I just didn't like turnips.

The well water tasted bad. (After years of our camp's complaining to the Health Department in Straubing, the government installed a hand pump.) Beer was our drink for lunch, dinner and in between. Milk was for babies, if it could be bought. Most women nursed their children clear up to two years of age, sometimes even to three. The Real German farmers always bartered with each other so they had fresh milk for their children.

When we were in Russia, I never saw men or women with goiters, grape-fruit-size growths usually located on the neck right under the chin, but here in Straubing I saw them all the time. Mama couldn't explain it, except to say it was the devil coming out of that particular person.

At the end of the summer, Papa's tobacco crop came in, about a dozen plants. He picked the yellowing leaves, strung them on a doubled sewing thread, and hung them in the big wooden box that we used as a smokehouse. When the box overflowed, he butchered all the rabbits and used their hutch to dry the remaining tobacco leaves. After the leaves were dried, he rolled them tightly into six-inch rolls and then cut them on Mama's bare wooden kitchen table with a special knife he made. No one was allowed to use his tobacco-cutting knife for anything else. When cigarette paper became available, Papa discontinued using newspaper or butcher paper.

* * *

On the pig's birthday, late October, when the first frost appeared, Papa asked one of our neighbors and his wife to help us with the slaughtering. The Schneiker's lived at the other end of our barrack and had seven children. For their help, our neighbors would be rewarded with some meat, sausages, and fatback.

This was a big event for all of us children. Papa honed our one and only kitchen knife to such a sharpness that the ultimate test was to put a long hair on the edge and blow. It cut the hair in two.

Just as soon as the sun showed its rays, everybody was up. Mama borrowed a black kettle, built a fire between two rocks, and started boiling water. Borrowed buckets and big soup pots were lined up on the ground. A small meat grinder was attached to a board that doubled as the table.

The pig, weighing approximately three hundred pounds, was a fighter. The two men first tied the mouth and nose together, then bound the front and hind legs. Mr. Schneiker helped to hold the fighting, screaming, wiggling animal down. Papa put his knee on the struggling front legs, then plunged the long, razor-sharp knife into its fat neck. I stood with my friends watching this spectacle and showing no emotion. Boys from the nearby barracks warming themselves around the fire were fascinated and wanted to help, but Papa said, "You are too young. At your age you must watch and learn." Mama caught the enormous amount of blood in a bucket. It seemed to me that the poor pig took a long time to die. My job was to draw and carry water from the well. Mutter tended the fire and boiled the water. The dead pig was lifted onto the makeshift table. The kettle of boiling water was poured over it in order to soften the hair on its body. Mutter continually rinsed it with boiling water until a smooth pink skin appeared. It was time to give it a shave with the sharp knife. Meanwhile, some of the men busied themselves with a homemade hoisting contraption that lifted the pig by its hind legs upside-down into a hanging position. The men in the audience carried on, smoking, laughing, joking, and recalling stories of years past when they were farmers and how differently they would kill a pig. They passed around a vodka bottle, which Papa provided. Whenever Papa needed a cigarette break, he stopped to roll one, then passed the small sack of tobacco around for the rest of the bystanders. While inhaling, expanding his lungs to their largest capacity, he ordered Mama to do this or that: get a rag, get more cigarette paper, get more beer.

Everybody stood silently in great anticipation of the most exciting moment. Papa made a long slit down the middle of the pig's stomach. The whole contents cascaded into the wash pot. To impress the teenage boys, the men commented all along on what needed to be done next. Extra care was taken not to cut the intestines. Mama reminded Papa that everything would be ruined. The intestines were full of waste, and if you cut them, even made a small hole, you contaminated the inside of the pig.

One of the boys said to Papa, "Herr Puder, will you give us the bladder?"

"What for?" Papa asked, as if he didn't know.

"To blow it up, let it dry, and use it as a soccer ball."

Papa did not give them the bladder. Mama had plans to use it as a container for blood sausages.

I did not have to draw and carry the water very far because the slaughtering was done close to the well. Nevertheless, as the day progressed, the buckets of water became heavier and heavier, not only to draw out of the well but to carry the few feet to the kettle. All the fat was collected separately in a soup pot and placed on the open fire to cook slowly into liquid grease. The heart, kidneys, lungs, and liver were washed and laid out on the makeshift table. Mama, Mutter, and Frau Schneiker then started opening one end of the intestines, squeezing all the waste into our wooden chamberpot. It smelled to high heaven. But it was useful, buried in the vegetable garden to fertilize the soil. When the intestines were being cleaned, I got sick to my stomach. Mama said, "What will become of you in life if you cannot stand a little smell?" Then, turning to Frau Schneiker, "Ella, with her nose, cannot even be a farm maid," which is one of the lowest occupations in life. I was embarrassed.

I kept drawing water until my arms went numb. I felt like running away. But Mama was intent on teaching me how to clean intestines just in case I became a farm maid or, even better, married a farmer. The intestines were turned inside out and washed and washed and washed. Then they were salted, put into a bucket of water, and set aside.

For a piece of meat, one of the bigger boys enthusiastically volunteered to peddle his bike into Ittling to get the meat inspector. Nothing else could be done to the pig until the inspector came, which was about two hours later. He was a bespectacled, short, stocky, balding old man in three-quarter-length leather pants, knee socks, and gray jacket, topped by a gray hat. In a thick Bavarian accent, he asked to whom the pig belonged, how old it was, and what it had been fed. Upon close inspection of each piece on the table, he placed his blue stamp of approval all over the carcass. Now the pig was officially dead, ready to be cut, cooked, or smoked. The inspector received a piece of meat and some money for his work.

Meanwhile, the fat had cooked down into a liquid. Little pieces of crisped fat floated on top, and Mama fished them out and passed them around to eat. After pounds of salt were added to the grease, it was poured into a metal container (which had been donated by an Ami to a neighbor, who handed it over to Papa) and covered with a cloth. After a few days it had set to the consistency and color of brownish paste. This was stored and eaten on everything daily throughout the winter. We spread it on bread. It was added to soup. Gravies were made. We used it as a substitute for meat. It was even spread on badly infected sores.

The pig was laid on a board and its body dismembered, first the head, then the front legs. The short segments of the legs were consumed first, within a couple of weeks. Mama salted all the pieces and kept them in a huge wooden barrel for a few weeks. The shoulders and upper hind legs were used for ham and salted separately. Mama and Mutter, with Frau Schneiker's help, worked until late into the night. Since Papa's work was done by dismembering the pig, he and his friends got a bucket of beer, sat around, and watched the women work. The men were drinking, smoking, and talking about the good pig kill.

Making sausage was the agenda for the next day. Early in the morning, before the sun came up and while the frost was still thick on the ground, Mama started the fire again. Once more washing all the leftover pieces of meat, skin, and entrails, she put them all through the little meat grinder. We took turns turning the handle while Mama stuffed the bits and pieces into the mouth of the grinder. Mutter and Frau Schneiker peeled and chopped onions, garlic, spices, salt, and red-hot peppers, all of which were added to the ground meat. Mama, with her sleeves rolled up, had her arms all the way to her elbow in the pot, mixing and mixing and mixing.

I was the runner, go for this and go for that, so that I wouldn't get sick to my stomach and throw up in front of all the neighbors, who stood around watching and talking. Mama was genuinely concerned about me. What would become of me? More than once I wondered myself. I was tall, very skinny, with no sign of getting breasts ever, and somewhat sickly. Farmer's sons wanted a woman who could work from dawn to dusk. A big strong German girl, who in a few years would become a hardworking, childbearing, obedient woman would be ideal. I was beginning to be concerned as well.

The nasty job of filling intestines with the sausage mixture was at hand. I asked Mama if I could stuff the intestines to show everybody that I could contribute without throwing up. The air was so cold I could see my breath. The noxious smell was diluted with the smell of garlic and onions. Mama took one intestine piece out of the soupy mix and cut it in lengths, measuring them from her wrist to her elbow. She tied one end with a strong thread. Putting the slimy intestine to her lips, she blew into it to see if it had a hole. She'd start the filling of one then hand it to me, and I'd push all the stuff between my index finger and thumb to the knot. After I finished filling the intestine, she checked it very carefully to make sure I hadn't left any air pockets or made any holes in it, because if there was a hole and you threw the sausage into the boiling water, all the filling would come out. Then she tied up the opposite end and tossed the link into a pot of boiling salted water. Whenever Mama decided it was done, she reached into the boiling water with a long wooden stick and removed one link at a time. After the links were air-dried, they were salted again and placed into an earthen pot in preparation for the next step, the smokehouse/box.

Weeks prior to killing the pig, Papa had built an airtight box about six feet tall, four feet wide, and four feet deep that had a door at the bottom and a removable lid. After a few weeks of curing the four hams in salt, they were ready to be smoked. Papa built a fire and let it burn down until it was just smoldering. He hung the hams from hooks attached to the lid of the smoker/box. At the same time, all the sausages were added except for the blood sausage.

It was my job to check on the coals. When they looked like they were about to die, I called for Papa. He kept the wood coals burning. Every night we had to bring everything in, afraid someone might steal the food, but the fire had to be kept going all night long.

The blood that had been saved in a bucket was now cooked with cut-up fatback, onions, garlic, salt, pepper, and spices. The pig's bladder was filled up with this thick mush and tied off; the process was the same as with the sausages except this one was the size and shape of a soccer ball.

Next, the knuckles and head were boiled. All the meat, including the skin, was removed from the bone, cut up, and added to the stock. Mama added carrots, onions, garlic, and spices (one of which was bay leaves) and boiled until all the vegetables were done. That mix was then poured into a bowl and set on the windowsill to congeal. After it set overnight, it was cut into squares and served cold with bread or boiled potatoes. We had a feast of pig knuckles and head, skin and all.

The hams hung in the smokehouse clear up to Christmas. Now we lived like rich Germans. We were the only family in camp who had smoked and salted meat aplenty. There were only two pigs raised in the whole camp in the seven years we lived there.

The day Mama made soap, which went hand in hand with the pig killing, I tried to disappear. I hated the soap because it stung my eyes. I did not want to learn anything else, especially how to make it. But Mama insisted that I watch and learn, as someday it may come in handy. She added fat to potash and brought it to a boil. This concoction was poured into a metal bread pan. After placing the pan under the stove for a few days, the soap was turned out and sliced like bread. The thick slices were laid out on a piece of newspaper and dried until they became hard. Sometimes the newspaper ink imprinted itself onto the soap, but with a few washings the ink disappeared.

I remember taking a complete bath only a very few times in the fall and winter. Papa made a bathtub out of wood. It looked like half a barrel. Mama had me fetch water. Three trips to the well, heat one batch really hot, then add the other two cold. In the wintertime, when I went to get the water from the well, I was so cold that by the time I came home there was only a half bucket full. With each step, it just sloshed out. My hand-knitted stockings and my dress were wet and frozen. I had to keep going until the barrel was filled. Then I changed clothes, and the wet things were hung to dry by the stove. The bath was taken in the kitchen. Starting with the youngest, Mama washed Brother Otto's hair then placed him in the tub, while Papa smoked and read an outdated paper. Then it was Sister Erika's turn. By the time it got to me, the water was cold and soapy, with no rinse water.

A big ado came when it was my turn to bathe. I didn't want to undress in front of Papa. I was self-conscious, but with Mama's threat of, "You better or you'll get it," I gave in. After a few battles, which I lost, I decided to take my bath whenever Mama and Papa were out taking a walk or going into town for food or food stamps. In the summertime, I went with my girlfriends to the Danube. We undressed and took our baths in the river. One of us was always on the lookout for boys.

1949

I had an insatiable thirst for knowledge. It didn't matter what subject. I always liked to read. Books and magazines in camp were rare; first, because few survived Hitler and the bombings, and second, because we didn't have any money. I would beg to borrow a romance novel from my friend's older sisters and wait until I could hear Papa snoring. Sister Erika slept at one end of the bed, I at the other. I read by candlelight in bed under my blanket. It felt so good to read about all those beautiful people and places. Nothing like that existed anymore, only burnt-out buildings, dirty streets, and people dressed in black. Actually, black was very practical to wear, it didn't show dirt and didn't have to be washed as often (per Mama).

This was an enjoyable time for me. Not only did we have plenty of meat to eat but we also found some relatives. Tante Lehman was Mama's mother's sister. She brought her daughter, Tante Ida, and Ida's husband, Stephan, a Russian, to visit us. My cousin was given the title "Tante" out of respect. She and her husband were Mama and Papa's age and seldom talked about how they got out of Russia. My tanten and onkel took a ferry across the Danube at Sand to shorten the two-hour walk. Tante Ida did not have children, and so we were treated as if we were adopted. They always brought us something good to eat. Tante Lehman entertained us with stories about Russia, her trials and tribulations of growing up in the small town of Stariska.

Here in Germany they lived in a tiny room over a cow barn and worked as servants for a rich farmer. The room held a stove, table, and two huge beds. Nobody knew when or where Tante Ida had married Stephan. We never knew anything about Stephan. They lived a very secretive life, like most of the Refugees from Eastern Europe. Some of them had questionable pasts. Sometimes they knew the people they lived with, bonded by things they did in the war. In some cases the men had served together or had secrets together in the war. That was what some neighbors said. Many farmers had single men or whole families living with them, doing chores for meals. If the men were single, they never married but lived with the farmer's family until they died. Sometimes family members who had served in the Nazi Party or the German army came home only to be banished to the mountains or the forest. The soldiers in hiding, who lived in the woods, hunted, fished, raised honeybees, and harvested mushrooms to dry and sell. They lived out their lives in obscurity, with only infrequent visits from family and friends. The past never caught up with them. Almost nobody even knew they existed. The neighbors or family members never questioned or talked about the past. Every time I thought about the war, I wondered about Papa's hidden past.

At least one weekend a month, in the spring and summer only, I made the trip across the Danube to visit Tante Lehman. They lived in Fürth, near the town of Bogen. We ventured out into the woods to collect mushrooms after it rained. Tante Lehman fried them with onions and boiled potatoes.

People from around the area attended the religious pilgrimage that was staged there once a year, at Pentecost, on the Bogenberg. A huge candle, over forty feet tall, was carried up the mountain, with all the Catholic faithful, mostly dressed in black, snaking their way up the slope to the cathedral that overlooked the Danube River valley. Inside the cathedral, the pilgrims lighted a sea of candles and placed notes of gratitude for miracles performed by the Virgin Mary. My girlfriend Herta and I attended this ritual once.

* * *

Four years have passed since we moved to Camp Hofstetten. Gerda is fifteen, Herta, Giesela, and I are thirteen.

Mama said one day, "It's time for you to attend Lutheran religious classes. You are screwed up about what you should believe; you'll be worshiping the pope in a couple of years."

Papa, who never went to church, was all for it. Dutifully, I attended religious classes once a week with my best friends, Herta, Gerda, and Giesela. The classes were held Saturdays for two hours at the pastor's house in Straubing. What a revelation they provided about God. I knew Him as an old man in the sky. I was fascinated by all the religious explanations, especially Martin Luther's Small Catechism. Christuskirche (the local Lutheran church) had been destroyed by bombs, so we attended Lutheran services at Straubing's St. Jakob Kirche, on Bahnhofstrasse—a Catholic church.

Mama produced many vegetables in her garden, one of which was cabbages. They were the size of soccer balls and very tight. We harvested them in the fall. Papa made a wooden barrel that Mama filled with shredded cabbages. After washing my feet, I climbed into the barrel and mashed down the shreds. Salt was added, then the barrel was covered with a cloth and a stone was placed on top of it. After a week or two, the smell of rotting cabbage permeated the whole house. Preserving sauerkraut took months. Mama also preserved cucumbers and green tomatoes the same way, alternating each layer with dill.

Sauerkraut soup began with a pot of water. Mama added a few potatoes when we had them. She peeled then diced and boiled them and added them to the sauerkraut. A few browned wild onions topped off the soup. Heated cabbage with a little lard was delicious on bread.

The gleaning season schedule year after year was early potato, then wheat, then late potato, then sugar beets. To exist was a daily struggle. Gleaning potatoes and sugar beets was completely different from gleaning wheat. The potatoes and sugar beets gleaned easier after a good rain. The rain washed the leftover potatoes or sugar beets, sometimes only pieces, out of the dirt, and all you had to do was pick them up. When it didn't rain but we knew by the drastic temperature drop each night that in a week or so the first frost would appear, we used a potato hoe. This tool was shaped like a hay fork with three or four bent prongs. When I ran the prongs through the soil, pieces of potato or sugar beet came up. Other times the farmer had done such a good job that it would take forever to find anything at all. Occasionally we came up empty.

The weather was cold early in the morning in the late fall. By noon, it became warmer and our outer wrap had dried off from the morning mist. My wooden clogs presented a problem. The wet dirt stuck to the bottom of the wood, accumulating two to three inches in an uneven height. I had to stop every couple of steps and scrape it off. My feet were forever wet and cold. I wore woolen socks but they never did dry out during the day.

We loaded the sack of potatoes or sugar beets on the bike. Both were heavier than the same sack full of wheat, and it took a lot more strength to push and steer the bike. With blisters on my hands, I prayed all the way home that we wouldn't have a flat tire.

The potatoes were not washed but stored in the corner of a newly acquired empty room. One of Mutter's old friends had died and left her a corner in her room, the other corners going to other old friends in the camp. The sugar beets were washed, dried, and stored next to the potatoes.

After a good cleaning, Mama peeled and chopped sugar beets and boiled them in a little water until the liquid took on the consistency of syrup. This was used in place of sugar on bread, in tea, or on pancakes. Other times Mama cut the beets into squares and dried them in the oven until they turned dark brown, almost black. She mashed the dried pieces with the bottom of a beer bottle then mixed them with hot water. Although Mama insisted the result tasted like coffee, I never did acquire a taste for it. Everyone else in the family was thrilled with the taste of this brew.

1950

My girlfriends Herta and Gerda had these horrific stomach pains once a month starting at thirteen, but not me. Their mothers heated a brick and put it on their stomachs. Oh, how they were pampered during this time with hot tea, spirits, and honey. They stayed in bed, moaning and groaning, for two or three days and then the blood flowed for a week. That was the safest time to have sex, their sisters told them. Between the three of us, after a lengthy discussion, we decided it would not be a good idea to have sex when bleeding. We were sure it would be a mess. I couldn't wait to start bleeding and to be one of them. Then my mama would tell me all the secrets I needed to know and pamper me as well.

Finally my time came. I was fourteen. My stomach hurt so badly that I doubled over in bed. After going to the bathroom, I noticed a dark brown stain on my underwear.

"Mama," I cried, "please help me, I'm going to die." It was the brown stain that frightened me. My girlfriends had said they had red stains.

Mama consoled me: "All women are plagued with this bleeding once a month. You can have sex during this time and not get pregnant. You must be very careful because husbands don't like wives who are always pregnant, even though it is a woman's duty to have children, just as it is the duty of the men to be soldiers and defend the fatherland."

"How do you keep from getting pregnant?" I wanted to know.

"You always do what the man wants you to do. Never complain, even if it hurts. Even if you are dead tired, if your husband is in need of it, you must adhere to his wishes. If you say 'no,' he will find someone else who will say 'yes.' A happy marriage is made or broken in bed."

I nodded as if I understood this.

"When he is finished," Mama continued, "he will fall asleep. You get up, squat down, put your finger into the second opening, not the third opening (I never knew there was a second opening), and try to pull out the whitish slime. If you don't get it all out, then you on your way to having a baby. No, you don't bleed when you are pregnant. It takes nine months to have a baby. During that time you don't have to be careful when having sex. As long as you nurse a baby for two years or so, you won't get pregnant either."

Those comments were the extent of sex education Mama was going to provide. But now that I was having my period, she made sure I had a pair of well-used underpants during this crucial time. She also showed me how to make rags for the bleeding. She took an old white cotton rag and cut it into strips as wide and a little bit longer than her hand. Triple thickness, she sewed them with a chain stitch around the edges and cut two buttonholes on each end. In an old pair of underpants she sewed two buttons, one in the front and one in the back. The two buttons were cut off of an old shirt. The strips of rags were buttoned to the underwear. Now I had a sample and could sew the other two by myself. That should last six days, and if you had your bleeding a few days longer, then you just used a regular rag. I was to put my used rags in the can with hers. It was my turn to wash, scrub, and rub until my knuckles started to bleed, making the pads white as snow. The boys always knew when any of us girls had our period and would make fun. The neighbor women made it a point to pass by on my washday to critique my laundry. For the first time in my young life, I felt a strong bond had developed with my mama.

* * *

After the opening of our school, there was no intermingling or any contact with the Real Germans, except when we went to the market, butcher shop, or bakery. Occasionally on a Saturday night, Mama and Papa would go to a nearby Gasthaus frequented by other Refugees. They drank a couple of beers, sang a few old songs, and came home around ten.

Being teenagers, we wanted to dance and sing and have parties too. Herbert Sapek, one of the boys, knew how to play the accordion. Many Saturday nights we met at someone's barrack, and while Herbert played, we would dance. Four of us girls, best friends, called ourselves "four-leaf-clover girls." Three of us always attended (without Giesela, who was not allowed out of the house at night). There were the same number of boys. It sure was a strange feeling being held by a boy. The kitchens were so small that only two couples could dance or comfortably move around. Once we found out what an erection was, we had fun talking about the boys. We discussed the feeling later when we were alone. The urge to kiss a boy became overwhelming at the age of fourteen. I was very careful because Mama said, "If you kiss a boy, what follows is sex, and then you become pregnant." God forbid I should get pregnant. Papa would kill me for sure. Not too long after this conversation with Mama, her theory would be tested. Gerda's brother Hansi had grown taller and very handsome. He kissed me twice, right on my lips. It didn't lead to sex. Oh, I would never wash my lips ever again! Nevertheless, I worried for three solid weeks before the blood flowed. No baby, thank God.

Finally, I decided now was the time to confront Mama with the word *abortion*.

"Whenever you need to terminate a pregnancy, all you have to do is visit a doctor. He will go in and clean out your stomach right there in his office," Mama said. "It doesn't hurt and there will be no baby."

All of us became very good dancers and looked forward to Saturday evenings when our parents allowed us to attend the dances in the school barrack. It was used as a classroom during the week and a dance hall on Saturday nights. Usually someone with an accordion played polkas, the favorite dance. Whenever Papa was in a bad mood, I was not allowed to attend the dance. Occasionally, I would go to bed fully dressed, wait until Mama and Papa went to bed, and climb out the window. Once, Papa locked the window and I couldn't get back in and had to wake him. Papa unleashed his fury, using his belt instantly and severely. Mama only watched. She never helped me or interfered.

After I had learned to dance the tango, polka, waltz and samba, I ventured into Straubing on Sunday afternoon by myself just to walk and look in shop windows. There was one particular Gasthaus by the zoo with a small band playing every Sunday afternoon for about two hours. I sat at a table by myself and wished that someone would ask me to dance. No one did. On the way home I passed through the center of town and admired the tall, huge tower that had five steeples, called the Stadt Turm. People were selling furs, old shoes, paintings, silver, crystal, and china. When I had an opportunity to steal one deutschmark (about 25 cents) from my mama by not giving her back all the change from buying a loaf of bread, I would see a movie. I seized every opportunity to spend two hours with Tyrone Power. To beat it all, he spoke German. I loved what I saw. America was heaven on earth. Every time I saw an American movie, I bonded to America by reverence, wonder, and adoration. I lost myself in the American countryside.

Prayer was supposed to make all your dreams come true, but who would ever pray about going to America? That was completely out of the question. It was like asking God to give you a mink coat with a pair of boots to match. God only had time for the sick, for the priests and the nuns. The hour walk home would be lost in daydreaming, completely detached from reality.

Mama: "Ella, where were you all day?"

"Oh, I spent the afternoon walking around Straubing."

This was partly true. It was only a small sin. God wouldn't mind. And stealing money from Mama—well, I could confide in our Lutheran minister before I went to Communion that I had sinned. He would tell me, "You are forgiven." But by then I had forgotten about all the small sins. My reasoning was, if God knew I was lying, stealing, and cheating, why should I have to tell Him? What would He take from me to punish me? I had nothing. His punishment would be to send some kind of sickness into my life. Whenever I got sick, Mama and Mutter would get me well. So there! And anytime I did get sick, Mama or Mutter would always say, "Your sins are coming out of you." After recovering there was a new beginning to sinning.

I envied Sister Lida. She lived with Mutter and always got the best of everything. The best food and the best dresses that Mutter made were all for her. She never had to do any chores. Mama, Papa, and Mutter never punished her. Sister Erika and I hardly ever included her in conversations or play, because if ever anything went wrong, Sister Lida would run to Mutter and complain. That would set Mutter on the warpath to inform Papa, who had to take action.

I could hear Mutter getting up with the birds. Through a small hole in the wall I'd see her eat a piece of dry bread and drink a little tea brewed the night before.

Mutter always wore a long black skirt, black blouse and kerchief, and never any underwear. I asked her one day why she never wore underwear and was told and shown that when she stood slightly bent over and held her long skirt out a bit she could urinate almost anywhere without people noticing. No one seemed to mind that Mutter smelled bad like all the other old people. Fall and winter around old people was bearable only because they wore many layers of clothing. When the days warmed up, the body odor mixed with the urine smell was overwhelming. I stayed away as much as possible from old people. Get close to any old person in the neighborhood and the stench was revolting.

"Mama," I said, "why doesn't Mutter take a bath?"

Her reply: "A bath once in a while is good, but if you take too many baths it is bad for your skin."

"Elsa, watch Lida while I'm gone," Mutter would tell Mama, then leave for the rest of the day. Not until she returned, toward evening, would we find out where she had been, either on the edge of the Danube gathering driftwood or somewhere in a forest collecting branches or uprooting a rotted stump. She returned with a huge bundle of wood on her back.

After one year of instruction, pages and pages of memory work, and having passed all the biblical questions put to me at the end, it was time for me to be confirmed. Our pastor was very old and strict, Herr Pfarrer Rohn (referred to formally as Mister Pastor Rohn). He had no tolerance and no forgiveness for breaking his rules. Bible reading and memorization of the Creed, including the Small Catechism and the Ten Commandments, had to be done perfectly and right on time. If you did not pass the examination, you got a beating from your parents and then were recycled into the next class. Anyone who came to the altar to be confirmed and who smiled, laughed, or giggled would be automatically excluded from the Lord's table and not confirmed. On the last day of instructions our pastor said, "Before you come to church for your confirmation, you must ask your mother and father for forgiveness for the unkind things you have said and the pain and sorrow you have caused them in years past. Your parents know what is expected of you, so you cannot tell me a lie. I also need your baptismal date."

"Mama," I asked, "was I ever baptized?"

"Of course," she said.

"Where?"

"In Kiev, in our basement apartment. We had a Lutheran pastor come and baptize you."

"Oma always told me there were no churches or pastors in Russia because of the Communists."

"He came from Stariska."

"How old was I?"

"You were almost one year old. I think it was the 10th of February 1937," she said. That settled that. I didn't have to worry anymore whether I was baptized or not.

The other requirement was to be dressed in black for the ceremony. We had no black dresses and no money to buy one. How would we pay a seamstress even if we could get material? We told the pastor early on in our class that we did not have black dresses. He looked at us with disbelief. The following Sunday after the service, a miracle occurred. He announced that those who didn't have clothing for confirmation should come to church the next day and pick out whatever they needed, black dresses for the girls and dark suits for the boys—shoes too. I must remember what Mama said about shoes: Always get them too big. I could stuff cotton into the front to begin with, then the following year the shoes would fit fine, and the next year they would pinch my toes. Because I wouldn't wear the shoes that often, Sister Erika could then inherit them.

The following day the four of us girls, with two boys tagging along, made the trip into town. At the annex of the church we were escorted by the secretary to a room where, to our complete amazement, we found tables piled high with used clothing and shoes.

"Where did all this come from?" I said to the secretary.

"From America," she said.

"From America? The same people who almost killed us just a few years ago?" I asked.

"Yes," she said, "and we should thank God that we have friends like the Americans who love the Lord and take care of us. If it were not for the Americans, you would not be confirmed."

I began to think more and more about Americans. They must be good people to send us food and clothing and give us candy and gum. Who could I ask about Americans? All the German men I knew from camp who had fought in the war had been on the eastern front. They never had anything to say about the war anyway. Nobody had fought the Americans or knew anything about Americans.

We spent hours looking over and trying on each black dress, followed by shoes, coats, and jackets. Finally, I picked out a really beautiful dress. It had a beautiful round neck and fit snugly to my waist, then it flared into a loose skirt ending below my knees. The long sleeves flared at the wrists. A perfect fit. Except for short white gloves, I was dressed from head to toe in black: dress, slip, stockings. The shoes were black patent leather, used but in good condition. The care instructions on my dress said, "Dry clean only." I had no idea what that meant. I resolved that I would never wash it. I didn't.

Mama took extra care when washing my hair the night before. Next morning she made a straight part down the middle, pulled my hair back, and braided two braids. She placed a little wreath made out of small white artificial flowers, interwoven with greenery, on my head. Mama had saved up a little money to buy the flowers and a small cross that I wore around my neck. She was beaming with pride when she saw me fully dressed.

"Now, Ella," she said, "from now on you must wash under your arms every time you wear the dress because you have grown quite a bit of hair there. If you don't wash, the sweat will permeate your dress and smell. Also, hang your dress outside to air after you wear it." Since it was the only thing of beauty and value that I owned, I followed her instructions exactly.

The day of confirmation had finally arrived. I approached my parents to ask for forgiveness. Papa took it stoically. Mama hugged me, held me close to her big breasts, and we both cried. Between sobs, I finally got out, "Forgive me, Mama." Mama reached up to her pierced ears and removed from them the only jewelry she possessed, her pure gold earrings. She cupped them in her hand, and then she stretched her arm out toward me and said, "Ella, this is the only thing of value I own in this world. I got them from my sister after my mama died. I want you to have them."

My reaction was not simple joy and a "Thank you Mama" but another river of tears. I could not speak. I was overwhelmed. Never in a million years had I expected Mama to give up her gold earrings. Never to give them to me. If she had given them to Sister Erika, I would have expected it and understood. But me? I was elated. I hugged and hugged her until she finally freed herself from my embrace and said, "That is enough."

Everyone in the family put on their best, including Papa. Mama had gotten hold of an orange parachute. She had a neighbor sew it into two Dirndls, the Bavarian woman's costume dresses. I was proud and happy.

Sister Erika wore her orange dress. Even Mutter and Sister Lida came. We picked flowers from our garden, which I carried all the way to the church. By the time we arrived, the flowers had wilted and I had two big blisters on my feet. I didn't complain. I had shoes. On the way, we met up with our neighbors and friends. The grown-ups talked about their own confirmations. I walked with my friends and flirted with the boys. Oh, the boys. How handsome they looked in their donated suits. Some suits were much too big, but they would grow into them. Others were too snug and good for only a few wearings. The church was a beautiful ornate building in the gothic style, with everything pointed toward heaven: the windows, the doors, and the altar. I was the happiest Lutheran in Germany, being confirmed in a huge beautiful Catholic church.

When we entered the church, the joy and happiness were automatically left outside. Our old minister, Herr Pfarrer Rohn, was dressed in black. He preached a very earnest sermon on our responsibility as believers in Christ. Then we received Communion. There were approximately fifty communicants from all over the city. On the way out, Herr Pastor Rohn presented each of us a certificate. Mine read, "Ella Elsa Schneider was baptized 10 February 1937, Confirmed 2 April 1950," with a memory verse: "Jesus answered, You are right in saying, I am a king. In fact for this reason I was born, and for this I came into the world to testify to the truth. Everyone on the side of truth listens to me" (John 18:37). After this ceremony, I was able to participate in Communion each Easter and Christmas.

Slowly all the Refugee families made our way back to camp. The Real Germans out taking their Sunday afternoon family walk in the predominately Catholic town stared and glared at us.

Mama had cooked the best she knew how with what she had. We had a horse meat roast, lumpy mashed potatoes with delicious brown gravy, and a tomato-and-cucumber salad. For dessert, Mama served freshly cooked, still-warm vanilla pudding with egg whites floating on top.

Papa took the water bucket and, instead of sending me to buy beer, went himself. It was a festive occasion. Papa even played a few songs on his dilapidated old accordion. Mama sang and we listened. It was not every day that there was such joy and happiness in our home. The rest of the day and evening I visited back and forth with friends. Then, as the darkness crept in on us, the families moved outside to continue the celebration. Many evenings people assembled in front of their barracks under starry skies to sit on their straight-back wooden chairs and sing songs of days gone by when they were young. Some people joined in parts from the other side of the camp and it sounded like a heavenly choir. This was how we celebrated holidays and special occasions. I learned songs from different countries and different melodies and in different languages. The grown-ups talked about many things but never the war. Never, never talk about Adolph Hitler.

"Mama," I inquired, "why doesn't anybody talk about the war?"

"Because there are too many Spionen [informers] among us," she replied. "Too many old Nazis. Then there are the Communists. We don't want any of them to know who and where we are."

The following day we went to the photographer. Mama had come up with enough money for one picture. Mama's admonition: Always save enough money for three pictures in your lifetime—confirmation, wedding, and a picture when you are lying in the casket.

After my confirmation, I went into Straubing every Sunday morning for worship service, even if I had to go by myself. I loved being close to God in that beautiful church.

* * *

When I made it to the seventh grade in the summer of 1950, to our total amazement and surprise, Herr Lehrer Mohr organized a trip into the Bavarian forest. I nearly died of shock when I saw a big Ami truck come into our camp. The "whores" were brought home by the Amis in jeeps. We ran to the truck. This was a new event. The soldier asked for Herr Lehrer Mohr. One of the "whores" came to translate. The Amis were here to pick up the kids to take us all to the mountains for a weekend. Herr Lehrer Mohr had requested transportation through proper channels. Herr Lehrer Bahle, a Bavarian, would never have asked the Amis to transport us to the mountains. Herr Lehrer Mohr must not have hated the Amis that much.

The Amis provided not only the transportation but also the food. It came in cans and was called "C-rations." Each meal tasted different—I could hardly wait for the next one. It was a fun-filled weekend. We sang while marching through the forest, picking and eating blueberries. We learned about the stars at night. All of us slept in the attic in a one-room cabin called "Die Fichtdacher Schi Hütte" (the Fir Tree Ski Lodge). The kitchen and living area were on the ground floor. We were a total of thirty-two. In the attic, the sleeping arrangements placed girls on one side and boys on the other. The three teachers slept down the middle. Herr Lehrer Mohr and Miss Dimmelmeier kept to themselves, smiling and talking in whispers. Before leaving, we celebrated our weekend with a huge bonfire. The outing was too short. After that excursion, Herr Lehrer Mohr and Fräulein Dimmelmeier got married and they moved into town, living in a house she owned across from the Straubinger Schlachthoff (meat-packing plant) on Heerstrasse.

Back in the classroom, we received our daily portion of oatmeal, which was donated by the Amis. An old woman was appointed to cook for us. She managed to burn the oatmeal every day. We could smell it all over the camp. It was prepared with powdered milk, and when it burned, it reeked to high heaven. We had to bring our bowls and spoons to school to receive a portion during the ten o'clock break. Daily, I forced myself to be grateful. Herr Lehrer Mohr reminded us to thank the Amis for taking care of us. We never saw any Amis in an official capacity to thank them properly.

In class, my assigned seat was right next to a window, which was permanently open during the summer months. It was a warm day. I daydreamed about the latest romance novel I'd read, my superlative imagination conjuring up all kinds of heart-throbbing scenes. Occasionally I followed a slow-moving, mashed-potato cloud until it disappeared from view. During one of those imaginative musings a goat raised up and looked into the classroom. Facing the goat about five feet away, I came out of my hypnotic state with a scream that must have been heard for miles. Everyone turned to see what I was screaming about. All they saw was a goat. After I regained my senses, I had to face the hilarious laughter of my classmates. I was completely mortified. My final few months in school that term were a torture, to the nickname of "Goat." The cruelty of my schoolmates seemed like it would never end. Being consoled by my girlfriends helped, but I could not find the rosy color when I tried to look toward the bright side of life when this teasing would stop.

I hated winter because it restricted my movements. Winters were incredibly harsh and long. The windows were frozen with an inch of ice on the inside. The water bucket froze on the cold stove. The snow was so deep that there was no way to walk to the next-door neighbor or to the well.

Once in a while, on a wind-free sunny day, Herta, Gerda and I made a trip to the banks of the Danube. Most of the time, however, Mama wanted me home to care for baby Brother Otto. Seldom was I allowed to visit my girlfriends in their homes. They didn't come to visit me very often either, because they thought my parents were too strict and not very friendly. School was closed for many days because there was no wood to heat the classroom and no one to shovel a path to the front door. There were no long winter nights sitting around the stove talking, since we had to be in bed when it began to get dark. The fire in the stove was damped right after Mama finished cooking dinner. After the dishes were washed and dried, it was time for bed.

Many times, I slept in whatever I had on. Since Sister Erika and I shared a bed, it didn't take long to get warm.

There was always something that had to be done. No idleness was allowed in our home. Mama had me unravel knitted socks or sweaters that were old but not rotten. We rescued them from the Real Germans' trash. After giving them a good washing and drying, Mama found a beginning and I rolled the thread into a ball. If the thread was too thin, I made two balls then combined them into one thread. The learning process started with two metal knitting needles for knitting a shawl. When I mastered that art, I graduated to the five metal needles used for knitting socks, mittens or gloves. Mama was a no-nonsense teacher. She showed me twice how to hold the needles and feed the thread through my fingers. I managed to knit all kinds of articles of clothing—socks, underpants, mittens, gloves, sweaters, shawls, hats, vests, and skirts—as well as to mend holes in socks. Our teacher, Herr Lehrer Mohr, would not permit any girl to graduate unless she handed in a pair of perfectly knitted gloves and a pair of socks. Not until the snow was falling and the icicles were a yard long hanging from the barrack roof did I appreciate the warm things I made. Joining Sister Erika in our cold bed in woolen underpants, socks, gloves, cap, and sweater, plus staying under the cover all night, made for sound sleeping. Woolen things were washed in the summertime only. Playing outside in the snow and getting my socks and gloves wet put me out of circulation until everything was dry. Heavy wool would take days to dry around our stove.

I was always an early riser, yet I never quite mastered the art of starting a fire without filling our rooms with smoke. I'd begin with balled-up paper and some kindling. Once this ignited, I'd add bigger pieces of wood. When the wind came from the wrong direction, the kitchen filled with smoke. Papa jumped out of bed and had a fit. Fists flew. I dodged as best as I could, while still more smoke poured into the kitchen. Mama, who stayed in bed until the thick smoke reached her bedroom and affected her breathing, would finally get up and remedy the situation.

The potatoes, turnips, carrots, and sugar beets we had gleaned during the summer and fall came in handy during these long, harsh winter months. The vegetables were covered with old blankets in our unheated extra storage room. Sometimes the frost was so severe it lasted for days and weeks, and then even the covered vegetables froze. Mama never threw them out but used them in soups. Frozen potatoes tasted the worst. They had a pungent, sickening sweetness. The only way I could tolerate eating frozen-potato soup was with a piece of dried black bread spread with cod-liver oil, which I hated, one bad taste covering another bad taste.

Grocery shopping was always done on days when the snowstorms had subsided. By midday the sun came out and melted some of the snow. There were no one-stop grocery stores. I had to go to the bakery to buy a few loaves of bread. Then on to the butcher. Another stop at the dairy store for milk, cheese, or butter. Buying candy was unheard of in our family. Money was in short supply.

Bread was sold by the bakery to each family with ration cards and had to last from week to week. It was brown, crusty, coarse rye bread called Schwarz Brot (black bread). Since we were such a large family, one loaf was never enough—and tomorrow the snow might be worse. Three to four loaves were the norm to last for a few days. Bread was never thrown away. It never got moldy, just hard as a rock. Mama reminded us that hard bread at least a week old was good for our teeth. I don't remember anyone having or using a toothbrush, but the hard bread took care of the yellow that collected on our teeth and gums. I ate my dried hard bread to ensure I would not have rotten teeth like some of the old women who lived next door. Mama and Papa had good teeth, so I couldn't go wrong. (In the fall, I stole some pecans that had fallen off a tree in a rich German's yard and used my teeth to crack them. My teeth, having chewed bread as hard as a rock, had no problem cracking the nuts.) When the bread became so hard you could not bite it for fear of breaking your teeth, it was added to boiling water to make bread soup.

Mama and Papa went to bed and did what they did with the bed squeaking and the funny sounds by Mama and the hard, harsh, unintelligible, untranslatable words by Papa. Sister Erika and I never dared to interrupt.

Sister Erika was never outspoken like I was. My siblings learned by my example. When Papa had a correction to make, I was the recipient. The others watched and remained obedient.

1951

One day while we were having supper, Sister Erika, leaving the table, started to scream and stomp her feet. Her face became quite distorted and tears were streaming down her cheeks. She was now about thirteen years of age. No one could understand what caused this outburst. Papa started yelling for her to shut up. Mama hugged her close, trying to hold her down. She was having a fit and completely out of control. It took some time before she stopped screaming and stomping her feet, all the while hitting an unseen object.

Mama, "Erika, liebchen, what brought this on?"

After several tries she finally said, "Mama, I saw the devil and I am so scared."

We were all completely stunned by this revelation. Papa had the solution: beat the devil out of her. Mama would not permit it.

"She is a child and will grow out of it," Mama said.

That should have been the end, but remember, the walls were thin. The following day Sister Erika was teased mercilessly by the other kids. When Mama washed her hair, it had a beautiful reddish sheen to it. The boys would yell, "Erika was bathing with the devil again." Poor Sister Erika, she suffered so much and cried a lot. This teasing went on and on.

* * *

It is June 1951, my birth month, and I am fifteen now. Finally, I finished the eighth row in the school classroom. It was the last and final row. Graduating from Volksschule, I completed the eighth grade with a marking of "Gut" (good), not outstanding or excellent, but just average. As far as I was concerned, considering the disadvantaged condition under which we were taught in our camp school, my education was excellent.

Every day I approached job hunting very enthusiastically. My new daily routine was to get up, put on my clean dress (I had three now), and make the hour-long walk to Straubing. My first stop was at the Bureau for Job Placements. The receptionist greeted me with a hostile glare.

"Yes, we have your name. We know you have completed Volksschule. Can you cook?"

This time I couldn't get away with a lie. The things I learned to cook from Mama I was sure the Real Germans would never eat.

"A little, mostly Polish." Well, Russian was almost the same. But the Real Germans didn't like the Russians or anyone who came from there, much less their cooking.

"Can you cook for ten people who are working on a farm? Three meals a day?"

"No, but I would be willing to learn."

In an icily efficient condescending voice she said, "Please come back next week."

Utterly despondent, frustrated, and completely helpless, yet always hoping for a miracle tomorrow, I returned home.

In 1948, the German government had given seven displaced families from Silesia parcels of land. This land reached from Hofstetten to the outskirts of Straubing. These were seven big (Catholic) families with many children, all interrelated. One of the girls, Regina Reitmeier, was my classmate; she had fourteen siblings. My pride suffered, but I would stop and ask if they had anything for me to do. Once or twice a week, I watched their cows graze or helped with bringing in crops like hay or wheat. Thankful for the work, I would get half a gallon of fresh milk and half a loaf of black bread.

My job search widened each week, with trips to the surrounding villages of Ittling, Bogen, Ober-Parkstetten, and all the way to Steinach. The question at the front door to a farmer's wife, "Do you need some help in the kitchen or in the garden, milk the cows, feed the pigs, run errands, work in the field? I will work for very little." If asked, "Where are you from?" I'd say, "Hofstetten," and that would be it. "No, I don't need anyone." End of conversation.

Mama's admonition: "Answer each question without giving much information." No luck. Mama again: "Don't tell them you are Volga Deutsche, either. They'll still hate you for being here, eating their food, taking up their jobs, and living on their land." Hard to know what to tell them, then.

It was the end of August 1951 and I still didn't have a job. Just seeing the words "Graduated from Camp Hofstetten by Straubing" was enough for potential employers not even to give you a chance. I spent many days worrying. Mama tried to encourage me: Something would turn up.

This was an ongoing daily reality that I faced. Where could I go to find a job or direction for my life? It seemed to me as if the situation of being unemployed would become the pattern of my existence. What was most depressing was to see others' successes. Gerda got a job as a lab assistant in Straubing. Herta went off to be a nanny seventy-five miles away, where no one knew about Hofstetten. Her brother, Herbert Schlolaut, who had come out of a Russian prisoner of war camp, worked on a ship hauling goods up and down the Rhine River.

Occasionally, Papa would get a carpentry job, which would last only a few weeks. Most of the time he didn't want one. Between odd jobs, he collected unemployment. Added to the child support money, that was enough. He didn't have to pay rent, could now afford cigarettes, and had an old bike to get around on. His philosophy was that he had everything and didn't need anything else.

Doing some volunteer work at the Lutheran church, helping with the kindergarten kids, did get me out of the house on weekends. The uncertainty of my future seemed overwhelming to me. At times like this, how I wished I were old enough to go to America, even if I had to marry a white, black, red, or yellow Ami.

The Real German graduates had no problems finding jobs or getting into job training. For me there was no room. They knew each other in their villages, where they and their families had lived all their lives for generations. When the butcher needed an apprentice, he called the friend of a friend. The job was filled before it even went to the Job Placement Bureau. It wasn't right, and the resentment was growing, not just in me but among all of the Refugees.

Papa came home one day after taking a walk on the banks of the Danube. "I talked to Kharakash," he said, referring to the native Russian family who lived at the opposite end of camp. "They're going to Canada next month." He let this news hang in the air a moment, then said to Mama: "It's been months since we registered to go to America. Nothing has come of it so far. What do you think?"

This was the first I had ever heard of this action.

"America," Papa continued, "would definitely strengthen our hope for a better place to live and raise our children, to be somebody in this world. Then too, we would get further away from the Communists. What do you think? Should we seriously pursue it? There is no life for us here in Germany. We will always be second-class citizens. What will become of our children? One thing is for certain, I will never go back to Russia. I will die first. Maybe in America our children will have a chance."

Mama agreed as usual. Papa became serious and sent a letter to the immigration authorities in Munich strongly reiterating our desire to be allowed to emigrate to America.

"Mutter," I said one morning, grinning with pride, "I had a dream last night that had a date in it. I got up, just like you said I should do, and wrote it on the dusty chest-of-drawers."

"What is it?" she asked.

"27 April."

"Remember that day. God is telling you something that will happen on that date," she said.

Fall was approaching, and with it my enthusiasm for getting a job diminished. Twice a week I reported to the Job Placement Bureau and finally was told not to come back, there were no jobs of any kind for me, and a letter would notify me when something turned up.

I talked it over with my parents and enrolled in the American-language classes that were given in Straubing next to the movie theater on Thursday evenings. A young German man who had been a prisoner of war for years in America taught the classes. He was not bitter. He was a very good teacher who liked Americans. The American language I memorized was referred to as "kitchen English" and had a very limited vocabulary. For instance: "How are you? My name is Ella. I come from Germany. Where do you live? Do you have a brother or a sister?" We memorized twenty words a week. Sentence structure was very important, since most German sentences have the verb at the end of the sentence—for example, "I will home with you go." Of course, the do's and don'ts were also important. Germans always shake hands when meeting and taking leave. They never say, "Hi, how are you?" when they are being introduced for the first time. On the other hand, Americans use "I'm sorry" for almost anything, even if they are not.

There were about twenty-five students in my class, the majority of them boys. Some Amis were still stationed in town. The boys hoped to land good jobs working for them, and some did.

Here I met my first boyfriend, Wolfgang. He was a Refugee from Hungary, living in Steinach, north of Camp Hofstetten on the other side of the Danube. He walked me home after our American class, pushing our bikes and trekking for an hour. His goodnight kiss was tender. That night I decided that not all men were brutes.

Papa made sure that I didn't miss one single American-language class. He was very proud of my accomplishment. Each day following a class, I had to relate to him what I had learned. All information was copied from the blackboard. I busied myself to put every word and every sentence to memory. Sometimes my sentence structure was all in disarray. I reasoned if I gave an American a cluster of words, he or she should be able to pick out what I was trying to say. I loved to hear, read, and discover the wonderful differences between Germans and Americans, getting to know Americans as hardworking, fun-loving families. To my surprise, I was told that there were whole towns of first- and second-generation German Americans living all over America. I could hardly wait for my next class.

I asked my girlfriend's sister, who had an Ami as a boyfriend, to get me some American magazines. Pictures alone tell a million stories. From then on, I lived in an unbelievable, indescribable dreamworld, America.

* * *

The Kharakash family was packing their things. They were leaving for Canada. They told Mama that while processing, they had heard that carpenters were needed in America. Papa had just about given up hope of getting a reply from the Immigration Office in Munich.

Mama and Papa discussed our dreams outside our front door in the evenings when the sun was setting.

Papa said, "I'm willing to sacrifice my life in order for our children to have a future." Mama added that her life probably would not be better in

America, because she needed to learn American, and she didn't know if she could learn a new language and new customs now that she was in her forties. They would both be giving up their friends and all the neighbors who had now become family after so many years of living together. It came down to the fact that only the children would benefit from emigration. As for themselves, they wanted nothing. Surely, the living, schooling, and working conditions would be better than they experienced in Germany as Refugees.

As soon as the news got out that we were thinking about going to America, we became the topic of conversation throughout the camp. Some neighbors laughed at our dream. Smiling, they said, "The Puders emigrating to America?"

"Theodor got it in his head he is going to America."

"Preposterous."

"Who wants a family with four children?"

We became the talk and gossip of Hofstetten. Only a few were supportive of our dream and dreamed with us.

After finding out from the Kharakash family where the Immigration Office in Munich was located, on a Monday morning in September, Mama and Papa took a train ride. They were gone about a week. Upon their return, we had a family conference. Papa instructed us from now on to tell the truth. I couldn't remember what the truth was anymore. His impression of the Americans was that they were smarter than the Germans and knew history and geography better. They had all of Papa's papers from the war, stating which army he served in, how long, and where. From then on, I respected Papa more. He must have been a pretty good soldier, whichever army he was in, because the Americans would not take a bad person with a questionable past. I never did get to hear the true, real story of his life or read any of the official papers.

The drill began again. I was born in Kiev, USSR. My real papa was taken by the Russians and we never saw him again. I came to Germany on one of the last German transport trains out of Kiev in the fall of 1943, with the retreating German army.

I was not to volunteer any information, only answer each question truthfully. I had been telling lies for years, so many lies that now it became very hard for me to sort out the truth.

Where am I from? Germany or Russia or Poland? Where were you born? What do you know about your father? Which father? What is his occupation? Was he in the army? Which army?

Since I didn't know anything about my present papa I could honestly say, "I don't know anything." These family sessions continued for weeks. I had become a talkative teenager, and Mama was always afraid I would say something that would destroy our hope of emigrating. Papa and Mama supposedly were telling the truth about their lives as well. Wish I knew what they said.

Weeks passed before the first batch of papers arrived. Papa dutifully filled out whatever was asked and personally took the return envelope to the post office. Finally, in late October, the paperwork stopped. An official-looking envelope came that summoned the whole family to the American Immigration Center at the Funk Kaserne in Munich for physical examinations and processing. Maybe, just maybe, if God was willing, we were really going to emigrate to America. I shared my excitement with everyone I met. My boyfriend was happy I was going to America and sad he wouldn't see me anymore. Papa talked to his mother. Mutter made no bones about refusing to go to America. She was going to die in Germany. Papa insisted that Sister Lida was coming with us over Mutter's strong objections.

With train tickets issued by the Americans, we made our way to Munich. After checking out our room in a barrack, my next stop was the bathroom. The ladies' room had a picture of a woman on the door. This was great—individual stalls with doors and toilet paper. The toilet paper was brown and rough but better than the butcher paper or the old newspaper we used in Hofstetten. There were bottles that dispensed soap, and tissue boxes next to the washbasins. Half a dozen showers stood against the wall with soap lying in the soap dishes. This world I liked.

We were interviewed separately and then as a family. The questions were the same ones Papa had drilled us about. If in doubt say, "I don't know." It worked. Two American soldiers asked all the questions in German. Between themselves, they spoke American.

"Ella, are you the oldest?"

"Yes."

"Are all these your brother and sisters?"

"Yes."

"What is your father's name?"

"Which one? This one is Theodor."

"When are your sisters' and your brother's birthdays?"

"Erika 31 May, Lida 26 July, Otto 31 July."

"Are you attending school?"

"No, I graduated from Volksschule in May."

"Why do you want to go to America?"

"I want to go to America to get a job."

"Do you speak English?"

"I speak a little American. Is it the same?"

"Yes."

Then it was Sister Erika's turn.

"Erika, how old are you?"

"I am thirteen and a half."

Turning to Sister Lida, he asked, "What is your name?"

"Lydia Puder."

"Do you like school?"

"Yes."

No questions for Otto.

When the two soldiers were finished, one took a stamp and stamped across our files "DP."

"What does that stand for?" I asked.

"Displaced Person," he said with a smile.

We were ushered outside and told to sit in the hallway chairs until our parents came out. I was so intrigued watching the American soldiers and German girls going back and forth speaking American and always smiling and laughing. One German girl asked us if we wanted something to drink. "Try a cola," she said. She brought a bottle of cola for each one of us kids.

Since it was a gift, I took it graciously. The first sip was not the best drink I had tasted, but by the time I finished the bottle, I liked it. Some soldiers passed by with purple drinks that had brown bullets floating around in the bottle itself. I asked a German girl, "What is that purple drink called?"

She said, "Purple Cow."

"And those brown things?"

"They are peanuts," she answered.

Mama and Papa took forever. When they finally came out of the office, they had very little to say except that if we were going anywhere it would be America, because the Americans were interviewing the people who were going to America. Papa didn't want to emigrate to Canada. It was too close to Russia and the Communists.

By the time we returned to Camp Hofstetten, the weather had turned snowy, wet, cold and icy. To my utter dismay, there was no way I could walk to the American-language classes anymore, or even make the trip on Papa's bike.

Two months passed. Our hope every day was that the postman would bring a letter telling us we would be going to America. Our neighbors and friends considered it an unobtainable dream. They greeted us with a sarcastic "When are you going to America?" as they passed us on the road. Christmas came and was spent as usual (except no Christmas mass for me this time). My best girlfriends had left the camp. The teenage boys had left the camp as well. It was a lonely existence for me.

1952

We almost stopped believing in our dream. At first, we had talked endlessly about America; now we talked about it very little, if ever. We were afraid of rejection.

Right after the New Year, January 1952, we received a big brown envelope stamped *Dringend* (urgent). The postman on his bicycle delivered it personally. Pages of precise instructions, what we should do and not do, pack or leave behind, in order to report to Munich to start processing for our trip to the land of our hopes and dreams. They gave us six weeks' notice. Sister Erika and I were jubilant beyond description, absolutely overwhelmed with great anticipation. It was all we talked about. Papa celebrated with a bottle of vodka. Sometimes we saw Mama smiling to herself. But Sister Lida and Mutter retreated into their apartment. A day or two would go by without a word from either.

We were the talk of the camp again. With snow still on the ground, the neighbors ventured out to get the information directly from Papa. Some were still skeptical even after seeing the official envelope and letter with train tickets. Even I approached our American dream with caution. With too much time on my hands, I went through the "What ifs?" What if it was all a mistake? Will the Americans like us? Will they consider us the enemy since they fought against Germany? Will the countryside be like Russia or like Germany? Did all the people look like Tyrone Power and Linda Darnell? On and on.

We were given a list of items to pack and the size of the single box we were authorized to ship. From the time we received our notice until we were ready to pack, our kitchen was covered in sawdust. Papa set out to build the most beautiful box. It was the size of a card table. The pine boards were polished smooth.

Mama loaded it with pictures, Papa's Hohner accordion, and the few thin summer dresses we owned. We had no shoes to pack. We wore the only shoes we owned. We took our aluminum pots from Russia, lace tablecloth, my real papa's embroidered Russian shirt (just in case he returned from Siberia someday). A baby comforter cover with pillowcase to match and some items that Oma had embroidered in Russia went in the box. I begged Mama to please pack the two books I had made from all those loose-leaf homework pages, the ones on history and science. Since Mama was so accommodating, I also handed her my Poesy book—a little remembrance book autographed by all my school friends in the eighth grade. Some wrote poems, others drew remembrances from our youth. I pasted little pictures of flowers next to each signature. Mama flipped through it and placed it in the box with a smile. Papa made sure his Bible was in the box. With the last money we had, Papa bought two suitcases to carry a change of clothing for each of us.

Needless to say, our neighbors were in a state of shock. For that matter, so were we. My friend Gerda came from Straubing to visit her mother and said she considered me the luckiest girl in all of Germany. All those movies we had seen like *The Mark of Zorro*, where Tyrone Power spoke German, would soon become a reality. The teenaged boys we had grown up with up with, who had left for work elsewhere but had come home for Christmas, took our emigration with mixed emotions. It would be great to go to America, but did they have restaurants there? They didn't like the American beer because it tasted bitter and sharp (the whores let them have a can of beer occasionally). Did America have German-made beer? They had seen the same movies as us and thought the American girls were too skinny and couldn't possibly be good homemakers. How can any girl who looked like skin and bone cook a good meal? Some of them, those who had found employment as farmhands, thought the American girls would never make it on a Bavarian farm. You had to be strong and cook three meals a day for at least ten people, plus having and raising kids, milking cows, washing clothes, and helping bring in the crops. No, no! German girls were the only girls to marry. They were big and strong, had many children, and most of all, were obedient.

The day of departure finally arrived. Papa hired a horse and wagon to take us to the train station. Some of our neighbors came along. Gerda came to the station to see me off. She hugged me and cried a lot, promising to write. I looked around to see, for the last time, the old, wrinkled, tear-stained eyes of our friends. The people at Camp Hofstetten had become extended family, not by blood, but by a shared history. There were no tears on my part. Sister Lida cried and Mutter cried. Papa and Mama smiled a lot. I was thrilled to see the happiness and relief on their faces. It all seemed so unreal.

At the immigration collection point in Munich, an American soldier who spoke very clear German instructed us to wait until the last train arrived. He said that when all of the Refugees were here, we would be transported by big trucks to a holding area.

While waiting, Mama and Papa became very uneasy. All around us were people from Russia, as well as from Romania, Czechoslovakia, Poland, and Yugoslavia, which were now occupied by the Russians. Surely they were not going to load us on trucks and carry us back to Russia like the Americans did to those people in that guarded camp near Passau? Even though it was 1952, none of us really knew what Americans were liable to do. No one wanted to go back to Russian-occupied lands and into slavery. They would rather die. So the worry started again. But the die was cast. It was too late. Whatever the outcome, we had no choice but to deliver our collective lives into American hands.

To ease their nervousness, Mama and Papa started talking about America. It was very unfamiliar territory to them. They had not been to a Tyrone Power film and therefore could not imagine what America looked like. I tried to share with them what I had seen in American movies: how we would be welcomed, have a house, a carpenter job for Papa, and a car. Mama would clean houses and we would go to school and learn to speak American. In Russia we were considered Germans; in Germany we were considered Russians. Maybe, just maybe, in America we would eventually be accepted as Americans. We would belong.

We would not write to anyone back in Germany, at least for a while, because the Communists might find out where we were and come and get us. Papa thought that there were no Communists in America; at least he hoped that this was the case. Mama knew, and voiced her opinion, that America was at the end of the world.

This was our final move. We could not run anywhere else. "Theodor, you better get used to it. America is our last destination before our graves."

Finally, a big army truck came to pick us up. We were transported to Funk Kaserne, the large transition camp where we had been processed last year. All the buildings were brick, about a dozen in all, three to four stories high. They had a few war scars in the walls but no major damage. We were given our building and room number, which was on the third floor. A couple of American-speaking German men carried our box all the way up. The room was a nice size. It had single green canvas folding army cots for each of us, with clean white sheets and dark brown army blankets. The room was nice and warm—the windows were not frozen even though it was still early March. Looking out, I could see the entire compound still covered in snow.

Daily we received information posted on a board outside the dining facility, what to do and where to go, starting with breakfast. Oh, what a good breakfast we had: pancakes, eggs and bacon, grits (new to us), sausages, toast, milk, coffee, and an orange or apple. We hardly had time to digest breakfast before we were served a huge lunch and then, for supper, hamburgers and hot dogs. We used forks and knives. Observing how some people ate hamburgers was shocking. They had no manners, putting such a big stack, held in their hands, to their wide-open mouths. No beer, to the amazement of all men there, only coffee and milk—and iced tea, also new to us; we never used ice, and this was the middle of winter. It was hard to understand how Americans could use ice in the winter. All of us drank milk to our hearts' content. On Sunday, we had ice cream, and it was really great. If this was the way Americans lived in America then I couldn't wait to get there.

Papa was still suspicious. They are fattening us up before the slaughter, he insisted. Mama's spirit wasn't dampened one bit. I had the run of the compound (no fence). As long as I was back for dinner I could do my thing: play ping-pong, read in the library, take long walks with my newly made friends. Henry Friedrich was an excellent ping-pong player. Ilse Schmidt, my age, was going to be a nun. I asked her, "Ilse, are you going to be in a cloister in America?"

"Oh yes," she said.

Sister Erika stayed and watched the kids. Mama and Papa had to go to the Immigration Office about half a dozen times while we were in Munich. We were given shots. One medication we took was dispensed on sugar, against something they called polio.

"Mama, what did you have to do today in the Immigration Office?"

"Ella, the less you know the better off we will be."

Our neighbor, who was emigrating with his elderly mother, asked me to go to Fasching (the Mardi Gras parade) in downtown Munich with him. I decided to go by myself since he was ten years older than I. After getting lost for the better part of the day, I finally made it downtown, wishing all along I had accepted his invitation. My eyes could not believe such parades existed.

Were these people crazy? Grown-ups drinking, drunk, dressed in all kind of costumes and dancing in the streets. This was a new and exciting world.

Around the first of April we were instructed to be on a particular train with other immigrants for our trip north to Bremerhaven and embarkation. It was rainy, wet, and cold. The train ride was long. When we finally arrived, we were met by American buses and transported to another holding area. The accommodations were just as nice as in Munich, including the three meals a day. To top it all, Papa was continually supplied with Camel cigarettes. No one wanted to go to heaven. It was great for us down here.

While we were waiting for our ship, Mama and Papa left for a day without telling us where they were going. We stayed inside and waited, hoping they would return and praying they hadn't deserted us.

They came back late that evening. Mama looked pale and sick. I prayed that whatever was wrong with her, she wouldn't die, not before we got to America.

"Papa, what's wrong with Mama? Is she sick? Why don't you take her to the camp doctor tomorrow?" My questions were left unanswered. I couldn't imagine what the big secret could be, not to share it with me. Years later, when I asked Mama where they had been all that day, she told me that she had been pregnant. The Americans would not take a pregnant woman. Mama and Papa decided that she would have an abortion.

I met Elisabeth Daniel and her brother Alfred, who were traveling by themselves. She was about my age. Her onkel was an American citizen who paid for their voyage. They were going to New Jersey. We still didn't know where we were going. I also met my second boyfriend, Otto Leukert. He and his mother were going to Philadelphia. Otto was a little taller than I, with beautiful blue eyes and blond, naturally curly hair. He was a very affectionate and considerate individual. The only drawback was that he was Catholic. My parents had no use for "servants of the Pope." We took many walks, posed for pictures taken with his camera, and promised each other to write. He gave me his address with the most gentle goodbye kiss. They took a plane. We took a boat into our new future.

On 17 April we embarked on the troop ship USNS *General Harry Taylor* (T-AP-145). As the ship moved very slowly away from land, I stood alone on deck in the fog, watching the waves dance together to the shore and crying uncontrollably. I was leaving the known and looking forward with anticipation and much trepidation to the unknown.

* * *

To me the ship was like a house. It had everything: bedroom, bathroom, playrooms, kitchen, shower rooms, reading rooms, and so many more rooms. American cowboy films were shown nightly in a huge auditorium on the upper deck. Our sleeping accommodations were located three flights of stairs below. I had seen beds stacked in twos, not threes. These were good mattresses to sleep on, not filled with straw. Sheets were dingy white and blankets dark brown. One great big bathroom had showers. We could shower with hot running water and good-smelling, non-eye-burning soap anytime we wanted.

Men and women were separated as soon as we boarded the ship. Mama always looked for Papa at breakfast. Sometimes I didn't see them for hours. They busied themselves with talking, walking on deck, and watching cowboy movies in the auditorium. Thank goodness Brother Otto was stuck to Mama's hand. I was busy with my friends. Elisabeth and I found a group of boys and girls our age who talked together in the library. How good it was to dream. One was going to be an engineer, another a doctor or teacher. Girls mostly wanted to marry, have a house, and raise children. Most agreed that our first responsibility was to help the family.

When we reached the open sea, the weather turned bad. The waves were so high that for days we stayed below. Even with the boat rocking back and forth, meals were served as usual. Who could eat?

Holding on to the railing, I made myself go to the dining facility. At the entrance of the dining room, the fragrance of coffee and bacon, which on land had always been so appetizing, caused me to become sick to my stomach. I was always on the lookout for the nearest strategically placed container. I was so sick that I went back to my top bunk and just lay there praying the rocking would stop. Food was not allowed out of the dining area, but Mama brought me a banana or an orange and a slice of American white bread. Oh, how I wished for German black bread. Nothing, but nothing, stayed in my stomach. I would eat it but not keep it. What a waste of good food.

All the others in my family were fine. Sister Lida was never sick. Sometimes she ate three boiled eggs and never once became sick to her stomach. After a couple of days Mama talked to one of the soldiers, who accompanied us to the doctor. He gave me a shot in my behind and some pills and told me to get out of bed. "There is no place to hide from the rocking," he told me. After about five days the rocking stopped. When I finally came on deck Mama said, "Ella, you look like you have arisen from the dead. You must eat or you will waste away to nothing."

The waves finally rested from their anger, and I was able to walk around on deck in the chilly but fresh April air. I scanned the horizon for signs of land or birds but saw no living thing, only choppy water. I felt better, looked better, and got my appetite back. When it wasn't too windy I spent a lot of time on deck during the day absorbing the beauty of the glassy sea, then evenings watching the moonlight shining obliquely through the cloudy sky.

One day an American spoke to me in the stairwell. He wore a white uniform with boots. Another soldier in the same uniform joined us. They were rather short, with tan complexions, straight black hair, and brown eyes. They looked more like boys than men. "Hi!" was used all the time. What an interesting word to greet each other with, I thought.

"Where are you from? Where are you going?" one asked.

I told him, "From Germany, going to America. You American?"

"No, no, Filipino."

I just smiled, not wanting to admit stupidity.

When I met my friend Elisabeth, I told her about Filipino not being American. We decided that was his name. When we saw him we always waived and hollered "Filipino." He answered with "Hi!" showing his perfect set of ivory teeth.

This little flirtation didn't go unnoticed by the real Americans in uniforms. One day during assembly we were told, "Do not talk to the workers." How was I to distinguish who was an American and who was a worker? Not to get Mama and Papa in trouble, I stopped waving and smiling altogether whenever I saw or ran into Filipino.

The days passed rather slowly. Elisabeth and I took advantage of the American magazines that were available. We looked mostly at the pictures, pondering beautiful wishful dreams with each turning page.

On the ninth day, the day before our arrival in New York, a long meeting took place in the auditorium. We were told what the procedure would be for disembarkation the following day. We were given colored nametags and told to always stay together as a family. Not to worry, someone would always be there to direct us. There was such excitement on board. Elisabeth didn't stop talking. How she looked forward to being reunited with her onkel. She made sure I had her onkel's address and would write her.

My enthusiasm was somewhat subdued. Nevertheless, I was determined to venture bravely and happily into the future. One last movie, a good shower, wash and roll my hair on strings of material, wrap the curls in newspaper, and by then, tomorrow was almost here.

America

After ten days at sea we stood at the railing of the USNS *General Harry Taylor* watching the skyline of New York slowly floating by. On 27 April (same date as in my dream), our troop ship sailed past the Statue of Liberty. We anchored in New York Harbor. It was early in the morning and everybody was on deck. People were shouting, dancing, and hugging each other. All wore their best Sunday clothing, including us (we changed into clean clothes, one of the two each of us owned). We were tagged with different colored tags. The loudspeaker delivered a recorded message in a half dozen languages, German, Russian, Italian, Hungarian, French, and American: "Families stay together at all times." Mama and Papa were still skeptical, but Papa said, "There is no turning back now."

No one in my family danced or hugged. There was a quiet resignation on my parents' faces. I was thinking how good God was to me so far in my young life. He let me live through all the bombings, gave me good health, and brought me to America. It must have been all those copycat repeated prayers in the bomb shelters during the air raids. I could not wish for more. But at that moment, for just an instant, I was afraid of the unknown. I viewed all those skyscrapers with fascination. How could people build anything so tall? I could not imagine living in New York City. Yet maybe that was our destination? Or maybe all this was just a dream? But if it *was* a dream, a dream come true, what a great life that would be. I resolved to become the best American ever. I would definitely do whatever it took to embrace the glorious image that I had seen in movies of the American way of life.

My ship friend Elisabeth Daniels, with her younger brother Alfred, had a different departure gate. Their onkel was there to meet them. Promising each other we would always be friends and write, we said a tearful "Auf-wiedersehen."

Finally, we were ushered off the ship into a small holding area. There, seated on wooden benches, we waited to be examined, first our papers then our bodies. Flashbacks of my earlier years haunted me. Was this another

Germany? Hopefully, we would not be placed into a new camp. I avoided looking at Mama, because I was happy and she looked sad. Papa showed no emotion. I was two months short of being sixteen. Sister Erika (thirteen) talked nonstop about the Statue of Liberty and the skyscrapers. Sister Lida (nine) was very quiet. Brother Otto (five) was permanently attached to Mama's hand.

We were directed to an area where all the luggage was stored. Papa had no problem finding our box. We stood around the box, our only baggage other than the two suitcases. He unlocked it for inspection. Papa's Hohner accordion was taken out of the box and the name was removed with a knife by one of the men in blue.

Chaos was everywhere. People were going in all directions. Children crying, with runny noses, were trying to find their parents. One man in blue had two little boys by their hands, towing them in the opposite direction from where our line was headed. The loudspeaker spewed out information on lost children and family members who were there to meet their husbands, wives, cousins, brothers, or sisters. The announcements came in waves, all in different languages. Finally in German, "Missing children can be claimed in section 15." That did not apply to us. The men in blue were checking the colored tags. Ours were blue. Mine gave my name, Ella E. Schneider, then Papa's name, Theodor Puder. A blue-uniformed, gray-haired man who spoke German asked to see our papers. After checking and rechecking, he was happy to report that they were in order.

"Leave your box and follow the blue line to the next station," he said.

"Ella, you bring up the rear so that we will not lose the children," Mama said.

I was proud of Papa. He handled the paperwork and conversations with the man in blue very well.

"I am pleased to see how well all this immigration service is organized," Papa informed him.

"We've had a lot of practice—many years taking in people from different countries," the man said as he showed us to the doctor's office.

We entered a large room that had chairs for everybody. The doctor called us up to his desk individually. He directed most of his questions to my parents. Only Papa spoke. Did any of us ever have TB? No. Nevertheless, the doctor listened to our chests, looked into our ears, mouths, noses, and even between our toes and fingers. While he was busy examining the rest of the family, I leaned over and asked Mama, "Why did he look between my toes and fingers?"

"To see if you have *die Krätze*," she said. "These are little broken-out places that itch and are very contagious." I later learned that the American word for this was "scabies."

No bloodletting this time, like the pricking of our ears when we had entered Germany.

After the checking was completed, Papa was given a packet with all kinds of papers. He was told, in German, that his responsibilities as an immigrant to America were to obey the laws, serve our sponsors for one year faithfully, and register with the local post office once a year. Papa asked, "Please tell us where were going." The uniformed man looked at the papers and said that a family in Mississippi who grew cotton sponsored us. Papa asked the man if he knew anything about Mississippi. No, except that it was very hot and the man never wanted to visit or to live there.

Papa wanted to know if I learned anything about Mississippi in the American-language night school. I hadn't. He wished for a map, but there was none to be found. I wondered why the immigration man had no use for Mississippi. It couldn't be so different from New York City. Comparing our train ride from Munich, in the southern part of Germany, all the way up north to Bremerhaven, the other end of Germany, the countryside looked much the same. America must look the same too.

At least we now knew that a family in Mississippi had sponsored us for one year. Someone got a taxi for us and instructed the driver to take us to the main train station. With Papa's help, our box was loaded into the trunk. The trunk could not be closed. It flapped in the wind. We squeezed in, Papa and me in front with the rest doubled up in the back seat. The taxi driver was a black man with beautiful white teeth. My family forever talked about the beautiful white teeth that black people had. He tried to talk to me. Try as I might, I couldn't understand him at all. I just smiled. Papa wanted to know what he was saying. I kept telling him I couldn't understand. His reaction: "You sure didn't learn much in that night school." At the train station a lady met us and directed us to the correct platform. She gave the conductor and Papa instructions (in American and in German) that we were not to get off until we were in Memphis, Tennessee. Each of us received a box lunch—slices of white bread with meat and cheese, or with jam and a brownish cream with a nutty taste not much to our liking. Each box also held an orange, a candy bar, a drink, and a bag that read "Potato Chips." It had something to do with potatoes.

As the train moved away from the Manhattan skyline, I realized with sadness that we were going somewhere other than New York City, maybe a different country. We tried not to draw attention to ourselves. People were pointing and staring at us, and some tried unsuccessfully to have a conversation with us. I was the only one who could come up with a few words, occasionally putting together a three-word sentence. A lady seated in front of me introduced herself as Mrs. Barr, a nurse by profession. She asked me where we came from and where we were going. The first part was easy. "Come from Germany, to Mississippi." At this point we still didn't know where, the town or city or village, we were going other than Mississippi. She asked for the packet Papa was given after processing. She opened and read it.

"You are going to Holly Springs, Mississippi. That is close to Memphis, Tennessee, where I live," pointing to herself. "Don't worry, someone will be there to meet you."

Mama didn't talk much during our train ride. She stared out the window. After hours on the train the nurse told us, "We are leaving New Jersey" (or Maryland or whatever state we were approaching or leaving). It was hard for me to understand all these states. Were they part of America? There were no checkpoints or border guards. Not having to produce some kind of identification was absolutely amazing.

The skyscrapers had long ago given way to shacks, houses, forests, and fields. People were working out in the fields, chopping some kind of plants. All were black and poorly dressed. Women wore kerchiefs wrapped tightly around their heads. Kids played on empty wagons. In some places it seemed that people lived outside their shacks. Furniture in various states of decay sat on porches or lay in the front yards. Even sofas were on the front porches, all tattered and torn. The front yards looked trashed out. No one was busily picking up trash like in Germany, where individuals, war or no war, swept the streets daily. Horses didn't look like any horses I had ever seen. Not in Russia and not in Germany had I seen horses like these—long ears, skinny bodies, dull coats, pulling huge wagons filled with black people. At railroad crossings cars stopped, occupied by white people.

"Theodor," Mama said, "I have a foreboding that leaving Germany was a mistake. We never saw pictures of Americans looking like these. At least in Germany the cleanup began right after the war. Here they must have had a war and then never got around to cleaning up afterwards."

I saw woods, fields, roads, farms, small and big towns. Now the countryside changed. On the side of the roads, green vines covered everything. It covered hills, trees, telephone poles, and telephone wires. I asked Mrs. Barr to tell me the name of the vines. "Kudzu," she said. When we got to Alabama, all of a sudden, tears began to roll down my Mama's pretty cheeks.

"What is the matter? You are in America. Don't cry," Papa wanted to know why Mama was upset.

"Look at the red earth," she said. "Only the devil could create such a red earth. God only creates good and pretty things. Remember the earth in Russia and even in Germany? It was rich and dark. Look, this is not even dirt. It is dust, red dust. How can anything grow in dust? It is a bad omen."

"Good omen or bad omen, what difference does it make now? There is no turning back. Wir können nicht wieder nach Deutschland zurück" (We can't go back to Germany).

It seemed like Papa was always searching for the right words to console Mama. He just couldn't find them. Her tears ran like quiet rivers down her face, which she wiped with her open hands. Not wanting to translate what was the source of Mama's tears, I told our new friend Mrs. Barr, "Mama happy America."

The sun had gone down long ago. The train made many stops to take on or discharge passengers. At one of the stops, a car came flying by with red lights flashing to the sound of air raid sirens. Our whole family was temporarily transformed into frozen statues except for Brother Otto, who was following the red lights. The sound of the sirens lasted only a few seconds from start to finish until it passed into the engulfing darkness. I sat very still. How can there be air raid sirens in America? Has the war come to America? What are we supposed to do? But everything looked normal, like before, people talking or reading, children playing. Mama with a heavy sigh said, "Mein Gott," followed by another torrent of tears. I asked our friend, "Mrs. Barr, rrrrr?" (attempting to mimic the sound of the siren). She smiled and asked for Papa's German/English pocket dictionary, given to him at the Immigration Office. He kept it on his lap, just in case. She looked up a word, then showed it to me. It read, *Krankenwagen.* Mama and Papa breathed a sigh of relief, including me. All of us smiled now. Mama's "Mein Gott" turned into a "Gott sei Dank" (Thank God). It was an emergency vehicle.

Arriving in Memphis in the dark, late at night, we were all tired, hot, and hungry. Our box lunches had long ago been consumed. Memphis wasn't anything like New York City. It had a few small skyscrapers but not anywhere near as tall. I was astonished by millions of glowing lights everywhere. I made a mental note to ask someone, do Americans ever turn off the lights?

A husband and wife met us. Mr. Dean was very tall, skinny, and quite distinguished-looking, with a straight military bearing and a full head of beautiful gray hair. Mrs. Dean was the complete opposite: short, stocky, bubbly, and homey looking.

They had come in two cars, one of which was a station wagon. We piled in. Our next stop was at a Dairy Queen. All of us had a hamburger. I asked for a fork and knife. Mrs. Dean said, "You don't need one. Just do as the other people do." We tried, with all of the lettuce and tomatoes and meat falling out of the bun. The chocolate-covered vanilla ice cream cone was tasty and brought back smiles to our faces. We piled back into the cars, with Papa's box in the back of the station wagon, and drove another hour to our new home. I couldn't sleep. I wasn't going to miss anything. We came to a sign that read "Welcome to Holly Springs," but we never stopped. Another half hour and we finally arrived.

* * *

When the headlights hit the shack, I could not believe my eyes. Were we to live here? A light was turned on in the front room and then another in the small second room, where a stove and refrigerator took up most of the space. Only those two bulbs hanging from the ceiling provided light. It was really hard to see the three double beds and broken-down fireplace.

After the Deans departed, all we could think of was going to bed. The beds were iron-framed springs with cotton-filled mattresses. In Germany, the mattresses were always bags filled with straw that smelled. Here were old, clean, used-to-be-white sheets and hard pillows that had no feathers in them, only cotton all smashed down. No feather comforters for cover, but old quilts that were lumpy and sewn together with all kinds of leftover pieces of material. Some had palm-sized holes in them. We pulled out some cotton to see what those little lumps were, only to find out they were seeds. Mama insisted that the blankets "never saw water" (had never been washed). All of them smelled musty. The only two windows in the front room had screens, and so did the front and back door. I had never seen anything like this before in any kind of movie.

The following morning we all woke before sunup and went outside waiting for the first rays of sunlight. When the sun did come up, we all were in shock. Complete shock! Even when we relocated from one camp to another during the war, we had never lived in anything as poor and broken-down or in such utter disrepair as this. It was a hopelessly dilapidated shack with a leaky roof (judging by the watermarks on the ceiling boards), a sagging front porch, and rotted-out eaves.

The shack was constructed out of single boards. Rusty tin sheets covered the roof. How would we ever survive wintertime with all the snow? I wondered. A huge water container shaped like a barrel sat next to the house, with a spout coming down from the roof. Mama said, "Surely we are not going to have to drink this water coming down the rusty roof? It will probably kill us." The water in the barrel had all kinds of creatures floating around in it. "Rainwater is only good for washing hair," she continued.

Examining the surrounding area we came across a well, just an opening in the ground fifty feet from the shack, about twenty feet deep and encased with cement. An outhouse was nowhere to be found. All of us descended upon a barn, which had no doors. It must have housed animals at some point because the floor was covered with piles of animal waste. The upstairs looked like it was used for storing hay.

It was almost noon and very muggy by the time we completed our survey. Sister Erika and I made our way down the red dusty road. After a while, not having encountered a soul, we turned and retreated to our new home. Mama looked into the well-stocked refrigerator, not knowing what to serve. We could not read the labels and did not recognize many of the things it contained except those that had pictures on them or were obvious anyway: orange juice, milk, and baloney slices. We had loaves of white bread, like the rich Germans, but at what price! We ate bread, baloney, and milk for lunch. Then all of us went back to bed. I kept thinking, when I wake again, all of this will be gone.

It was very hard to fall asleep in the stifling heat. The windows and doors were covered with screens and remained opened all the time. With no wind the shack felt like an oven. Soon mosquitoes found their way in and began making meals of us. It was time for me to face reality.

America, as portrayed by the movies in Germany, sure was different. I did not think anyone back in Germany would believe me if I wrote to them of our living conditions. At this point, it seemed my future was sealed: I was destined to spend my life in this Godforsaken kudzu-covered Mississippi jungle. (Since we were so isolated from humans and surrounded by woods, my parents referred to us as living in the jungle.) My American dream died.

We woke up to witness an incredible bright orange ball starting to disappear into the trees. I was hoping this nightmare would go away, but it was here to stay. I was saddened and so disappointed that I did not speak very much. I did not want to face Mama and see the anguish in her eyes.

* * *

That evening the Deans came in two cars and drove us to their house about two miles away. Their whole family was assembled in the front yard. They had a daughter, "Puddin'," a beautiful child, about six or seven. She talked back to her parents and mouthed off whenever she had an opportunity. "No!" was her favorite word or, "You can't make me do it!" I was embarrassed to see her in action, stomping her foot, making faces at her parents when their backs were turned, and not using a very loving tone when talking to them. They must have loved her very much because she did just as she pleased. This impressed me. It would never work in my family, particularly when we had company. Then there was Hal. He lived next door with his wife. He was Puddin's much older brother, in his mid-twenties.

"This [unrecognized words] Bar-B-Q," Mrs. Dean explained. Meanwhile, a heavyset black lady busied herself with carrying dishes from the house, never saying a word. Mrs. Dean told her to fetch something out of the house. "Yessum," she answered. I wondered if she had prepared the food. We had the choice of chicken, hamburgers, or hotdogs. Mama always said that, if in doubt about how to eat something, wait until other people are eating and then imitate them. So we did, eating chicken with our fingers. The potato salad was not to our liking. It tasted different from German potato salad. Mama had a dab of sweet pickles, commenting that it didn't taste good. We were offered iced tea and ice-cold colas in bottles. I said, "Please," shaking my head from one side to the other and pointing toward the ice. Mrs. Deans reply, "In America [unrecognized words] ice." We took the plastic container of iced-down drinks. It didn't take long for the ice to melt for us to drink. It was a sultry evening. Even in the shade, it was very humid. Papa mumbled, "Ich hatte gerne ein Deutsches Bier" (I sure would like a German beer). Mama smiled. Apple pie for dessert, our first. Papa and Mama didn't like it. I thought it was delicious.

"Invited guests should be sitting at a table and eat in a civilized manner instead of fighting the flies, ants, and smoke. Balancing the plate on our laps with a drink, dogs and cats underfoot, and dodging an undisciplined child running around is an uncivilized way to eat," Mama concluded. Poor Mama didn't realize we were *not* guests.

We spoke in German among ourselves during the meal. If Mama and Papa liked something they ate, they indicated with a simple smile and with the word *gut*. The Deans talked American with one another. They yelled at Puddin' when she started running around as if she was possessed. Once in a while they addressed a question to us. When that happened, I looked up the word in Papa's dictionary and acted it out in pantomime. Otherwise, it was a quiet Bar-B-Q.

The Deans gave us a house tour. We were impressed. The air in the house was cool, almost cold. Papa was completely intrigued by this temperature change.

"Ella, ask where this air comes from and how it works."

"Mrs. Dean, where cold?" I asked as best I could.

She took us to the window, where a box was installed.

"This [unrecognized words] air conditioner."

Papa wanted to know how it worked. I interrupted, "Papa, I don't know enough American to ask all you want to know." He was visibly disappointed. Mrs. Dean, with her bubbly personality, continued her rapid explanation of different pictures, picking up heirlooms, knickknacks, standing around the rooms and pointing out furniture and rifles that her husband used. Papa took the stand of a soldier shooting a rifle, saying, "Bang bang."

"Yes, yes, Mr. Puder, dogs, bang bang!" Mr. Dean volunteered.

My quick check in the dictionary . . . ah, *Hunde*. Papa mused in German, "Why do they shoot dogs?"

"Dogs?" he said in American.

Placing her hands around her own neck, Mrs. Dean indicated a killing action. "Sheep."

"Elsa," Papa said, "The dogs kill the sheep and he shoots the dogs." Mama nodded, "Ja, ja."

Mrs. Dean talked way too fast for my understanding, with big words and an accent that was hard to decipher. They even had a box that showed movies. We inspected both the front and back of it thinking we would see a projector. None there.

"Ella, ask what do you call this box?" Papa said.

"TV," Mrs. Dean answered. "Television."

Papa marveled at this creation. Mama had no opinion. Sister Lida and

Brother Otto took off with Puddin' to see her room. The rest of the family tagged along behind Mrs. Dean. Mr. Dean joined the B-B-Q outside and tended the coals. Their house had two indoor toilets, bathtubs and showers with hot and cold running water, a beautiful kitchen with running water, no feather comforters on the beds, just lightweight blankets, walk-in closets, his and hers. Puddin' had her own room complete with a walk-in closet full of clothing. I bubbled over with excitement.

"Mama, can you believe what you see, so many dresses, shoes, and toys everywhere? These people must be rich. Someday we will have all these things too."

Her soft, sad, sighing reply: "Ja, ja."

We entered a large screened-in front porch with two rocking chairs and a swing, not like our broken-down porch we were afraid to walk on because the boards might give way under our weight. Back out in their yard, we watched the sun sink slowly out of sight as a red ball behind the trees. Evening settled in and the mosquitoes descended upon us in droves. Each of us shook hands and said, "Dankeschön." We piled into the two cars and were driven back to our shack by Mrs. Dean and Hal.

After seeing the luxury the Deans lived in, my heart ached. Oh, how I wished we were back in Germany in our refugee camp. The windows and the doors of the shack were open all night in order to get some air circulation. We had no air conditioning or even a fan; no TV or even a radio; no phone, newspapers, or magazines. The unbearable oppressive heat, the humming of the mosquitoes, the noise of crickets, frogs, and other night animals prevented us from sleeping until the early morning hours. By then, it was time to get up.

God! It was all His doing. I really didn't have to pray anymore. Sure, He realized our wish and brought us to America. But look where He put us. What should I thank Him for? Surely not for this shack. Nevertheless, I prayed faithfully that He would watch over us and bless us, whatever that meant here in America. The only way I could go to sleep was to think about the beautiful German countryside, the Danube River, and my precious years of growing up in our last camp.

Mama and Papa sat in the dark with voices barely audible talking about our situation. Papa kept reassuring Mama that things would get better. This would be a temporary arrangement until we paid back our passage. "Wir müssen es nur ein Jahr aushalten" (We need to endure it only one year).

* * *

Next morning Mama was up early trying to figure out how to use the electric stove. By turning the knobs in every direction she finally got it started. First thing she did was to open all of the boxes. I got out of bed to help with the meal. Mama asked me to open a can with pictures on it. I could not. The harder I tried, the hotter I got, perspiration running down my face.

I finally told Mama, "I just don't know how to use the can opener."

"If the duck can't swim, there must be something wrong with the water," Mama said.

Raising her voice to make sure Papa heard, Mama called, "Theodor, if you want something to eat, you had better get up and open this can."

Dutifully Papa got out of bed. Mama handed him the can opener and a can. He tried so hard to figure out how it worked, to no avail. In desperation he got his small pocketknife, that he brought from Germany, and used it to open the can, partially anyway, so Mama could pour the sliced peaches into a bowl.

The mice and rats moved in with us, or we moved in with them. Mice had already invaded some of the bags, like sugar, rice, and cereal. How do we eat cereal? We ate it dry. Mama tried to put as much of our food in the refrigerator as fit, mostly things in burlap bags. Bread and packaged things she placed in the oven. Try as she might to hide the food, the pests always found something to get into.

As if the mice, rats, spiders, and mosquitoes were not enough for us to battle, we had bugs that even found their way into the oven. Some were as big as my finger. I asked Mrs. Dean what they were and was told they were roaches.

Within a few days, early one morning, Sister Lida came running in the shack. "Mama, Mrs. Dean just pulled up."

We all ran outside. Mrs. Dean was getting out of the pickup, which her son Hal had driven. To the truck was hitched a trailer. Hal opened the trailer door. After much pulling and yelling, a cow finally backed herself out of the trailer. Mrs. Dean made a milking motion toward Mama. Mama just smiled. Hal led the cow across the road, opened the pasture gate, and unfastened the rope from her neck. Meanwhile, Mrs. Dean reached into the truck and came up with a large box that she handed to Mama.

"Chickens," she said.

I said, "Thank you."

There were four chickens in the box. They were glad to be released from their confinement.

As soon as the truck left our yard, Mama told me, "Ella, get the bucket that we use to draw water from the well, and a bar of soap. Be sure to bring a rag." Everyone was excited. All of us accompanied Mama to the pond, where "Sterna," as Mama named the cow, received a good wash down.

"Elsa, that is a pretty sickly looking cow. Skin and bone," Papa said.

"I don't care, as long she gives milk. I'll fatten her up," Mama answered.

★ ★ ★

Mrs. Dean checked on us daily the first few days.

"Mrs. Dean snakes here?" I asked one morning.

"Oh yes, many are poisonous," she answered. I busied myself to look up *poisonous.*

When I translated it to my parents, Mama's reaction was a resounding, "Auch du Lieber Gott" (Oh, dear God).

I also asked Mrs. Dean, could she please help us get rid of these creatures that were flat, black, and as long as Papa's middle finger: "Roaches." Well, she explained, she could do something about the mice and rats by giving us some poison for them. As far as the roaches, snakes, and spiders were concerned, there was nothing she could do; in the South people were plagued with insects and snakes and we just had to learn to live with them. I wondered if Mrs. Dean had all these creatures living in her fine house, but I didn't ask. Could she buy us something for lice? Where were they? On our heads. Within a few days Mrs. Dean brought us a bottle of powder to put on our heads, leave it on for two hours, and then wash it out. That took care of the lice. Mama was so afraid of the poison for the rats that she set the packages under the house rather than in the house.

We showed Mrs. Dean our legs and arms that were scratched red.

"Yes, those are chiggers. Nothing can be done. They're in the grass."

She explained about the other little red or black bugs that were filling up with our blood. They were called "ticks," she said, and we had to remove them. Using my leg as an example, she demonstrated the removal of a tick. "What you do, you put Crisco on them, then pull them out between your fingers. Make sure you get the head."

I was thinking, what an exchange! German fleas, bedbugs, and lice for all kinds of new American pests.

★ ★ ★

For the first few days, Mama just sat on a bed with her hands in her lap after cooking and sweeping the shack. She took on a hypnotized appearance. The occasional gladness and happiness that I had witnessed in Camp Hofstetten over the years was now completely gone out of Mama's eyes.

"Mama, sei doch nicht so traurig" (Mama don't be so sad). "Can I help you do something? Let me peel potatoes."

"Ella, there is not enough work for me to do." She looked at me with so much pain in her eyes.

Sister Erika sat on the bed looking at the Sears catalog we had found in the shack. Sister Lida and Brother Otto were playing in the dust right outside our front porch.

"Theodor, you must do something about the toilet situation. The kids and I cannot use the barn for fear of being bitten by a snake or spider or stepping into animal waste. Come Monday, when you go to work, you must mention to the Deans that something has to be done about a toilet. It will become a health problem in this heat."

In order to relieve ourselves, to tinkle, we could just go out the back door. However, for bowel movements, Papa decided that we should not use the barn. It was too dangerous and nobody could relax from worrying that a spider or snake would bite you, God forbid. Hal came early Monday morning and called, "Theodor!" Papa raced out the door into the waiting pickup truck. When Hal brought him home for lunch, he carried two boards and a pick.

"Papa how did you get the pick and wood?" I asked.

"I found the boards while cleaning out their horse barn. I just picked them up and brought them home. Hal didn't say anything, so I guess it's OK," he smiled.

That evening Papa dug a hole at the edge of the jungle, as we called the overgrown, kudzu-covered backyard, about fifty feet from the back door. The whole family stood watching Papa, who was wet from perspiration from head to toe, using the pick like an ax to dig a hole in the hard red ground. He placed the two boards, with a space in the middle, over the hole so we had something to stand on when relieving ourselves.

"Whenever the hole is full, I will cover it with dirt and dig a new one," Papa said.

All of us hoped that none of us had to go at night. Our only nightlights, the single 60-watt bulb hanging from the kitchen ceiling, the other in the living/sleeping room, were not enough to light up the backyard. The designated toilet spot was totally dark. Many times I could not go and just returned to the shack because I was too scared.

Mrs. Dean provided us each with secondhand shoes.

"Ella, you must go with Papa tomorrow and ask Mrs. Dean for a good board and a piece of canvas. Papa can make us some outdoor shoes that we can slip on when we go out and then leave outside when we come in," Mama said.

I looked up the words in the dictionary that I needed to use. Toward evening, before Papa was to come home, I headed toward the Dean's place, cutting across the pasture. I arrived so soaking wet with sweat that she asked me, "You OK?"

"Yes, OK. Mrs. Dean, Papa want wood board and canvas," I said, showing with my hands about half a yard.

"What for?" she asked.

"To make shoe."

"You all have shoes."

"No, no, shoes toilet."

"I don't know what kind of shoes you wear to the toilet. When I drive into Holly Springs, I'll get you the board and canvas."

"Is Holly Springs a city?"

"Yes, a little one," she said.

A day or two later Papa brought home the requested items. He had a hammer and some nails. Papa traced his shoe on the wood, then cut it out with his German pocketknife. He shaped and carved a pair of flip-flops by nailing a piece of canvas across the middle section of the sole. After making a pair of wooden clogs (one size fits all), he placed them outside the kitchen door for us to use. History was repeating itself. These were the same clogs we left behind in Germany. Papa announced where the new hole in the ground was located. Judging from remnants, it looked like someone else used it before us. The previous occupants must have left the Sears catalog in the shack. The pictures were so pretty it was heartbreaking to have to tear the pages out in order to use them for toilet paper.

Papa tried to be upbeat about life in general and our living condition in particular. For one thing, he was thankful for the jungle. The Communists, still pursuing him, would have a heck of a time getting him out of America if they found him. His daily encouraging phrase for Mama was "Elsa, wart doch, es wird besser werden" (Elsa, wait and it will get better).

* * *

We could have heard Mama's scream a mile away. The question was, what had befallen her? Bucket in hand, she came screaming into the shack.

"Theodor, there is a big snake in the well."

She cried out to God, whose fault it was that she had to go through all this, saying she would be better off dead. She started begging to be taken back to Germany or even Russia.

Papa went to the barn, emerging with two long boards torn from inside it. Nailed together they looked like long scissors. With that he reached into the well and brought out the snake. After he killed it, he estimated that it was about five feet in length. Papa hung it on a nearby shrub so all of us could take a look. The snake was a good meal for the flies. It baked for days in the sun. When Mrs. Dean stopped by to pick up Papa to do some work at her house, I asked her what kind of snake this was. She said it was a "water moccasin" and that they were very poisonous—you could die if one of them bit you.

The well was our only source of drinking water. We kept praying that we would not die from it. The big barrel that stood right by the kitchen door, which the rain from the roof filled, we used for bathing and washing dishes. The water tasted foul. Papa wished for a beer.

In Germany we never drank water. The water in Germany was bad and might give a person a goiter from iodine deficiency. We drank beer or lemonade, which came in small packages as a powder to which some kind of sweetener was added. Papa had me ask Mrs. Dean if she could get a few bottles of beer the next time she was buying groceries in Holly Springs. She became very hostile and upset. In a longwinded explanation, of which I understood very little, she made it very clear in Mississippi there was no beer. No buy, no drink beer. The police will arrest you. Dry state. We looked it up but it meant nothing. Two words Papa understood, "No beer." He tried to argue with Mrs. Dean. Luckily, she could not understand him and he could not understand her. With Papa speaking in German and Mrs. Dean speaking in American, communicating didn't go very well.

Mama was happy she had brought her aluminum pot all the way from Russia through Germany to America. She continued to scour it, using the red dirt outside, just like in Russia and Germany. She complained in between scrubbing and rinsing that the red dirt was like powder and didn't have enough substance or grit in it to get her pots shining clean. Dishwater was thrown out the back door. Mama was back to our refugee camp recipes. Being unfamiliar with the groceries and not being able to read American, she cooked what she knew best. Soup was our mainstay, along with baloney sandwiches. Cutting up apples and baking them in the oven was a waste of good fresh fruit. No apple pies.

Mrs. Dean brought over a huge tub so that we could take a bath. She tried to explain that it was necessary to bathe daily because of the heat. She did not want to tell me we all smelled bad. As the days became hotter, we washed in the same tub—hands, arms, and faces, including the neck—always fearing that we would run out of water and have to walk to the snake-infested pond to finish.

Washing clothes was a problem. Since the water level in our well was getting low, we had to conserve water. The cistern was almost empty and there still wasn't any rain. We had a choice: haul water from the pond, about a hundred yards from our shack, or take the clothes to the pond and wash them there. Papa built a pier about twelve yards long into the pond so Mama wouldn't have to stand in the muddy water and stir up the dirt at the shore. Papa's job on washdays, which were always on Mondays before going to Mrs. Dean's, was to walk out into the pond and stir the water with a stick to see if there were any water moccasins around. Most times there were snakes in the pond, but they always swam away. Between Mama and me, doing the laundry took half the day. Mama washed, rinsed, and handed clothes to me to hang on the nearest shrubs. Sometimes the humidity was so high that it took the wet clothing three days to dry. In Germany, in Camp Hofstetten, Mama had prided herself on the whiteness of her whites, but now she was embarrassed and happy there were no neighbors to see the gray sheets and pillowcases. Mrs. Dean supplied us with old clothing that we gratefully accepted. Some of those old dresses didn't last through the first wash. They shrank and no one could wear them. If I found a dress I liked in the batch, I wore it for days until Mrs. Dean objected to the odor. I told her that washing some dresses ruined them. Oh yes, those dresses were to be dry cleaned only.

"What is 'dry clean'?"

"This means you have to take the dress to a special store in Holly Springs that does laundry and dry cleaning."

"Cost much?" I asked.

"Oh yes," was her reply.

With no money and no car, how was I going to get to the dry cleaners? It was easier to wear a dress a few times then throw it away.

Papa drove dozens of nails into the wall so that we could hang our clothing. The rest was folded and placed under each mattress. Trying to find a particular piece of clothing caused a complete uproar in the family.

* * *

I think Mama was happy cooking for us. We had a cast-iron frying pan that came with the shack. With plenty of time on her hands, she placed a pound of bacon in it and then slowly stir-fried it until we had a frying pan full of grease with bacon strips swimming in it. To this she added a couple of sliced onions, followed by a dozen eggs, beating one at a time into the concoction, stirring all the while. Salt and pepper were added to taste. Mama put the frying pan on the box/table, and we ate the mixture in sandwiches. It was hard to hold onto the sandwich because the grease soaked through the bread and dripped down our hands. Oh, was that good! Mama passed around one of her handmade sack/towels to wipe our hands clean. We dipped extra slices of bread into what was left in the pan.

While the bacon/onion/eggs were bubbling, Mama filled our soup pot with milk, and when it boiled, she added a cup, maybe more, of sugar, then 1/2 to 3/4 cup of instant coffee. All this had to boil awhile, until it had a nice light brown color. It was served in stained and chipped enamel coffee cups. When cold it developed a thick skin and I'd have to use a spoon to punch through the skin to the coffee itself in order to get a cup.

On cool mornings I liked to sleep in. Sleeping in meant staying in bed, not actually sleeping. In a small room with six people moving about, how could I sleep? On those mornings Mama always saved some of the egg concoction for me. I spread it on my bread like butter. Sometimes, after we had eaten the eggs, onions, and bacon, Mama poured the remaining grease into an empty coffee can that permanently sat on the stove between the burners. Those bacon drippings were used in almost everything, from green beans to boiled potatoes and soups. When any of us became hungry in between meals, we always ate a sandwich spread with bacon drippings. The jar of peanut butter was never used. It was opened, tasted, and never touched again. Mama had the amounts of food for meals down so patently that there were very few leftovers

My days were taken up by helping Mama with whatever she needed done. Mama's days were spent repairing clothing, taking care of Sterna the cow, milking her twice a day, tending the four chickens, and cooking. When I was on my hands and knees washing the kitchen floor, I could see daylight through the boards. There was no end to the dust. I cleaned our house spotless, but the next time a truck went by, the red dust settled on everything again.

Papa was a heavy smoker. Mrs. Dean made sure he never ran out of cigarettes. She provided cartons of them for him.

"I will admit that the Amis make the best cigarettes," he said.

I was extremely grateful to America because I didn't have to go and pick up old used cigarette butts like I did in Germany. We lived under a cloud of smoke, especially on rainy days when Papa was home.

When it rained, it was good for the cistern but bad for us. The tin roof leaked in five places one time, and the next time in six or seven. Mama placed tin cans all around the room to try to keep the bedding from getting too wet. It didn't matter in the kitchen because the water just dropped on the floor and disappeared between the cracks.

"Mama, how do you know when to get up to empty the cans at night?" I asked.

"By the sound. Drops of water falling into an empty can sound different than that of a full can."

Poor Mama, she must have listened to the raindrops filling the cans all night long.

In the morning when it stopped raining, we hung everything that was wet on nearby shrubs; that included most of the bedding. Between the humidity and the rain, we rarely got everything dried out.

Try as we might, the red clay mud would be tracked into both rooms. At first, Mama wiped it up just as soon as we came in, but after a while, she waited until it stopped raining and then washed the floor on her hands and knees.

"No, no. I'll do it," I said.

"I need to keep busy," she replied.

* * *

Our first Sunday in America, after breakfast, we all sat outside on the decaying porch in the cool of the morning, watching all the horses and wagons filled with black people go by. They rattled down the road, leaving a cloud of red dust behind. Women had handkerchiefs on their heads; some young men were bareheaded, others wore hats; there were little girls who had a dozen pigtails on their heads. The black soldiers I had met in Germany all had short hair. Their heads looked almost bald. I wondered if these were the same people or even related. They stared at us. There was no "Hello" or even a friendly wave. Shortly thereafter, we heard beautiful singing and clapping hands to drumbeats coming from the same direction. I was scared. In the movies I had seen in Germany, that was how it started. First the noise, the drums, the singing in the jungle, then they attacked and killed all the white people in the area. The people doing the killing in the movies wore feathers. Surely the Deans would not expose us to something like that? I must remember to ask. That drumbeat and shouting continued all through the day and stopped only just before the sun set. Then, throwing up a cloud of red dust, all the traffic returned from where it came.

The very next day, Sister Erika and I walked in the direction the black families had headed, and to my surprise we came upon a huge barn, except it had a cross on the roof. The building was made of dark brown boards. It had screens for windows. The door was open. Inside was a dirty wooden floor. A small table at the far end, and the place was furnished with long wooden benches. This must be a church, and Sunday morning was a service. There was no comparison with the big stone and brick cathedrals in Germany. It all must be a bad dream. We were less than two weeks in America, and we were frightened by all we had heard and seen. Surely, God had better plans for us. After all, we had lived through so much.

Papa kept reading the Bible in German and then looking up nouns and verbs in the dictionary. Little by little he started to put together a new language.

"Just give them all the words. They can put it together or pick out what they want," Papa often said.

Trying to teach Mama even a few words was a hopeless task. She would not cooperate.

* * *

We made a list of questions we wanted to ask Mrs. Dean the next time she came. Papa looked up *church* and, gesturing toward us, asked our landlady, "Church go?"

"No, there are no churches around here that you can attend."

"Black church?" Papa asked.

Waving her hands in the air Mrs. Dean shouted, "No! No going to church with niggers! No talking to niggers! You are white. Black and white don't mix in America. No good. You understand?"

My American language was rapidly improving. No church, no blacks, no whites in America, no good. Each sentence Mrs. Dean uttered ended with "You understand?"

We didn't understand, but we did know enough to see when she became upset and redfaced. We always said, "OK."

We started to copy words that we needed out of the dictionary. Papa had me ask Mrs. Dean for an American Bible, which she provided the following day. He read the Bible and came across a word like *watch*. Papa said this word was used a lot by Mrs. Dean. "Theodor, watch this or that." Many words had several meanings. All of the meanings were written down. Since from an early age I spoke German and Russian, the American language fascinated me; for instance the words *fixin'* or *ot to*. Papa heard those words often, but he could not understand them either. They were not in the Bible, and I, who should have been a pro by now (per Papa), couldn't translate them. Most of the time it was all very confusing.

Sister Erika and I began to have daily American-language sessions. Papa joined us after work. Mama had no interest. She said it was too hard. Two languages, Russian and German, were enough for her.

With Papa's help, I put a sentence together that lasted Mama and Papa forever: "Please speak slow, little words."

* * *

Sister Lida was inconsolable. She missed her mutter so. Days passed with her wanting to know when she could go and visit Mutter. Papa tried to tell her that it was too far away, but she couldn't imagine just how far. Even if we could make the trip, we didn't have the money. She was quiet most of the time, looking at pictures in the Sears catalog before they were used as toilet paper. Mama rummaged through the kitchen shelves again. She stumbled upon a few rolls of white paper. We looked it up. It was toilet paper. It was very different from the rough brown sheets Americans used in Germany. The remainder of the Sears catalog was saved.

Brother Otto played with rocks and sticks on the broken-down front porch. Our little chickens were happy living, sleeping, and laying eggs under the shack. Mama was getting ready to milk Sterna when all of sudden her yelling awakened us. The whole family jumped up and out of the front door just in time to see a few feathers come floating down from the sky.

"Elsa, what is the matter?" Papa shouted.

"This big bird swooped down from the sky like lightning, grabbed up one of my chickens, and flew away."

"I guess we need to have one of the kids watch the chickens," Papa said.

When Mrs. Dean came over to drop off our groceries, I asked her about the chicken-grabbing bird.

"We call that bird a 'chicken hawk,' " Mrs. Dean explained. "They circle way up in the sky, and when they see a chicken they come down and get their meal."

Sister Lida was given the job of watching out for chicken hawks. When she saw a bird in the sky, she would shoo the chickens under the shack until the danger passed.

Mama wanted a small garden, but we didn't even have a shovel. When Papa came home one evening after working on Mrs. Dean's farm, he brought one with him. He tried to turn the dry red ground over in order to plant a few potatoes that Mama had kept from the last batch we received. She cut each potato into four parts. Each piece must have an eye in order to grow, so I was told. After much hard work, Papa finally turned over a small plot. Mama planted the potatoes in the hard ground. She was all smiles when she saw the first green leaves peeking through the soil. After days of no rain her hopes died. The green leaves turned brown, shriveled up, and died, never to come up again.

Sitting around the room during a rainfall, between the rusty cans catching leaks, Mama wanted to know how people here in America lived when they couldn't even grow potatoes. Papa had no answer.

Mama's conclusion to questions that Papa had no answers for was that America was created by the devil. Red was the devil's color. Were people also possessed by the devil, just like the red earth? Why had God brought us to such a land? We had been through so much. Mama concluded that the reason was to punish us. For what? Papa had the answer. The Bible said the sins of your fathers were handed down to the third and fourth generation. It must have been something our forefathers did for which we had to suffer. God said it, my parents believed it, and that settled it. It was God's plan. What would become of us only God knew. We didn't pray anymore. For what should we pray? God had spoken.

Papa read the Bible aloud and applied the Old Testament to our family. We had to sit and listen to stories about a God who was angry most of the time and punished nations and people for disobeying His instructions. No discussions or questions were allowed. It was plain and simple what God said.

Nights were short. It didn't cool off until way past midnight, and 5:30

A.M. was wakeup time. All of this was hard on me. I was always tired. I woke up at night hearing the jungle sounds of noisy night animals and thought about those years in Camp Hofstetten. I wished I was back there with my dear friends. Slowly, a few weeks passed.

* * *

Mrs. Dean had stocked our kitchen with a good supply of groceries before our arrival. I'm sure she did the best she could. We didn't know what all those things on the shelf were and didn't know enough American to ask her, since she always stayed for only a few questions and demonstrations. We now used toilet paper, soap to wash our clothing, good-smelling bars of soap for bathing, sanitary napkins (to Mama's delight), and good Chesterfield cigarettes for Papa. There was no avoiding canned goods. We had a can-opener that no one could use. Until Mrs. Dean demonstrated how it worked, Papa used a screwdriver and a hammer to open the cans.

Papa was on the lookout for beer. He pressed the issue.

"Ella, ask Mrs. Dean why there is no beer or whiskey here in America for sale in the stores. I would like for her to buy me some," Papa said.

"Papa," I said, "I asked her that before."

"You ask her again," he ordered.

"You see," Mrs. Dean said, "we have a law here in Mississippi that prohibits the sale of liquor of any kind. There are people who make their own whiskey, and sometimes they sell it. If you are caught, you go to jail. Everybody goes to jail, those who make it, those who sell it, and those who drink it. You understand?"

"The law, no beer, no buy, no drink." I looked up the word *jail* and that was all Papa needed to know. I made a mental note not to bring the beer subject up again.

Mama used the cotton bags that the flour, rice, and sugar came in to make an apron, pillowcases, and curtains, which she chain-stitched by hand. The material was also good for washing dishes and the floors when the rags got too worn out. To cover her beautiful hair she now adopted the custom of wearing a handkerchief on her head; the handkerchief was made out of cotton bags as well.

From his daily contact with the Deans, Papa's American language improved considerably. He spent all his free time at home reading the Bible, which was only after work and all day on Sundays. First he read verse by verse in German, and then he cross-referenced it in American. I tried to help him as much as I could with the pronunciation of the words I knew, but to no avail. The words never came out right. The sentences he did learn he became pretty good at, but with a heavy German accent. He memorized a formidable vocabulary, including putting many Bible verses to memory. After a few weeks, he was able to piece together short, understandable American-language sentences.

Mama, on the other hand, never learned English beyond "How are you," "Fine," "Did you work hard," "Yes." Most questions she answered with a smile and OK.

We didn't talk much about Germany because it made Mama cry. We sat on our beds watching Mama's pain; rocking back and forth, with her hands in her lap, her eyes would fill again and again. The tears would make two streams, reaching her chin, and unite as one river, dripping on her chest and disappearing into her dress. The journey of tears was accompanied by no sound. Whenever she thought it was enough, she wiped her face and chest with her apron, and with her voice barely audible said, "Mein Gott, mein Gott." It was a pitiful sight. Occasionally, Papa played his accordion hoping to cheer her, and we sang along, but not with as much gusto as we used to back in Germany.

I was grateful for one thing: After leaving Germany, Papa didn't beat Mama and me anymore. Sometimes he yelled at the top of his lungs when things didn't go his way or when Mrs. Dean gave him a hard time. He was frustrated with Mrs. Dean. "Theodor, do this . . . Theodor, do that." At home, he told us of his daily trials.

For example, according to Papa, Mrs. Dean said, "Theodor, paint the fence." But as soon as he started to paint, Mr. Dean came to get him to wash the car. Mrs. Dean came out, pointed to the fence, and said, "Theodor, no finish yet?" That's how it went daily.

* * *

The start of our third week, Mrs. Dean laid down the law of do's and don'ts. The whole family was assembled in our front yard.

The entire family, including the children, was to be ready for work by 6:00 A.M. daily. She gave Papa a Big Ben wind-up clock. No one was to stay home. Mama was to make sandwiches for everybody and take whatever we usually had for lunch. Mrs. Dean demonstrated with her hands, two slices of bread with a piece of baloney in between. No mayonnaise. What is mayonnaise? You spread it on bread like butter, except in the heat it goes bad and you might get sick. Right, we had an unopened jar in the refrigerator.

When the weather was bad we could stay at home, except for Papa. He had work to do on her farm.

"I carpenter, no farmer," Papa said.

"That's OK, Theodor, we'll teach you all you need to know to become a farmer," Mrs. Dean asserted.

"Children, school," Papa said.

"Y'all came over here to work for me, so now you work for me, your children also," Mrs. Dean explained. "No school. Work! Do you understand? You and your family will live here with us for one year. That was in your contract." (The contract was in American, which we couldn't read, much less understand.) "You will chop and pick cotton for one year to pay back the money we invested in bringing you and your family from New York to Mississippi. So settle down and start working."

Out of this whole conversation, the things I picked up were "no school," "everybody work," "contract," and "one year."

After Mrs. Dean left, we sat in silence. Papa asked me for a translation, and I picked out the words I knew and pieced them together.

"Papa, as I understand it, all of us will have to work every day in the field for one year. We are to work with cotton."

We had no choice. We had no money. In fact, we hadn't even seen any American money. The few bills we had were worthless German money. We had no place to spend it. Would Americans even take German money? How were we going to get into town to buy anything?

Mama spoke up. "We made our bed. Now we must sleep in it."

She was crying again, her chest shuddering as big streams of tears fell from her eyes. Occasionally she wiped them with her crude apron.

We were busy looking up words: *cotton, chop, pick.* With "chop" we had no problem, but "pick" was less clear. There were no pictures of cotton trees in the dictionary. The German word for cotton is *Baumwolle*, literally "wool tree." We had no idea what picking cotton would be. All of us were discussing what cotton trees looked like. I assured Papa I had seen no cotton trees on the way to the black church.

Early Monday morning a tractor with a trailer hitched to it clattered up outside with Hal in the driver's seat. Mama made sandwiches for everyone. We all climbed in the trailer and rode about five miles down the dusty road. There we were unloaded and given a big can of water and hoes. Hal showed us what we were expected to do. Go down each row, remove the weeds, and thin out the cotton plants enough that they wouldn't choke each other as they grew. He unhitched the trailer and told us he would be back in the evening.

We started to chop cotton. (This process, contrary to our expectations, was what "chopping" referred to.) Each of us had a hoe. Little brother Otto played in the rows with his oversized hoe. Mama didn't want to leave him in the shade of the trailer because she was afraid a snake would bite him. We started off with much enthusiasm. As the sun climbed higher and higher and the humidity increased, we came almost to a standstill. We were not prepared: no hats, no gloves, and no handkerchiefs, except for Mama. Our faces and arms turned red and hurt. My hair and body were dripping perspiration. My hair hung down in my eyes and I had to keep pushing it back to see what I was doing. It had rained a few days before, and the red clay stuck to the hoes and our shoes. I removed it with my fingers, only to get my hands all dirty without a place to rinse them clean. Red mud caked my face and hair.

I wanted to talk to Mama about all this, our lot here in America, but what would I say? She looked so depressed and hurt, and Papa was disillusioned as well. The noon sun beat fiercely down on us. It was too hot to continue. I got an excruciating headache. Every stitch of my dress was wet, and every breath I took caused such head pain. We walked back to the wagon and sat under it for shade. From the can Hal had left us, Mama poured a little water on our hands to get the mud off. We dried our hands on the inside hems of our dresses.

Mama insisted I eat my sandwich. Oh, for a piece of black bread! The sandwich consisted of butter, pickles, and baloney between two slices of bread, but the bread was soggy from the sour pickle juice. (The next time she packed our lunch ingredients separately, pickles in the jar, baloney in tinfoil, which she washed and saved for reuse, and the bread left in its wrapper.) We each got an apple and a tasty cake.

Mama encouraged me to eat, hoping my headache would go away. No such luck. It hurt so badly I could hardly see. I could not find a position to relieve the throbbing. Leaning over to chop made it worse. I could not remember ever having a headache before. Sister Erika voiced her opinion that I didn't want to chop cotton and was complaining in order to get out of working. Sister Lida and Brother Otto hoed some, but the hoes were bigger than they were and almost impossible for them to handle.

As the day progressed, the rows began to look longer and longer. Would there ever be an end to this?

We rested for the second time. Papa even took a nap. Soon it was time to start again. Mama thought I had better stay under the trailer and rest a little longer, what with all my moaning and groaning. My conscience bothered me and I started to chop again. Mama and Papa were up front. I tried to stay just out of earshot behind them. I didn't want my cries of anguish to be heard by parents or siblings. Even lying down between the rows for a few minutes didn't help.

It was getting to be late afternoon, and the mosquitoes were out in full force. We heard a tractor in the distance and knew that, for this day only, our salvation was at hand. Hal, without saying much, loaded us and drove us back to our shack. With a "See y'all tomorrow," he was gone.

We washed up outside as best as we could. Mama started a pot of some kind of soup. Papa retrieved Sterna from the fenced-in pasture. I brought a bucket of water from the well so that Mama could wash the cow's udder to milk her.

"Ella, you need to learn to milk a cow. That will help me a great deal when we return from the field."

"OK, Mama. Show me how."

I watched her for a few minutes. It looked easy. I sat on a small log we used as a milking stool. But Sterna sensed I was new at this and would not cooperate. She moved her hind legs so that it was difficult for me to lay my fingers on her udder. Not only did Sterna lose her patience, but Mama did as well. I was too slow. She took over. I rinsed out some gallon pickle jars and she poured milk into them and set them on the shelf to make clabbered milk.

The days passed and my head continued to hurt. I spent more time under the trailer than chopping cotton. Mama tried some home remedies, rubbing Crisco on my forehead, then tying one of the cotton sacks tightly around my head. It still hurt. After two weeks of unbelievable pain, I started to throw up. Papa made a trip to Mrs. Dean's house one evening after work. She brought him back in her car. She asked where it hurt, and I told her my head. She told me to get my clothes. I didn't have much to pack. I grabbed clothes off the nails and stuffed the clothing that was mine in a pillowcase.

"Tell your parents that you will be going home with me until you get over the headache," Mrs. Dean said.

* * *

At her house Mrs. Dean gave me a BC Headache Powder dissolved in a glass of water and told me which of the bedrooms was mine. All I could think about was lying down anywhere in that beautiful cool house to sleep and sleep.

When I awoke it was dinner time the following day. My headache was now a dull throb. By the next day it still hurt but not nearly as badly as before, and I wasn't sick at my stomach anymore.

"Mrs. Dean, I go doctor?"

"I don't think so," was her reply. "You just had a little too much sun, and I can take care of that. You understand? Stay out of the sun. No outside, stay in the house."

It took almost a week before I was myself again. Now I had time to look around and enjoy all those pretty things, all the while thinking these people were really rich. They had horses and three dogs. I could not imagine the amount of food they ate. In addition, they owned two cars and a tractor. They had everything I saw in the movies about America. I thought, Will we ever have anything?

Papa came every day to check on me. They had finished chopping cotton. Mrs. Dean mentioned that it was only five acres we chopped. After a week of recuperation, my guilt set in. I hadn't seen my family in a whole week. I had my own bedroom and bath. Mrs. Dean was very kind and helpful. She made sure I drank a lot of juice and water. Now that I felt somewhat better, I spent a lot of time in the kitchen watching her prepare food or direct the black woman as to what she wanted done. Mrs. Dean was a very good cook. Most of the dishes she prepared were new to me: tasty turnip greens, corn cakes, apple pie, pecan pie, lemon icebox pie, and many more. She never cooked soup or the same meal twice in a row. Some kind of meat was served at every meal (but not horse meat). Fried chicken with rice and gravy were her husband's favorite. Every day there was a new dessert. The table was set with napkins and beautiful dinner plates. I hoped I would be able to cook as well as Mrs. Dean. We always drank iced tea (no beer!). I had tea without ice because the cold might give me another headache.

One evening a neighbor came over. They introduced him as their friend Mr. O'Dell. The three of them sat on the screened-in front porch drinking martinis. I could not imagine what that was, but I did like the pretty glasses with a green grape in each. I tasted the leftovers before I washed the glasses. Nasty.

Mrs. Dean gave me a batch of secondhand dresses. I had never seen her wear them, and besides, she was a heavy-set woman. Someone else must have given them to her. The dresses were made out of printed material so thin you could look through them. I only wore underpants, since I had no need for a bra.

My first visit home, everybody was eager to hear about all I had seen, heard, and experienced. I had to tell them. Mama cried, but the rest of the family was envious. My heart hurt. I wished I could take each and every one of them back with me to my room. Next time I went home, Papa grilled me on my American vocabulary and what I had seen on the movie box. I had seen an old bald man named Eisenhower everybody was crazy about.

"Why?" Papa asked.

"I don't know. They say he was some kind of general who won the war against Germany."

I decided to be selective about what I shared with my family because I could not stand Mama's tears. I wished I could share all my newly acquired knowledge, but that was impossible. It would just hurt them—Mama in particular. They worked so hard every day while I was having a good, cool time. I still suffered from headaches, but not as often. I was forbidden to go out into the sunshine. Days stretched into a week, then two. Cotton chopping time had ended.

I was well again, but Mrs. Dean had no intention of sending me home. Away from my family, I had to speak American no matter how badly I butchered it. The Deans always corrected me in a very kind way. Every day I learned new words. Mrs. Dean provided me with my own personal German-English paperback dictionary, which became my lifeline. I was determined to be a first-class American whatever it took.

Evenings contained long discussions, of which I understood only parts.

"Here in America," Mrs. Dean would start, "you can be anything and do anything and have anything as long as you are willing to work hard. Americans may not understand what you are saying, but they can tell by your work what kind of person you are." She continued, "You don't have to have much money in America, but you should make many friends. You will find that Americans are very friendly people. So be friendly to people you meet. You understand?"

Wow, I thought. What a difference friendliness would be compared to the majority of Real Germans, who had been so unfriendly. I was also thinking, How in the world am I going to make friends living here in the jungle with no people around and having met no one except Mr. O'Dell?

We had come to America in April. It was now the end of May. Living with the Deans, I had learned many things. Mrs. Dean had taught me how to use the vacuum, dust, clean the bathroom, and do other general cleaning-lady chores. I had inadvertently found a career. I became the maid of the house. Mrs. Dean laid out my daily routine, from using the vacuum to mixing a cake, from using the washing machine to polishing silver. Each new chore I soaked up like a sponge, for which she praised me. I would have loved to have had this job in Germany.

My American language improved daily. I was absolutely fascinated by the telephone and television. I was grateful for Mrs. Dean's interest in teaching and helping me, and told her so.

I learned all the things I needed to be a good maid and was very grateful for that, always showing my appreciation and much thankfulness to our landlady for paying our way to Mississippi. Mrs. Dean mentioned that they had sponsored another family the year before but didn't say anything else about them, including where they came from or where they went.

* * *

Not far from the Dean's house, about a quarter of a mile, stood another shack just like ours. Little black children played outside. The Dean's big house was separated from the shack by a row of pear trees. I made a mental note to be sure to ask Mrs. Dean for some pears when they came in season. One evening I was outdoors when the black family came home from the field on a mule-drawn wagon. They stopped, and a young black man said, "Hi! You, Germany?"

"Yes." I said.

"I fought in Germany during the war."

I understood "war."

"Where?"

"Berlin."

"You like Berlin?"

"Yes. Do you like Mississippi?"

"OK."

"Got to go. Bye," he said.

I was elated that I had talked with someone who had seen Germany. I couldn't wait to tell Mrs. Dean about our conversation. She listened carefully, then informed me, "White people don't talk to blacks, especially white girls. Remember, Ella, in the South whites have nothing to do with blacks. They are not called black"—my translation of the German *Schwarze*— "but are called 'niggers' or 'colored.' They have their own schools, toilets, water fountains, and eating places. You understand?"

I was too scared to ask why. As soon as I could, I shared this vital information with my family. I didn't want them to do anything wrong in this new country. From then on, I avoided all contact with the black people next door.

* * *

"Well, Ella, we need to have a talk about cleanliness," Mrs. Dean began. "As you can tell, here in Mississippi the weather is very hot and muggy. We expect you to shower and wash your hair, use shampoo and conditioner. You understand?"

I thought, What is conditioner?

"Bathe either in the morning or at night. We also want you to shave under your arms and your legs." She demonstrated with the razor. "In America it is not the custom for girls or women to grow hair under their arms or on their legs. Men yes, women no. You understand?"

I understood why she wanted me to shave under my arms. It was hot. But my legs? It never made sense. I never asked.

"I bought you a razor and you can shave yourself in the shower or bathtub. You should also change your sanitary napkins more often. That is another reason you must shower daily. People can smell you"—holding her nose—"and that is no good. You understand?"

The sanitary napkins box was brought out of the bathroom. She used a clean napkin to demonstrate, including the elastic belt.

"After use, it has to be rolled and wrapped in toilet paper and placed back into the box. Whenever your time is over, you throw the full box of used napkins in the trash to be burned. You understand?"

Everything Mrs. Dean said was followed with a demonstration and "You understand?"

"It is important to use deodorant under your arms daily," she continued. "Whenever you run out, let me know, and I'll get you some more. I'll give you a home permanent so that you'll have curly hair. You don't need to wear any makeup yet, only a little lipstick. You can use one of mine for the time being. Keep your fingernails short because they accumulate dirt. Wear a clean dress and clean underwear daily, and put the dirty one in the wash. You understand?"

Now I was the proud owner of at least half a dozen too-big, see-through, thin, floral-print dresses.

"But I no dirty cleaning house," I protested.

"Ella, you don't understand. It's not the dirt on your dress, it's the sweat that smells. We call it 'body odor.' It is very offensive. While we are on the subject, I bought you a toothbrush, and you need to brush your teeth every morning and night. People don't want you around when you have bad body odor and bad breath. You understand?"

Going home Sunday afternoons to visit became increasingly difficult. The shortcut through the pasture took about thirty minutes. The heat was unbearable even with a newly acquired hat. I passed through a dry sandy creekbed that was covered with snake skins. What happened to the snakes? I wondered.

The first thing I noticed after arriving in our shack was Mama and Papa's body odor. I didn't have the heart to tell Mama to shave under her arms or take a bath in the pond every day. Mama wore the same dress for days, and no matter how hard she scrubbed under her arms while having a birdbath, she always smelled. Up until then, I had never noticed the foul body odor of my family. Now I could hardly stand it.

Finally I mustered up enough courage to suggest to Mama that she should bathe, shave her legs and under her arms, use deodorant, and put on a new dress and underpants daily.

Mama became pretty upset. "Where I come from, only whores shave under their arms, their legs, and elsewhere. As if I have nothing else to do except play the pretty lady all day. I do not have the time to wash clothes in the pond daily, much less bathe. With the shack to keep clean, take care of three kids and a husband, cook, milk the cow—and you not here to help."

I resolved not to mention to my parents my newly acquired American customs. None were appreciated or followed. They found fault with all of them.

One day I was wearing a sleeveless dress and Mama noticed I had shaved under my arms. She turned to Papa and said. "She has already started the American custom of shaving under her arms. Where else do you shave? Your legs? Are these Americans Christians? Do men shave under their arms also? I don't know if it is a very good thing to do everything Americans do. God created each part of our body for a purpose, including hair under the arms and on the legs. Really, Ella, people can talk you into anything. I find it sad, but since you want to become a real American, you must go along with the customs here. Whatever custom you adopt, remember your roots, where we came from and what we have been through. Don't expect us to go along with everything Americans do. Never, never be ashamed of your parents, because we sacrificed our lives for you."

I promised myself never, never to be ashamed of my family.

I could not convince Mama of the virtues of shaving under my arms, much less my legs. Of course, in the long run, it was all considered to be the devil's work.

* * *

I always watched when Mrs. Dean cooked. When I went home to visit my family on Saturdays or Sundays, I told Mama how to cook the bacon and eggs and make coffee the American way, and about other things Mrs. Dean cooked, like turnip greens.

"Just think, Mama, in Germany we always ate the turnips. Here in America they eat the tops of the turnips, the greens. They taste bitter, but with bacon drippings on them, they're pretty good. Mrs. Dean also bakes bread—cornbread, like we tried once in Germany. Next time we go to the grocery store, we should buy some of this corn meal and make some bread. It's really good."

But Mama had her own way of doing things and didn't appreciate my advice. "No, we don't need that," she replied. "Some things that the Americans eat or do are not always good for you. Right now, Ella, you are very impressionable, but as you grow older you will see what I am talking about. Be selective." I never had turnip greens or cornbread at our house.

It was now time to ask Mrs. Dean to show me about money. I had never seen American money. I had seen Hitler's money and, after the war, the devalued deutschmark. Whenever I asked a question, she was always very eager to answer and teach me. With great patience she repeated, explained, and gently corrected, for which I was always very grateful. She took time to show me all the bill denominations, which were not hard to learn. It was the coins that gave me trouble.

Every day I practiced with pennies, nickels, dimes, and quarters. On my Sunday visits to my family, I carried my change to teach Papa. Mama wasn't interested. She said, "I have enough children who will speak for me." Papa and the rest of the family participated in playacting with the coins until we all got it right.

They expected me to tell them everything I did. I continued to be very selective in what I told them because I felt so guilty that I had so much and my family had so little. Guilt was my constant companion. Since the cotton was chopped, the family stayed at home, but Papa reported daily to Mrs. Dean to do different chores. He was a carpenter by trade and a very good one at that, but after a few months of practice, he became a farmer. He had a gift in being able, with few instructions and little effort, to fix anything. With my rapidly growing vocabulary, I became the main translator. I realized that I could translate whatever I wanted, leave out whatever I wanted, and no one would be the wiser. Neither party would get upset. There was no telling what Papa would do, with his temper, if I actually translated verbatim. I translated only those things that Mrs. Dean wanted to hear and what my parents wanted to hear. Mrs. Dean was the "enforcer," as Papa called her. We hardly ever saw her husband.

*　*　*

It was almost six weeks after our arrival before we made a trip to Holly Springs. Our first shopping trip to buy groceries at the store was a memorable one, seeing Americans other than the Deans. Mrs. Dean brought us to town in her station wagon, just Papa, Mama, and me. This was the first time we had ever shopped in a grocery store. We were to get what we needed and no more. Mama started with flour, sugar, lard, onions, potatoes, canned sauerkraut, baloney, yeast, noodles, canned peaches, canned beets, eggs, fatback cut in neat, thick slices (bacon), oranges, a few apples, and instant coffee. We basically ate the same food we had in Germany, except for the black bread that we hungered for. How absolutely ironic. Now we ate white bread like the rich Germans but wished for even a crust of black bread. Mama tried in vain to make black bread, even starting sourdough herself, but it never looked or tasted like the bread we left behind. (Our shack was as hot as hell when Mama was using the oven to bake bread.)

Our total grocery bill came to $10.

Our regular shopping day from then on was set by Mrs. Dean for Saturdays. The town was completely inundated with black people. We saw very few whites, and those we saw were poorly dressed. The white women had their hair pinned to their heads with hundreds of bobby pins. Poor white families came into town in the backs of pickup trucks. Their speech and mannerisms fascinated me. Women and children standing around had little success trying to brush the red dust off their clothing. The majority of white men looked emaciated, their pants were too big and had to be gathered by a belt around the waist. Their pants and shirts looked like they had never seen water. Most of them had a rifle or two inside their beat-up pickups.

"Mrs. Dean, are these white Americans like you?"

"Yes. They are Americans, called 'sharecroppers.'"

"What is 'sharecroppers'?"

"They work on someone else's farm and the owner pays for everything. They work the land and receive a share of the combined sale of cotton, sweet potatoes, tobacco, or whatever crops they are tending. When the crops come in, they are expected to pay off what they owe the owner, and the rest of the money belongs to them."

I would look it up later. It was becoming hard to keep all the explanations and new words in my head.

"Black people?"

"The niggers work for landowners and are paid very little money, but their houses are free." She took this opportunity to remind me: "Everything is separate for niggers: eating places, including the toilets, water fountains, churches, and schools. If you see any sign that says 'colored,' avoid it. 'For whites only' is for you. You understand?"

"Will black people be like you?"

"What do you mean?"

"With money, nice house."

"No, I don't think so."

"Will my family ever be like you?"

"Probably. Hard work will determine if you ever amount to anything," she said.

More and more black people arrived on the square. They came in mule-drawn wagons. Each wagon seemed filled to capacity. Little girls had pigtails all over their heads and were barefoot. Women had handkerchiefs tied around their heads, and little boys and men had very short-cropped hair, some wearing straw hats. Everyone looked so poor. The biggest black crowd was around the courthouse that stood in the middle of the square. Blacks did not even mix with the poor whites. In fact, poor whites didn't assemble in groups at all. I wondered where I fit in.

The only well-dressed white people I saw were those in the stores. We stopped at a hardware store where Papa picked up nails and other things that Mrs. Dean needed. People in front of us in the checkout line didn't use any money at all. They just said, "Charge it."

"Mrs. Dean, what is 'Charge it'? No pay?"

"No, no," she said. "The store owner will write down how much money you spend every time you come in the store. Whenever you get paid or get some money, you pay him back. We call it 'credit.' You understand?"

"Pay later?" I asked.

"Yes," she replied.

After sharing this information with Papa and Mama, we talked about it but couldn't understand the whole system.

Watching Mrs. Dean write a check I asked, "Is money?"

"Yes," she said. "A check is as good as money."

I watched her writing the check but could not make out the amount until the clerk said, "Mrs. Dean, your groceries are $10. Your check is for $20. Do you want the change in a ten or two fives?"

"Two fives will do," she said.

Since I knew the most American words in our family, I tried to interpret for Papa what was being said by the black people we overheard. Most of the words I didn't know. Those I could understand within the context of a sentence I didn't have the German word to translate. I had problems with words and phrases like *fixin, ot to, ain't, sho-nuff, reckun so, Goodness gracious! Mercy me!* and *honey chile.* Finding them in the dictionary was "pert-near" impossible. Try as I might, I could not understand black people at all. To me they sounded as if they spoke a foreign language, not American. The poor white people were hard to understand too.

Our next stop was Armor's Drugstore, where Mrs. Dean bought epsom salts, paregoric, hydrogen peroxide, Carter's Little Liver Pills, Kotex, BC Headache Powder, talcum powder, and other items for her family. When I returned to her house, I looked all those things up in the dictionary.

Mrs. Dean also bought each of us a nickel's worth of ice cream and a small cola. Mama and Papa liked the ice cream but not the cola. It was too sweet to quench their thirst. I was busy looking around for people my age. I noticed behind the counter two teenage boys and in the back a teenage girl. They were beautiful people, the boys with nice white shirts and pants, the girl in a nice skirt and blouse, hair worn in a ponytail. They laughed and joked among themselves and always were friendly to customers. I wished I had left my hair long and didn't have that homemade permanent. It always looked bushy. I washed it and let it sun dry. I promised myself that someday

I would look like the girl in the drugstore. I resolved to grow a ponytail. On the way out I heard one of them say something about the German girl.

Returning from our shopping trip, I spent the night with my parents after we unloaded sacks and sacks of groceries. We put whatever fit in the refrigerator and the oven. The rest was at the mercy of the mice and rats. Whatever they didn't eat, we finished off. That evening Papa retold the happenings of the day blow by blow. Inevitably, no matter what subject we were on, Papa managed to remember something from the Bible and he'd go off on a tirade complaining about how things were in America. According to Papa, Mama didn't know anything because she was a woman, and children were simply too young to know anything at all. Papa complained about: women bossing men around (as Mrs. Dean did); buying things on credit; pickup trucks with guns in the back window for everyone to see; children driving cars; sharecroppers working for very little; black people working for even less; our family working for nothing. He had become an expert on American culture after a few weeks of odd jobs on the farm. Since he was happy in his one-way discussion, we let him have his say on all subjects. No one wanted to start a verbal disagreement.

* * *

My head didn't hurt anymore, so I was allowed outside. In the sticky heat of a Sunday afternoon in early August, wearing a hat and walking on the side of the road where it was shady, I came upon the main unpaved road. A well-kept white house sat on a green lawn, not all brown and burned up like ours. An old lady was sitting on the screened-in front porch. She called to me, "Sugar, would you like a glass of iced tea?"

"Yes."

"It is too hot for man or beast to be outdoors," she commented.

I introduced myself. "I am Ella Schneider."

"I'm Mrs. Brown, and you must be the little German girl who lives with the Deans."

"Yes. I am German girl."

She was a widow (I looked it up later). She wanted to know about our living conditions and I told her, "The Deans' house is beautiful. My mama and papa live in a bad house."

She nodded her head and mumbled something like, "I thought that much." She asked, "Are you going to be attending school?"

"No school, Mrs. Dean pay back money. Picking cotton," I said.

"You children must go to school. If you don't go to school and learn, you will forever chop and pick cotton."

I knew what chopping was but not picking. She offered me iced tea.

"No ice please," I said.

She smiled. "Would you like a piece of homemade lemon icebox pie?"

"Yes, thank you."

It was delicious. After I shook her hand, I thanked her for her hospitality.

"Ella, please come back to visit next Sunday," she said.

"OK," I said.

The following Sunday I didn't tell Mrs. Dean where I was going, just out walking. She said, "You should stay inside or you'll have another bad headache."

"I am OK," I replied.

A pickup came by and threw up a cloud of red dust. I prayed that I wasn't covered with too much of it. A second pickup even stopped and the driver asked if I was lost and needed a ride, that it was too hot to walk. "No, thank you."

Mrs. Brown had baked a beautiful chocolate cake, and I had tea without ice on her front porch. She told me that she had telephoned the school board and told them that there was a German family living close by who needed to enroll their children in school. She said she had taken care of everything. She kept repeating, "Don't worry, I took care of it. Just wait and someone will get in touch with you as far as transportation is concerned." She explained that it was not too soon to enroll because school in Mississippi started in mid-August. The farmers needed to have their kids at home to pick cotton in October, which meant time off from school.

Stopping at our shack on the way back to the Deans,' I told Papa that school would be starting early in Mississippi because the kids helped with picking cotton. Papa and I, the interpreter, marched over to Mrs. Dean's. He told her that his children must go to school. She got into an argument with Papa, saying that she hadn't paid all that money for the railroad tickets to bring us to Mississippi for us not to work. Translating for Papa, I asked her if she paid for the ticket from New York City. Yes. Who paid for the ticket from Germany to New York City? That was the Lutheran Church in America. (This was a revelation to us.) Papa kept telling her that he didn't mean to be ungrateful, but his children would go to school.

He said, "We very much thank you." He added that we would need to know how to get to the school, since we lived in the jungle. Of course, I didn't translate that exactly.

Mrs. Dean insisted, "I paid for all those hands, for the whole family. Little some of them may be, but come cotton-picking time I will get my money's worth out of you." With a short "Goodbye, Mr. Puder!" we were dismissed. Papa left disappointed.

* * *

Evenings at the Deans' air-conditioned house, I would get lost in the few photos Mama had brought out of Russia, and the pictures my friends had given me of themselves before I left Germany. I had brought these pictures to Mrs. Dean's because they filled my heart with warm memories. How I wished I was back in Germany. I was pondering our unbelievable living conditions here in America: snake-infested, broken-down shack, leaky roof, chopping cotton, and picking cotton yet to come. It was a nightmare. I spent a lot of time examining my real father's picture, wondering what had become of him. Was he still living somewhere in Siberia, or dead? Would he be able to find me in the middle of the jungle? My friends in Germany would not believe the life we started here in America. They probably would think I was lying. Besides, Papa thought it best not to write anyone for a while. Let our friends and tanten continue to envy us. Although Papa didn't permit me to write to Germany, he did agree that I could write the friends I had met in the processing camp in Munich and the embarkation camp in Bremerhaven: Otto Leukert, who lived in Philadelphia, and Elisabeth Daniel, with brother Alfred, in New Jersey. Mrs. Dean paid for the envelopes, paper, and stamps. With sadness, I received my friends' enthusiastic replies recounting their wonderful first impressions of America, completely different from mine.

The Deans had two horses and two mules. The mules looked funny, with small bodies, long ears, and unkempt coats. They were also slow to react. I had never seen a mule in Germany. The phrase "stubborn as a mule" came up in conversation one day to describe someone. I looked up the word in my dictionary. *Stubborn* explained it all.

One of the horses was a beautiful animal that the Deans' young daughter was learning to ride. I asked if I could ride it. "OK." Mrs. Dean came up with a pair of riding pants that must have been hers when she was young, a white blouse, and a cowboy hat. After saddling the horse, never knowing if I did it right or wrong (it looked so easy in the American movies in Germany), I tried but could not mount the animal. It kept moving in circles. Finding an old chair in the barn, I finally got into the saddle. Slowly, I rode into the community of Laws Hill. The first white building I came to, old men were sitting on the porch in rocking chairs, spitting frequently onto the red dust. Must remember to ask Mrs. Dean about the significance of spitting. Above the porch a sign read Smith's Groceries. I got down off the horse, tied it to the porch railing, smiled, and said, "Hi."

"Howdy, ma'am," was their reply.

A smell met me at the door, burned meat and very strong onions. The store was one big dirty room. Its shelves were filled with canned goods all around the room. The floor was covered in sawdust and looked like it was never swept. A big cast-iron potbellied stove sat in the middle of the room, surrounded by empty rocking chairs.

A heavyset white lady emerged from behind a partition. She cleaned her hands on an apron that should have been condemned years ago. From the smell it was obvious she was preparing hamburgers in the back. Moving long strands of wet hair out of her face, she said, "Honey, can I help you?"

I didn't have any money even if I wanted to buy something.

"No, thank you."

"Go look around and holler if you need help."

"OK," I said.

I looked around a little more. Most things on the shelves were in cans. There was a glass-encased box displaying some kind of meat, pieces of sausage, and cheese. By then, pickup trucks were accumulating in the parking lot. I surmised they all were there for lunch. They must have been farmers, wearing dirty blue pants attached to a square piece of material held up by straps, which served as suspenders. Funny-looking pants for a man, I thought. Each was topped by a well-worn straw hat. The men stood on the porch, and as I walked past them I overheard one saying something about "German girl" and "Come back to see us." I kept going.

Because I didn't have a chair to step on, I could not get back in the saddle. After a couple of failed tries to the loud laughter of the men, I just took the bridle and walked, in the noonday heat, the three miles back home. Never did try that again.

* * *

Sunday I visited Mrs. Brown again. She had been a very busy lady. In her slow, sometimes hard-to-understand southern drawl, she told me that she called the superintendent of the Holly Springs High School. She was told that Laws Hill, the small community down the road, was at the end of the bus route. Laws Hill had an elementary school. Sister Lida and Brother Otto would attend school there. Sister Erika and I would attend Thyatira High School over toward Senatobia.

I began to worry that Mrs. Dean would get mad if she found out what was going on behind her back. There was no telling what she might do. There was going to be a big confrontation, and I was afraid of the consequences. We had no idea what we could or could not do, what our rights were—in fact, did we even have any? On the other hand, maybe it wasn't such a bad thing to be deported back to Germany. Everybody in the family would be happy, Mama most of all. We had no money, no friends, and no car.

Mrs. Brown assured me that it was the law in Mississippi for children to attend school. "You will go to school," she said. "The school board will take care of everything. Mrs. Dean should know better. She has had many other families over the years working for her."

"Did Deans pay people?"

"Oh no," Mrs. Brown said. "All those people were indentured servants, just like your family. They come over, chop and pick cotton, then they are gone."

I made a mental note to look up "indentured servants."

* * *

Within days, a very sour-looking Mrs. Dean told me to inform my family that all the children were to attend school. It was mid-August. I could hardly contain myself. Papa was happy because he thought he had won, making his first stand here in America. There were numerous questions I needed answered. How would we get to school? School bus. What is that? Time to get on the bus? What kind of clothing should we wear to school? We didn't have much to choose from. Do we need coats, gloves, and hats with cold weather coming? Does it snow? School pencil and paper? On and on.

Mrs. Dean started to become short with me. "How many times did I tell you to always empty the vacuum bag? . . . By now you should know how to make tea . . . Are you not finished with the dusting yet?" I now found myself in a very hostile environment.

Nonetheless, I got up enough nerve to approach Mrs. Dean about school.

"Mrs. Dean, I have many questions."

"Yes, what is it?"

"Would you be kind and buy us what we need? We need shoes, clothing, paper, and pencils."

"Don't worry, Ella, I will take care of whatever y'all need."

"I hope I did not hurt your feelings. You have been very good to us, bringing us to America, and we thank you. Papa says we must go to school."

"I understand. We are not going to talk about it anymore."

"OK," I said.

On the next shopping trip to Holly Springs, all of us went except Mama. Mrs. Dean paid for our school supplies and new shoes.

On the way home she said, "Ella, I think it will be best if you move back home to live with your family."

I didn't ask why, I already knew. My disappointment must have been written all over my face. All I choked out was, "OK." I packed my belongings in a box and was dropped off by Mrs. Dean herself.

The day finally arrived when Sister Erika and I walked from our side road to the main dirt road and waited for a small truck to pick us up. It was not even seven o'clock yet, but it was already hot and humid. The truck was driven by an elderly gentleman who had two of his lower front teeth missing. He chewed and spit dark-brown stuff out of the open truck window. I reminded myself to ask somebody what he was spitting. We climbed into the back of the pickup. The truck started slowly enough, but every time the man shifted gears it moved faster and faster. We bounced around; even holding onto the benches didn't keep us from bouncing. We finally arrived at the main paved road, and the truck stopped. We just sat there waiting, trying to brush off the red dust that had settled on our hair, clothing, and faces. After a while a big yellow school bus came charging down the road. Sister Erika and I were the first passengers. The bus driver was a friendly man and tried to start a conversation, but after a while my vocabulary of "Yes," "No," and "OK" must have gotten old.

We turned off the main road onto unpaved roads in the countryside. At each stop more students got on the bus. None of them had book satchels or backpacks. They carried their books and notebooks under their arms. Each addition was greeted with a smile and an introduction by the bus driver: "These are the German girls living with the Deans." The usual reply was a smile and a "Howdy." The girls my age were pretty. Some had home perms that looked just as bushy as my hair did. Others had ponytails, what they called their "hairdo." I thought that was very apt. They wore skirts, some with poodle-dog appliqués on them, blouses, socks, loafers like mine but with dimes in the front slot (I need to put a dime in mine), a lot of makeup, and beautiful pink lipstick. The boys were loud and boisterous. Bits and pieces of words and phrases were all I could understand. Girls talked about summer camp, boyfriends, dances, PJ parties (must remember to ask somebody what PJ parties are). All the boys sat in the back of the bus and out of earshot.

At 8:00 A.M., after innumerable stops, we arrived at the school, a big H-shaped building beside the paved highway. Two other buildings housed a gym and a cafeteria. We had no names. We were introduced to whomever, always, as the German girls. Mary Lee Worley was assigned to make sure I did not get lost. Another student was assigned to Sister Erika. The first day, no one knew what to do with us. By now, I had a very good working vocabulary and most people I spoke to could understand me. But Sister Erika knew words that were not connected at all. Finally, after consultations with half a dozen teachers, a decision was made. Since I had finished German school, Volksschule (I even had my diploma with me but the teachers and principal couldn't read or understand it), I would be in the tenth grade. I was sixteen. Sister Erika, fourteen, was placed in the ninth grade.

Cheerfully and with great enthusiasm, I threw myself into studying the different subjects. It was very difficult to learn a language and learn a subject at the same time. I was determined that I would not chop and pick cotton for the rest of my life.

Lunchtime came and everybody descended on the cafeteria. We had no money for lunch. Graciously, we were treated to a free lunch. Before going home I was summoned into the principal's office and told that we would be given free lunches if I worked in the cafeteria during lunchtime. I was grateful for getting a job and not being dependent on handouts.

The teachers were very helpful, and so were the students. One of the first corrections made by my American teacher, who came prepared with her own English-German dictionary: "Ella, here in America, we speak English, not American."

She was very helpful and explained, "Remember when students or teachers correct you, that is not a criticism. Please come to me any time you have a question."

I told her I needed help with some of the words that were not in the dictionary but used in many different sentences, like *fixin'*, as in, "I'm fixin' to go home."

She explained, "These are southern expressions. 'Ain't' is not a good English word. Don't start a sentence with 'How come?' Keep in mind that words and phrases in the South sometimes have an altogether different meaning, which is not always the meaning Mr. Webster used."

The girls were friendly, smiling, taking me from class to class and asking all kinds of questions. I did as best I could with my answers. Not speaking German every day helped me to improve my English. Since I had always liked to sing, I joined the glee club. I also went out for basketball, beginning as a forward. What a turn my life had taken. It was a joy to be in school five days a week. I was sad having to go home every afternoon to our dump and my downhearted parents.

In school we became a novelty. The girls were impressed that we came from so far away. The boys were not interested at all, as their lives revolved around hunting, fishing, local football games, and girls who were "easy." *Easy* was not translatable. "Easy" meant "light;" girls were "light"? Must remember to ask my English teacher what is "easy" when applied to a girl. Embarrassment on both sides set in when the female English teacher explained.

"Easy girls will have relations with any boy. Some may get pregnant and leave school. Pregnant girls are not allowed to attend school."

"Mrs. Teacher, please tell me, what does the driver spit out of the pickup truck?"

With a smile she said, "Chewing tobacco. You put a piece of tobacco, a 'plug' they call it, into your mouth and chew but don't swallow, then you spit it out."

Sounded revolting to me.

I had looked up *indentured.* It meant you worked for the wealthy, all your time for someone else's benefit. Didn't make much sense. "Please explain, indentured servants?" I asked.

Her definition was "people who pay off money they owe by working." In our case, to pay back the price of the train tickets from New York to Mississippi. I got it. So, we were indentured servants. The only difference between our indentured servants' status and slavery was that we could, after paying off the debt with a year's work, establish ourselves elsewhere. After telling Papa about it, we tried to figure out what the status of all the black people was who worked out in the fields. Were they slaves, indentured servants, or hired hands? Later we found out that some were sharecroppers, as Mrs. Dean had mentioned, but that most were just plain workers.

* * *

I was learning in school about the atrocities the Germans had committed during the war. It was the first time I had ever heard of such things. Fascinated by this revelation, I was too scared to ask questions. I just knew the teachers were making it up because they didn't like the Germans. Pictures of Jews being led to gas chambers were in the books. Some pictures showed them in their homes, and to my surprise, the men all wore little black caps. When someone asked if I had seen any of these events, of course I said I didn't know anything, which was the truth. Somehow being from Germany, I was supposed to know all this and testify to it. Also, this was the first time I heard anything bad about the Nazis. At school in Germany, nothing was ever mentioned about so many Jewish people being killed. There were no books or pictures, and no one discussed the war at all. Shortly after one of those Jewish discussions in class, I was going through our pictures from Russia again when I was absolutely stunned by the sight of my real papa's picture. I noticed a cap on my papa's head. All kinds of pictures of my real papa being Jewish were parading across my mind. Mama never told me anything about my real papa, or grandfather or even grandmother on Papa's side. Where were they from? What did they do? I didn't remember ever going to any of my real papa's relatives' houses.

Papa was out working when I mustered enough nerve to ask Mama, clear out of the blue, "Mama, was my real papa Jewish?"

Mama was completely taken aback. "Why do you bring this up? Why do you want to know? All these things should be forgotten." Then very curtly she said, "No."

"But Mama," I continued, "Look at this picture. Papa is wearing a cap. That is what Jewish men wore. He must have been Jewish."

She became very agitated with my questioning. Turning away from me she said, "He wore a cap only to keep his long hair out of his face."

Then I remembered that I had asked this question before, when I was much younger. The answer had not changed.

I never mentioned the subject again.

When Papa came home we had dinner. I asked Papa, "Is it true that the German people killed six million Jews, then burned them?"

"Where do you hear such stories?"

"I read it in a book in school. I even saw pictures. Did you see anything like that when you were in the war?"

"Ella, you are so gullible, you will believe anything. No, I never saw anything like that. Furthermore, I would appreciate your not bringing that subject up again. What's done is done."

* * *

Late one Sunday afternoon, I had to get out of the shack to be alone and think. I took a different direction. I didn't go toward the main dirt road but went past the Deans' house. After a mile or two I came upon a nice-looking house with a big front porch. A huge flower garden fronted the house. An elderly man was working in a flower bed.

I said, "Hi, how are you?"

He came to the fence, took off his hat, reached for his red-printed hanky, and wiped the sweat off his brow.

"I'm fine, how are you?" he replied.

"OK," I said and introduced myself.

He already knew: I was the German girl. His name was Mr. Marvin Rutledge. He lived here with his wife, Mae. His wife came out and invited me in for a cold glass of freshly made lemonade and peach cobbler. They talked about their two married daughters, Katherine Mackie, living in Holly Springs, and Corrine Russell, two hundred miles away in Jackson, Mississippi. They missed seeing their grandchildren, particularly Sue, who lived in Jackson. I had much to tell about how many were in my family, where we came from and how I liked America. I don't know how much they actually understood. They never mentioned the Deans or asked me questions about our living conditions. They never said anything derogatory about the Deans and neither did I. It was a very interesting afternoon. Over the months my visits became more numerous and uplifting. Then one Sunday when I dropped by, I met both daughters and their families. They had come to spend a weekend with them.

* * *

It seemed like we were in school only a short time before we were on our way to pick cotton in the same field we had chopped in the spring. School was closed so that the students could help their parents with the cotton crop. Hal, Mrs. Dean's son, came with the tractor and wagon about mid-morning.

"No come early? No hot," Papa asked.

"Because the cotton is wet in the morning. It has to dry off from the dew," Hal said.

He made sure that we had hats, drinking water, and lunches. We were given large dirty white bags. Nearing the field, as far as I could see, it was covered by a white blanket. Cotton did not grow on trees.

Hal unhitched the wagon, which was now screened with chicken wire to a height of ten feet. Demonstrating, he put the strap over his head and one arm so that the opening of the bag was in front of him, like an apron with a hole in it. The bag extended in sort of a cone about four to five feet long. Then he just reached out and picked the cotton out of the casing. When the bag was full, he said, Papa needed to weigh it, write the weight down, then empty the bag into the wagon. With a "See y'all later," he was gone. We started off with much determination and enthusiasm. It only lasted a couple of hours. The sun blazing down on us had no mercy. My hair, dress, and even my underwear were drenched. The rest of my family fared no better. When Papa took his shirt off, rivers of sweat ran down his muscular tanned body. Mama's scarf, made from a flour sack, was matted to her head. Whenever I raised up, I felt like my back was breaking in two. My siblings made out a little better: since they were only as tall as the cotton plants, they did not have to bend over.

Using both hands, we pulled the soft white cotton out of the pods, which were as sharp as needles at the tip ends. My bag was half full and hard to lug. After two more hours, the tips of my fingers began to bleed. It instantly colored the white puffy cotton red. The whole operation stopped. We retreated to our wagon, trying to figure out how to administer first aid. Mama removed her bandana from her head, tore it into strips and bandaged my bleeding fingertips. Later in the afternoon, she used the remaining torn bandages for her own fingers and the rest of the family. It was a long back-breaking day. Papa weighed each sack. Mine was 85 pounds. In total, we had picked a little over 300 pounds. This first day was a good day as far as we were concerned.

Over the following days, with everybody's fingertips bleeding, we did far less. We bandaged our fingers before we left home. Every time I thought my fingertips were healed, I re-injured the same one or two again. The hard dried spikes came through the material. We picked until the first week of November.

"How many bales of cotton did we pick?" I asked Mrs. Dean.

"Enough. This year was a bountiful cotton harvest," she replied.

"What happens to the cotton now?"

"Well, we take it to the cotton gin in Holly Springs. There, the cotton is separated from the seeds, baled, and sold. Five hundred pounds make a bale. The seeds are sold separately and used for animal feed or squeezed in a press to produce cottonseed oil."

* * *

After cotton-picking time was over, we went back to school. The next few weekends I spent with girlfriends at PJ parties ("pajama parties," I knew by now). Instead of going home on Friday afternoons, I would go with a new girlfriend on her bus to her home. I looked forward to a weekend invitation. Each weekend was with a different family. Monday mornings came too soon, and we would take the bus back to school.

Most families lived in nicely painted houses, but very isolated from their nearest neighbors. I was treated like royalty. After dinner, their fathers would be interested in my life thus far. Where did we come from and where had we been? Some had even fought in Germany during the war and were interested in that aspect. The same questions came up in all the different homes. Conversations were constantly interrupted to look up words in the dictionary. The women were interested in what we ate and how we cooked. It was impossible to explain our German black bread. They were astonished that everyone drank beer, even kids.

My new friends were very generous. I was thankful for their secondhand clothing. Papa was proud of our report cards—no grades, only comments like "advancing nicely." It didn't matter because now we would amount to something, in a land for which he sacrificed the good life he could have had in Germany. The learning process was monumental. Our job, his children's job, was to go to school. That is all he asked from us. Go to school, learn, and get a good education.

During the PJ parties, I was exposed to the American way of life. I experienced how people lived, talked, worshiped, and worked. Once I was invited by an upper-middle-class family. It seemed to me as if they just tolerated me. It was the blue-collar and farming families who opened up their homes and hearts.

Shopping in Senatobia on Saturday mornings, my girlfriends rolled their hair on rollers before going into town. Later that evening the hair came down, the whole family piled into the car or on the back of the pickup and headed for the drive-in movie. Mary Lee Worley, whom I visited most often, gave me a home perm. It looked worse than the last I got from Mrs. Dean, totally bushy. Mary Lee lived in a half-finished house with three brothers and sisters. Her father was working on it when he found time. Sometimes her parents dropped us off downtown at the movie theater, where other girls and boys congregated. Some even had dates at fourteen. Boys my age were not much interested in dating. The older boys worked in filling stations and on their own cotton farms. They had steady girlfriends. I found it interesting that the older men who had been in the army found me fascinating. Some talked about fighting in Germany. Others talked about how easy the German girls were. I interrupted, "Not all German girls easy."

Mary Lee's boyfriend, who was older, about twenty-two, fixed me up with a friend of his who had just returned from the armed forces. We drove several miles to an adjoining town for a hamburger at a drive-in restaurant. I couldn't understand why he would drive to another town to go to a movie. I was thinking we would go to Senatobia and that I would be able to show off my date. It finally dawned on me he did not want to be seen with "the German girl." After the hamburger, the necking started. Kissing, I didn't mind. I would not go "all the way." He brought me back to Mary Lee's house before 11:00 P.M. Just saying "See ya," off he went. I never dated that boy again.

Double dating was popular. I felt safe going on a double date. Most of the time a date consisted of a movie, a milk shake, and a goodnight kiss. The few dates I had were arranged by the girlfriend I was spending a night or weekend with. I was never asked out by the same boy twice. After a few "NO!s" on my part with different dates, I thought enough is enough. Not knowing what "all the way" meant, I was too afraid to go there. Was it kissing, necking, petting, or sex? If it meant sex, what if I should get pregnant? I'd have to leave school. I would never disgrace my family, never! I needed an interpretation and explanation of so many things like, if he says he loves you, does that automatically mean you have sex? Mary Lee took a deep breath and told me everything in almost one sentence. Nice girls didn't go all the way, which meant having sex, same as easy girls. If I should get pregnant, I would be the talk of the town. No nice boy would marry me. In fact, I might not ever get married. And the shame my parents would have to face every day! A nice boy would not marry a girl who had a baby.

Friday night was football night. I was sad that all the girls had dates after the games. Me, I took the school bus home. Besides, my parents were very upset. In Germany and in Russia, nice girls didn't go out with different boys every weekend. Those who did were called whores. An honorable girl had a boyfriend and married him after a short courtship. All the explanations in the world about how American culture was different from German and Russian wouldn't change my parents' minds. As for me, I was determined to be a good American. I soaked everything up around me like a sponge, and I loved the culture. I even learned all the songs mothers sing to their babies. Little Jimmy Dickens was my favorite singer for a while. I imitated the English language and began to get very good at pronouncing the words. But I never quite mastered the southern drawl. Most people thought that I came from New York. The biggest problem I had was with the *th, v* and *w* sounds because the German sounds for those letters are different. Some words like *thing, through, thought, volley,* and *water* are still problematic to this day.

* * *

Visiting the small one-room library at our school, I checked out books written for elementary-school children. That was my reading material on the school bus. When I arrived home, the homework had to be done right away because the 60-watt light bulb hanging from the ceiling didn't put out much light in the evenings. In fact, I could hardly see to write on our box/table. Papa was always very interested in our homework, which meant spending extra time explaining what we had learned that day. Most kids did their homework on the school bus on the way home. My dictionary was in constant use. Reading and writing were my most difficult subjects. Mama never had any interest in school work. Papa took the time to ask questions and then give his opinion. Mama sat and crocheted using a needle from Germany and thread Mrs. Dean bought, looking through a pair of donated glasses. There was no TV or radio. The only sound was the staccato racket of insects and frogs coming in through the screen window and doors as evening fell.

Returning to the shack after a weekend away from home, I would be more determined than ever to learn everything I could to become a good American. I dared to dream that maybe it was a good thing coming to America. And if I tried real hard, I would someday amount to something. Whatever it took, I would be known by my given name, Ella, and not always as "the German girl." Someday I would be one of them.

The whole family always spoke German. Whenever Mama or Papa wanted to keep something from the younger kids, they spoke Russian, which I understood. Once we kids got in school and learned some English, we discovered we could speak privately in front of them. We used words of which Papa could comprehend only a few and Mama could not understand at all.

* * *

I can hardly wait for the weekend. Mary Lee Worley has asked me to spend it with her again. She is engaged to be married following her graduation from high school. As we spent Friday night getting ready for Saturday, she said, "Ella, let me roll your hair"—with a million bobby pins—"so you'll look nice tomorrow."

Oh brother (the favorite expression of the time), here comes a sleepless night, I thought.

"Are we going to downtown Senatobia again?"

"Yes sirree. My boyfriend, Max, will drop us off. We'll, shop, eat, then see a movie."

"I don't have any money."

"Don't worry, I've got plenty," she replied.

Waiting in line at the drugstore, I noticed this nice-looking boy in front of me. He was tanned, handsome, and muscular. The T-shirt showed off every muscle in his upper body. Wow! When he opened his mouth to say what he wanted, I knew he was from somewhere other than Mississippi. He had a very thick accent.

"Where are you from?" I said in my broken English.

"I am from Hernando."

"Before Hernando?"

"Latvia."

"Where is Latvia?"

"By Germany."

"Do you speak German?"

"Ja, ja," he said.

After we introduced ourselves in German and shook hands, we told each other where we lived. Yes, he knew where Laws Hill was. No, I did not know where Hernando was.

"Can I come over and visit with you, so we can talk more?" he wanted to know.

Could he come over the following weekend and pick me up Sunday morning? I would be back home Sunday night. A whirlwind of questions left me blushing with anticipation of Sunday to come.

I was stunned and extremely happy to actually meet someone from Europe. To relieve my loneliness I said, "I would like that."

He wrote his name, Markus, and address with his phone number on the back of the receipt he received for his purchase. We didn't have a phone.

"Oh, do you have a swimsuit?"

"No, but I'll get one," I said.

"Good, bring it. We may have time to take a swim," he said.

After a handshake and a smiling goodbye on both of our faces, he turned and headed for the exit, looking back once or twice. Mary Lee, a silent bystander, who didn't understand a word we were saying, thought it was great for me to meet someone from "the old country," as she called it.

"Mary Lee, can I borrow your swimsuit, for next weekend? I guess we're going swimming."

"Sure," she said.

The rest of the weekend was spent imagining Markus, with all those muscles, in swim trunks.

As soon as I got off the school bus Monday afternoon, I couldn't wait to tell Mama about Markus. Mama's first reaction was, "I am so happy for you." Then she admonished me because in the old country, girls go out with only one man, and that man they eventually marry. Girls who dated more than one boy were called whores. Maybe this Markus was raised by the old country rules. I wondered myself how different our cultures were. Here in America, girls dated around before they decided who they liked or loved the best, then they picked the one they would marry.

Sunday finally came. I fixed my hair, put on the blue gathered skirt I had made in home economics class, with a white blouse, my loafers with a dime (donated by Mary Lee) inserted in the front, and white socks.

Papa and Mama were home and met Markus. We spoke in German.

"Be sure Ella is back home early tonight because she has to get the school bus first thing in the morning," Papa said.

Markus assured him he could count on me being home on time.

Once on the road I asked, "Where are we going?"

"We'll spend the day in Memphis. It's about sixty miles. Have you been there?"

"Yes, when we came to America back in April. Our sponsors picked us up in Memphis. I didn't see much though. It was at night."

"Memphis it is."

He talked about himself. His whole family had come over about five years ago as indentured servants. He was the only child. They lived on a big farm and took care of the cows only. The house they lived in was furnished by their new landlord. I gingerly approached the question of age.

"Did you go to high school here in America?"

"No, I was too old to enroll. They would not take me."

Quick math. He must have been at least twenty when they came, so now he was about twenty-five, if not older. Oh brother, I was dating an old man. I had just turned sixteen a few months earlier.

We spent the day riding around Memphis, even crossing the bridge into West Memphis, Arkansas, and back.

"Is this the Mississippi River?" I asked as we crossed.

"Yes."

"Why, it's no bigger than the Danube."

He had never seen the Danube, so he couldn't say.

On the Memphis side again, we passed by the Peabody Hotel, then stopped for a hamburger and shake before getting on Highway 51 South to Hernando. It was late afternoon, the sun was ready to call it a night when we arrived at Markus's home. His dad was drinking beer, watching TV, and had very little to say. His mom prepared a nice dinner for the four of us. She was a short, stout, strong lady who reminded me very much of my mama. We talked mostly about Europe. Since I never heard of Latvia, I was very much interested in that part of the world. His father, like Papa, had many gaps in his life's story.

After a lovely dinner at which many bottles of beer were consumed by all except me (I had one; it had a very bitter taste I didn't like), Markus said, "Mom we're going for a swim. When we come back I'll take Ella home."

In his car, it took us just a few minutes to reach the pond. I changed into my swimsuit while Markus took his first strokes.

"Ella, hurry up! The water feels great," he yelled.

Mary Lee's swimsuit was a one-piece, size small. I was desperately trying to work my medium-sized body into it. It was an extremely tight fit. I gingerly wandered into the pond. The water looked glossy from the reflection of the full moon. I could not see Markus. He caught me completely of guard by surfacing and pulling me into the deep end of the pond. I did not want to get my hair wet. Too late. He pulled me to his muscled and well-proportioned body and kissed me as hard as I had ever been kissed. His kiss tasted of beer. When I finally came up for air, I tried to push him away.

"Markus, you hurt me."

"So what? I like you."

His embrace felt like I was in an iron clamp. Markus was taller than I was. I had no choice but to hang onto him, or I would be under water. Every muscle in his body was tense. Now I was beginning to worry about the situation. Being so close, I could not distinguish if it was mine or his heart thundering through my chest. All I could think of was to get out of the water. My first and only opportunity came when he stepped on something sharp.

"Damn, I bet it's a beer bottle, sure hope I didn't cut my foot."

As he turned me loose to inspect his foot, I propelled myself half swimming, half running, toward the shore. In just a few seconds he caught up with me. He grabbed me from behind in his iron grip and carried me kicking and screaming, "Let me go, let me go," to his car.

He put me back on my feet, holding onto both of my hands with my body pressed against the back fender. With his free hand, he opened the back door. I was terrified. With tears streaming down my face, I began to beg, "Markus, please don't."

"Do you like me?" he asked.

"Yes, I like you."

"Since we both like each other, there's no problem," he said.

He pushed me head first into the back seat. Enraged, on my back, I kept kicking and screaming, "Please, stop!" Then just, "Stop! Stop!"—hoping against hope that someone heard me. With one hand and part of his body he held me down, with the other he quickly wiggled out of his swim trunks. His beer breath kept trying to find my mouth.

"Markus, please don't. I'll get pregnant and not be able to finish school. My parents will be very upset."

There was no reasoning with this wild beast with a contorted face. In short sentences, while trying to get my swimsuit off, he said, "I got you, I like you, I'll take you, and I'll marry you."

My kicking feet were now firmly held down by his. He tried to pull my swimsuit down from my shoulders. It wouldn't cooperate. Being wet and one size too small, it felt glued to my body. My cooperation was required. To have it removed by anybody else was humanly impossible. With his enormous weight on my body, I almost suffocated. My lungs were squashed and hurting. I was gasping for air. Droplets from his sweaty face and wet hair were falling on my face. I felt like I was struggling for my very life.

"Ella, can't you see? I need you. Won't you cooperate?" he stammered.

"No! I don't want to have sex with you, not tonight, or ever. Take me home right now!"

"You're going home when I get good and ready to take you home," he said.

With one hand he held my arms back until they hit the open door, my legs were hanging out of the other side. With his free hand, he tried to get into my suit, between my legs. He pulled, tugged, cursed, and sweated to no avail. Frantically, I tried to defend myself. His rage was out of control. He got as far as to put his index finger between my suit and my skin.

Then, suddenly, his grip on my arm loosened as he collapsed from sheer exhaustion on me, saying, "Damn, I lost it. I lost it."

I lay very still so as not to arouse this wild animal again. He got up, took his swim trunks, wiped himself with a towel, then put on his regular pants and shirt.

"Get up and get dressed. It's time to go home," he said.

Shaking, I put my skirt and blouse over my wet, messed-up bathing suit. I sat next to him in the front seat. As he took a turn, which was not the way to my house but to his house, I said, "Where are we going?"

"Home to bed."

"You have got to drive me home, please."

"You're not going home tonight. You're going to spend the night at our house, and I'll take you to school in the morning."

"My parents will worry. We don't even have a phone to call them. Please take me home."

"No," he said.

I entered the living room, where his mother was watching TV. She said something to Markus in Latvian that I didn't understand. There must have been some disagreement, by the tone and body language. I kept thinking, What do these people think of me? I was ashamed and scared.

She said to me, "Ella, you can spend the night in Markus's bed. He will sleep on the sofa in the living room."

With a half finished bottle of beer in his hand, his father said nothing. Feeling frazzled and nearly dead from exhaustion, I went to the bathroom, locked the door, and took off all my clothes. I dried myself with a towel, then rolled the bathing suit in the towel and twisted it until it was completely dry.

His mother knocked, "Ella, take these."

She handed me a pair of men's pajamas through the bathroom door. As I climbed into the bed, wearing my swimsuit and men's pajamas, I was shivering, shaking, mentally and physically fatigued beyond measure. I closed the door, which didn't have a lock. I prayed and promised God all kinds of things if Markus would not enter the room during the night.

I could hear him arguing with his mother. Lying there, I promised myself I would never get in this kind of predicament again. Waves of anger, then disappointment, and finally shame flooded over me. I had stopped shivering but couldn't sleep. Between his snoring and his father's snoring and being worried as to the outcome of my dilemma, I stayed awake to see the first sunrays come through the thin sheer curtains.

His mother opened the door and said, "Ella, come and have breakfast. We have to go and milk the cows. You stay here until Markus gets finished with his chores. Then he'll take you home."

I dressed, over the swimsuit, combed my hair with a comb that was laying in the sink and full of black hair, then joined the family assembled at the breakfast table. Avoiding Markus's eyes, I sat down and quietly ate my breakfast of eggs, bacon, grits, and toast, washing it down with strong black chicory coffee. His mom must have noticed something was wrong. My face, I am sure, reflected pain, fear, and unspeakable anger.

"Ella," she said, "are you OK?"

"I'm fine."

"Yesterday you were all bubbles. Today you are very quiet."

"I'm just concerned about missing school today and my parents worrying about what has happened to me."

"Well, your mother will understand. Young people cannot tell time when they're having fun."

"Yes," I agreed.

Markus and his father ate in silence. After the table was cleared, with all the dirty dishes piled in the sink, they left to milk the cows across the road in the barn. Markus's mother went with them. I was alone.

I had to do something to keep my mind busy or my imagination would drive me crazy. No telling what Papa was going to do, as protective of his family as he was. He would never believe that nothing happened. He probably would not believe I slept alone.

The wall clock announced nine. It was too late for school. It would take an hour to get home, clean up, and get my books. No transportation. Oh brother, who would take me to school? I busied myself washing and putting away the dishes and making my bed. I was straightening up the couch when Markus and his parents returned by the back door.

Markus and his father had a beer and sat in the living room. His mom started to prepare something for lunch. I sat on Markus's bed, just waiting.

A car came into the drive. I ran to the window, pulled back the sheers, and saw Mrs. Dean, her husband, and Papa getting out of her car. I was scared out of my wits! I just knew Papa had borrowed a gun from Mr. Dean's collection and would probably shoot me. Or at the very least beat me for disgracing the family.

Mrs. Dean knocked on the screen door. Markus's mother came out of the kitchen to answer. I heard the introductions.

"I'm Mrs. Dean. This is my husband, and this is Mr. Puder, Ella's father. Is Ella here? We would like to see her."

I came out of the bedroom. Papa roared at me in German, ignoring everyone in the room. I stood there wordlessly staring at Papa as he vented his anger.

"How can you do such a thing to us, staying out all night? You are not a whore. You are only sixteen years old. Ella, what were you thinking? When you didn't come home last night, Mama was sick with worry. I stopped by Mrs. Dean's early this morning to ask her to help me find you, since you left his address at home. How am I going to hold up my head? You should get the beating of your life right here and now, but I will spare you for the time being."

Markus spoke up in German. "Mr. Puder, we spent the day in Memphis, came home, and I had a few beers and was unable to drive another hour to take Ella home. Nothing happened."

"She slept in Markus's bed, and he slept on the couch. We took good care of her," his mother added.

Mrs. Dean, noticing the two empty beer bottles on the coffee table, said, "You know, I should call the police and have all of you arrested, first for drinking beer in a dry state and then for abducting a minor."

Papa broke in, "No police. Ella OK, we go home."

There were no friendly handshakes on the way out. We passed the pond. It had looked so romantic and inviting the night before. Now it was revolting, with the cows standing in the water up to their knees quenching their thirst.

The hour-long drive home was taken up by Mrs. Dean's explanation of why, in America, girls didn't run around with men who were older than they were and why a sixteen-year-old could not spend a night with a strange man who she just met. As Mrs. Dean droned on, I reflected on my misbehavior. Mama always said, "Each experience in life will teach us something." I examined my experience and decided that all men were brutes. Smoldering inside, I dreaded facing Mama. Arriving at our shack, from the front passenger seat Mrs. Dean turned and said, "Ella, I want you to promise me that this situation will never occur again."

"I promise."

Mrs. Dean let us out at our shack. Mama met me at the door. She looked hurt and disappointed. I stepped inside. She reached over and slapped my face. Turning away, she left by the back door and went out into the yard. I sat on the bed and cried. Nothing more was said on that subject.

Mary Lee kept asking me to go home with her, but I hesitated. I was afraid that if I had a confrontation on another date I wouldn't be able handle it. I never said a word to anyone about Markus. The shame I carried in my heart. Somehow it was all my fault. It was no fun sitting home in our shack with the family and books. I wanted to have fun. Soon the Markus episode was filed somewhere way back in my brain.

"Ella, come on and spend the weekend with me. We'll go downtown Senatobia to a movie."

"OK."

Papa was very reluctant to let me go.

Mama said, "We can't keep her locked up forever."

At the entrance of the theater stood this handsome, six-foot-tall, curly-haired, beautifully featured boy. Mary Lee knew him from school. She introduced him as Lawrence.

"Can I sit with y'all?"

"Sure," she said.

He sat next to me, but we never touched. Back home Mary Lee gave me all the details. He was four years older than I was. He had graduated from Thyatira High and worked at his dad's filling station in Laws Hill. We were in Mary Lee's bedroom when her mom yelled, "Ella, you have a phone call." It was Lawrence, asking me if I wanted to go out the following Friday.

"With pleasure," I said.

When I told my girlfriends Monday morning in home room, "I was asked out on a date by Lawrence," in unison they screamed, "That redneck!" None of them could explain to my satisfaction what a redneck was, except that farmers had red necks (sunburn) between the end of the brim of the hat and where the collar of the shirt started.

Lawrence drove a jeep and had a motorcycle too. He picked me up at our shack in his parents' car.

Mama said, "Ella, just remember your last experience. I know I cannot keep you home in this Godforsaken dump. You are young and want to have fun, but remember the consequences of your actions."

"I will, Mama," I said.

We had a hamburger with a malt and saw a movie in Senatobia. After the movie we parked on the side road not far from my shack and talked. I started to get out of the car, and he asked me if he could kiss me.

I told him, "Yes, but no funny stuff if you plan to date me again."

He laughed and laughed. We dated pretty steadily. Our dates ended with a goodnight kiss only. I was happy that I had a boyfriend and could attend ballgames with him. I now played guard on our girls' basketball team, and he always came to our games and rooted for me. Sometimes he picked me up at school and drove me home—I didn't have to ride the bus. He taught me to drive a stick shift using his jeep in the cow pasture at night by moonlight.

Right before Christmas we were parked in our driveway, listening to hillbilly music on the radio and not saying very much. He handed me a beautiful box, which read "Evening in Paris." The box was covered in blue foil paper, the most beautiful I had ever seen. In it were perfume, powder, and all kinds of assorted items. Since I had no money and no car, there was no way I could reciprocate with any kind of gift.

Sitting there in his mom's car after he gave me my present, he took my hand and said, "Will you marry me?"

I was shocked.

"I love you Ella. I promise I will be the best husband to you."

"Lawrence, I'm sixteen years old."

"That's OK. We can run off and get married."

"I must finish school. I must help my family. I have no money. Where will we live?"

"Don't worry. My parents have a house next to their own. We'll move in next door."

"Lawrence," I said, "I must finish school."

No, no, I didn't want to get married. I had to finish school. Girls didn't go to school who were married or pregnant. I needed to help my family as much as I could. He wouldn't take no for an answer. He didn't kiss me goodnight on the porch but said, "I want to talk to your parents. I want to marry you"

"No, Lawrence, we cannot get married."

He opened the door and went inside. I followed.

He said, "Mr. Puder, I want to marry Ella." I had to translate.

Papa looked at Mama dumbfounded.

"Marry Ella?" he said.

For Mama's benefit, I kept saying, "Nein, nein. Ich will ihn nicht heiraten" (No, I don't want to marry him).

Mama, who was not impressed with the American dating system, encouraged me to marry him. "Ja. Ella, heirate ihn. Da kommst du aus diesem kram raus." (Marry him, then you will get out of this mess.)

A big debate started between me and Mama, in German, as to the benefits of marriage.

"You will have a home, a car, a husband who has a job, who loves you, and someday some land."

"But, Mama, I don't love him."

"What does a sixteen-year-old know of love? Rich people can afford to be in love. You are poor. In order to better yourself you must marry someone who has land. Land is everything. Lawrence has land. His parents are farmers."

While all this controversy was under way, Lawrence was left standing by the door. At one point I just sat down and didn't say a word. To the embarrassment of my family, Lawrence started to cry. Papa gestured for Lawrence to come outside with him. I followed. Papa was saying to Lawrence, "You good man. Ella school. No marry."

Papa then turned and went inside, leaving me with Lawrence on our dilapidated front porch.

I told him, "Lawrence, I'm sorry. You are good man, but I'm too young to marry."

"OK, OK," he said. Lighting up a cigarette, he finished with, "Someday you'll be sorry," and left. I never saw Lawrence again.

* * *

Papa was still working for the Deans every day while we attended school. Mrs. Dean was disappointed because she had signed up to have four work- ers. Instead, Papa was the only one to work. Papa mended all the fences, painted her house, built an addition to the barn, and did all kinds of odds and ends, but there was little field work at this time of year. We really couldn't do much until cotton chopping time came around again. Mrs. Dean was wasting her money on us. I told her that as soon as she released us, we wanted to start a new life in Holly Springs. She was all for it. But she didn't offer to help us find a place or move.

The weather turned rainy and cold. Mama kept the broken-down fire- place going all day long. Does it snow in Mississippi? Mary Lee says she's never seen snow. Good thing. We didn't have to worry about freezing to death. We had no Christmas tree. No place to put it. No decorations. No money for presents. A few days before Christmas, Mrs. Dean came by and took the stove. Mama was totally surprised. Papa helped Mrs. Dean put it on her truck. She would fetch the cow later, she said. Her explanation: "You can leave whenever you want, now that the cotton is done. You won't be needing the stove or the cow." All of us sat sad-faced on our beds, in a smoked-filled room, with a heavy rain making a hypnotic sound on the metal roof, waiting for the coffee cans to fill. This was the saddest Christ- mas ever. I was thinking that we had prayed so hard for God to let us come to America. Our prayers were answered, but we were worse off in America than we had been in Germany or Russia.

On Christmas Eve a car came into the drive with the headlights reflect- ing the driving rain. A man in rain gear and hat came to the door and knocked. Papa got up and opened it. A man asked, "Is this the German family?"

"Yes," Papa said.

The man introduced himself, then he turned and went back to the car. Within a few minutes he came back with his wife, carrying huge grocery bags. It took them three trips to the car before everything was unloaded.

He said, "We come from the Holly Springs Methodist Church to wish you a blessed Christmas."

Mama cried. Papa was embarrassed. Me, I was transformed into a speechless column. Finally, I got my voice back. Papa and I shook hands with the couple, thanking them profusely. They looked around our room, staying only a few minutes. Christmas came early for us. Going through all of those grocery bags, we came upon a huge frozen turkey. Never having seen or cooked a turkey in her whole life, Mama didn't quite know what to do. After thawing, it went cut up into the soup pot and cooked in the fireplace. The presents were clothing and sweaters. Papa got a beautiful pair of pants and shirt. I received a sweater, Mama a dress, and the rest of the siblings clothing as well. On Christmas Day, Mrs. Dean brought us each a small gift. I can't remember what I or anybody else got.

1953

The first part of January, on a cold, rainy, miserable late afternoon, there was a knock at the door. It was the same lady from the Methodist church who had brought us the groceries and gifts for Christmas. She wanted to know just how long we were going to stay with the Deans.

"We're supposed to stay until April, but Mrs. Dean said we could leave whenever we wanted."

"What are your plans to move and where to?"

"Mrs. Dean told me it was OK for us to move to Holly Springs, but how are we going to move with no car? And where can we move without money?"

"Don't worry. I'll take care of you all. I'll be in touch with you in a few days," she said.

She was going to take care of the move and the apartment. Mama and Papa talked about this strange woman, wondering how helpful she was really going to be.

Mama said, "It remains to be seen."

How unusual these Americans were. Complete strangers helping us get into school, a couple of people bringing us gifts from a Methodist church. Papa commented that he only knew of Roman Catholic and Lutheran churches. He didn't know if Methodists were Christians. Within days the lady came back and told us she had rented an apartment for us on Salem Street, one of the oldest streets in Holly Springs. Our landlord and his wife were a very gracious, helpful, and loving elderly couple. They had no children. They had converted part of their house into what would be our apartment.

The furniture in our new home was all donated by church members. The following week someone with a pickup came to move us. We left the shack as we found it, except for our box/table and two beat-up, roach-infested suitcases. Before we left, Papa and I went over to the Deans' to thank them for everything they had done for us and tell them how much we appreciated their paying for our way from New York to Mississippi. Either they were not at home or they didn't want to answer the door. I never saw the Deans again.

I'm not sure who paid for the apartment that first month, the lady or the church. We moved into a beautifully furnished four-room apartment with an extra bedroom upstairs. Papa built collapsible stairs after we moved in. Sister Erika and I lived upstairs. We had a living room that served as my parents' and Brother Otto's bedroom. Sister Lida had her own small bedroom that held only one single bed. There was an eat-in kitchen with electric stove, refrigerator, a table, and four chairs. We had everything we needed: pots and pans, plastic dishes, silverware, bedding, sheets (used but in good condition), towels, shampoo, mop, broom, plus a well-stocked cupboard. Mama even received a donated secondhand wringer-type washing machine. She washed clothes almost daily. Our donated secondhand TV became a new world my parents lived in, particularly Mama. The whole family was glued to the TV, never missing the *Lawrence Welk Show*.

* * *

After settling into our new apartment, Mama got a job as a cleaning woman at the Escridge house. Mrs. Escridge had the patience of a saint, teaching Mama how to use the vacuum, explaining, demonstrating, in some instances correcting each step of housecleaning. Mama's smile and "OK" were the extent of her English. Papa was looking for a job. He stood waiting at one of the corners around the courthouse until someone needed a handyman for a day or a few hours. When people found out just how good a carpenter he was, he became very busy. We children attended school in Holly Springs. I started looking for a part-time job as well.

In fact, I found two, one at the Western Auto Hardware Store after school and the other at Armor's Drugstore on Saturdays.

The daily learning process was slow and sometimes funny. When I started to work after school, it was unbelievable the things I learned and how fast my vocabulary increased. My tasks increased as well. People asked me to babysit for them at 50 cents an hour. I wouldn't just babysit—I cleaned their homes, did the dishes, and took care of their kids. One of my steady clients was Katherine Mackie, a married daughter of the Rutledges, whom I had met when we still lived on the Deans' property. I spent many weekends together in her home telling about my future plans and my dreams. The money from babysitting was essential until Papa obtained full-time employment.

Our local sheriff, Sam Coopwood, came by our apartment and said that he knew of a good-paying job for Papa that didn't require much English. It was in a brick factory in the northern part of town. Papa was grateful. After the first week he said, "It is a good warm place to work in the winter, but it probably will be hot as hell come summer." He was right. Working around brick kilns was not a good job for summer in Mississippi. He didn't complain, though, because he was making pretty good money.

When the Western Auto went out of business, I worked at Armor's Drugstore after school as a soda jerk. I worked with Nell Johnson, who became one of my dearest friends, and with Charles Ames, one of the handsome boys I had admired a few months earlier on one of our Saturday shopping trips with Mrs. Dean. We were in the same grade and now we were working together. But Charles didn't allow for any chitchat or girl-boy conversations. I was from the wrong side of town.

Mr. Armor, the pharmacist, was a tall, skinny, serious but loving man. "Ella, you're not to work anywhere in the store except the soda counter." He personally took time to teach me to make milk shakes, sandwiches, and ice-cream cones—"Nickel or dime?"

One Saturday morning the town was filled with people. Cars and beat-up pickups were parked next to the courthouse. The drugstore was packed. I was behind the counter making shakes. An elderly white gentleman ordered a chocolate malt with a raw egg in it. I did exactly as I was taught. He tasted the thick shake, using two straws. After a few sips he said, "I been having chocolate malts in this drugstore for ten years, and not a one ever tasted like this." He put the shake on the counter, gave me a tip, and left. I couldn't understand. What in the world did I do wrong? I retraced my steps and realized, to my absolute horror, that I had pressed the root beer button instead of the chocolate button. I was totally embarrassed when he returned the following Saturday. I apologized profusely, and he received his chocolate malt compliments of the store.

Having overcome my first mistake, I resolved to do better and be more careful. White women were always addressed as "Ma'am," but black women never were—though I was to be friendly toward both black and white.

The store was wall to wall with customers. I forgot about staying behind the soda counter. I felt like I was ready to work the store. A black woman approached me and wanted some "rubbers."

"Do you know where they are kept in the store?" I asked.

"Sure, right in the back. I have been getting them here for years."

I walked to the back of the store looking for rubber gloves, finding a bunch. No, that was not what she wanted.

"What size do you want?" I asked.

"Don't make no difference, I is going to a picnic this afternoon," she replied.

Well, I didn't want to leave her just standing there, me with the rubber gloves in my hand. I walked over to Mr. Armor.

"This woman wants some rubbers, not rubber gloves. Could you tell me what they are and where they are so that I can sell her some?"

He looked up from filling a prescription, peering over his glasses. Red-faced, he smiled a great big smile. "Ella, go on back to the soda counter. I'll wait on her."

After the rush was over, I asked my friend Nell Johnson what this "rubber" bit was all about. She was somewhat embarrassed but, out of earshot of Charles Ames, explained in great detail the use of this item.

"That is what men use in order not to get a girl pregnant. They are actually called 'condoms.' Boys usually carry some in their wallets," she said.

Sister Erika started working at a clothing store adjacent to the drugstore. It was owned by the sheriff and sold jeans and work clothing for men. One day she came home yelling, "Why doesn't someone tell me the difference between zippers and buttons? I had to find out the hard way, and now I'm the laughingstock of the store."

"What happened, Erika?" I asked.

"Well, this black man comes in and wants blue jeans. So I go back and get him a pair. Well, the size was too small. He tells me he don't want no buttons. I make another trip to the back with him following me. I find the size and hand it to him. 'No, no, Miss, I want a zipper.' I asked him, 'Where is the zipper supposed to be?' He pointed to his pants, to his private opening. I was totally embarrassed and so was he and so were all the people standing around, including the owner of the store." Sister Erika was still steaming. It didn't help when we laughed as well.

* * *

What a difference between Thyatira High School and Holly Springs High School. I felt like country had come to town. Starting over in a new school would be fun; new teachers, new friends. I was hoping I would be called by my name, Ella. To my sorrow, I still had no name. I was still "the German girl"—sometimes, affectionately, "the little German girl." I was active at Thyatira with basketball, the glee club, visiting my friends' homes and going with them to the drive-in movies. Sunday mornings I went with friends to church. In the Baptist church people sang with much gusto and raised their hands praising the Lord. Ministers wore suits, and sometimes they even took off their coats and rolled up their sleeves. How different it was from Germany, where one was afraid to speak or move in church. Here, families always prayed before meals. The other churches I visited, first the Methodist and then the Presbyterian, were very formal. Everybody dressed in the most beautiful clothing, hats and purses to match. I didn't really fit in.

At Holly Springs High everybody was friendly, but I was seldom included in any weekend activities. PJ parties were held at different homes. All the girls were dating or double dating. When Monday morning came with everybody meeting in Mrs. Lee's home room, I was a bystander listening to their weekend exploits. No one was interested in me or my life. It was a sad and lonely existence.

I went out for basketball. All the other girls on the team had already lettered in basketball and had their sweaters. It would take me too long to letter. I bought yellow yarn and knitted myself a sweater with *Holly Springs, Mississippi* in black wool letters on the back. It was a conversation piece. I joined the Future Farmers of America and the 4-H Club, hoping I would become an insider. It never happened.

After a couple of months of practice, I quit the basketball team and devoted myself to school and work. We needed the money.

Only two girls, Betty Dale Buford and Sue Johnson (Nell's sister), extended the hand of friendship. Sometimes one of the girls used her parents' car to stop at our apartment and ask me to go riding with them (around and around the courthouse). This was my mental high for weeks to come.

The girls from affluent families had very little to do with the girls whose families were from the working class—girls whose parents were sharecroppers or gasoline station attendants or worked as clerks in stores. I was maybe even lower than that because these girls at least had dates. I had none.

I met John Ositis at school. He was a year or two younger than me. John told me his parents were from Latvia and they had also been indentured servants a few years back. They lived in Holly Springs. My parents were over-joyed to know somebody could identify with them. We were delighted to meet them. Our common language was Russian. They had gone through life experiences and ordeals similar to those of my parents. Our families became good friends.

Holidays were spent in each other's homes, with many European dishes, black bread (that Mrs. Ositis baked, which was not 100 percent German but close enough), beer, and whiskey.

The Ositises invited us to attend the Latvian Lutheran church in Sena-tobia. Mr. Ositis drove us, with his wife up front and Mama and Papa and me in the back seat. Mama and Papa had finally found someone with whom they could talk. It was a little white church located in the middle of town. We were warmly welcomed. The church service was held in both English and Latvian. We loved it. Mama was lost, but Papa could understand English pretty well by then, having dealt with people on a daily basis, and he trans-lated what he could for Mama. There were many young people there, high school kids, just like me. I was introduced and received warmly by all of them. Janis Dukas was the handsomest, at six feet tall and slender, with blue eyes and blonde hair, easily my favorite. Attendance at church every Sunday was essential, in order for me to talk to Janis. The only problem was that he was not there every Sunday and we didn't have a car.

Attending football games on Friday nights made me feel dejected. All the girls had their boyfriends. After the game there were always parties to go to at somebody's house. I never got an invitation. Walking home my soul hurt. I wanted to belong. Since it was a waste of time, I stopped going to football games altogether.

1954

After a few months of hard labor and having to walk a good distance to work, Papa wanted to go the local car dealer and see if he could get an old car on credit. Mr. Ositis advised him on cars. Since Papa's friend had come to America a few years before we did, he already had two cars. Well, we should put some money down. We didn't have any. However, the dealership made an exception and sold us a '48 Chevy for $600 at $25 a month and payments for years to come. Now we knew about credit. It was hard for Papa to comprehend that car payments were one thing; repair payments were not included. It took a considerable amount of money to keep the car running. We soon found out that it drank oil—we carried extra cans in the trunk at all times. I got my driver's license the same week we bought the car and was now the main operator/driver. The driving instructions I had received from Lawrence in the cow pasture at night came in handy.

Papa was very hard on the American way of life. He always knew better, and better was the way it was done in the old country. No, no one had to teach him how to drive. He assured me, "Driving a car is just like driving two horses and a wagon." He had done plenty of that in Russia. Only thing though, a horse has more sense. One morning he said he was going to drive us to school and then take the car to work. Until now, I had driven Papa to work, then myself to school. All went well on the way to school, but just as I walked into home room the school secretary came to the door and asked for me to come to Principal McKenzie's office. When one of the boys was called out of class to see Mr. McKenzie, it meant trouble. I just knew I had done something wrong. Well, a policeman was there and told me Papa had run the car up a tree. He wasn't hurt. We needed a new radiator, he thought. But I needed to come to the sheriff's office to fill out papers. When I arrived, Papa was trying to explain that he never saw the tree and if he were in Russia with his horses, it would never have happened. Everyone there was having a good laugh.

The sheriff came in and wanted to see just me, Papa, and the policeman who came to the scene. No, Papa didn't have a driver's license. No, we had no insurance on the car. The sheriff, who employed my sister at his store, made a decision. He would make an exception, this time only and for this particular wreck. He would not charge Papa with anything, provided he got a driver's license and insurance. Actually, he helped Papa take the driving test and arranged to get the car fixed on credit.

The second encounter with the police, a few months later, was also car-related. Mama and Mrs. Ositis got pregnant just a few months apart. Mama went to Doctor McClatchy just once in her nine months. We knew she was pregnant. However, I was too embarrassed to talk to her about having a baby at her age. Mrs. Ositis had given birth to a wonderful girl, Nora. Mama gave birth to a beautiful girl, Sister Susan, on 13 March. After Mama delivered Sister Susan, Papa and Mr. Ositis went to celebrate with heavy drinking, European style, at Ositis's house. Returning home in the wee hours of the morning, Papa drove into the neighbor's driveway. They promptly called the police, who took Papa to the local jail. The next morning I had to go the police station and get him out. Again, our sheriff had a little talk with Papa. In America, people don't get drunk except in their own homes. But because

Papa had been celebrating the birth of a new baby, Sheriff Coopwood would not charge him with anything. From then on, Papa was careful not to have anything to do with the police or with things that would land him in detention again. His reaction to this whole affair was that the police must be conspiring with the Communists.

Sister Susan would become the apple of Mama's eye, particularly in Mama's later years. Sister Susan was almost a year old before Papa allowed us to write letters back to Germany announcing her birth. Mama said that our neighbors and friends back home in Germany would say that I had gotten pregnant and we were covering it up.

Now that we had a car, we faithfully attended the Lutheran church in Senatobia. A traveling pastor served it and two other churches with very small congregations. Papa talked to him about getting Sister Erika confirmed before she left home. She had to attend religious classes and received instructions in Martin Luther's Small and Large Catechism. The confirmation was a beautiful and memorable service. Sister Erika was dressed all in white and carried a big bouquet of flowers; I remembered my own confirmation, dressed all in black clothing donated by Americans. Mama invested in a small inexpensive camera and recorded it for posterity.

Once Janis Dukas, the boy I liked at church, overcame his shyness, he asked me for a date. I had never realized he drove up from Jackson, two hundred miles, with his family to visit his sister. After seeing each other about half a dozen times, he asked me to go steady. He had graduated from Forest Hill High School on the outskirts of Jackson and was attending Mississippi Southern College in Hattiesburg. I had a boyfriend and his class ring! Could heaven be any better? He asked me to accompany him and two other girls for a short visit to Chicago. My Sister Erika and I went and had a wonderful time in the "Windy City." We stayed with his friends and attended a Latvian banquet with music and dancing, just like in Germany. I knew then that I would never stay in Mississippi. All of my friends at this time were from Europe, people like me, with parents like mine. Janis was a swell guy, very loving, attentive, and smart. All that mattered was that he cared for me, liked me, and we enjoyed each others company.

Even in Holly Springs, Papa was still obsessed with Communism. We had all fled the Communists when we left Russia. Germany was too close to Russia, and if ever war broke out again—and he knew it was coming, just a matter of time—the Communists would get us and ship us to Siberia. The Germans would hand anyone over to the Russians in a heartbeat, one way to be rid of Refugees. The only place to hide was in America. Yet even in America, in the Mississippi jungle, he believed the Communists still hounded him. The first year in Laws Hill, we were not allowed to write letters back to our friends in Germany because the Communists would find out where we were and send someone after us.

Papa impressed upon us to keep quiet and have as few friends as possible. He had only one, and Mr. Ositis was in the same boat as Papa. We watched TV and could see throngs of people at Times Square in some kind of parade or celebration on New Year's Eve. Papa knew that the Communists were instigating the people. Whenever the phone stopped working after a thunderstorm, it was the Communists' fault. When his vehicle would not start, for sure, there were Communists in the area. And so it went.

*   *   *

For me came the hustle and bustle during every class break: Who was going with whom to the junior-senior banquet? It was to be held at the high school. I was determined to attend, even without a date.

I attended wearing a secondhand formal dress, a donation from one of my upper-class classmates. In fact, I would get bags of dresses from the girls who were a year ahead of me, who graduated and were going off to college. I inherited their high school wardrobe, always thankful. My hair had grown out and I wore it in a ponytail most of the time. I was becoming Americanized, except when I opened my mouth. Try as I might, it was a dead giveaway that I was not a southerner.

We were thirteen boys and seventeen girls in the junior class of '54. One of the boys I had a crush on was a great football player, Wyman Winter. He didn't know I existed. Yet I was happy because I sat by him at the banquet. He had very little to say and didn't even ask me to dance. The biggest surprise and highlight of the banquet for me was when I was asked to dance (rock-and-roll) by two of the most popular boys, Fred Belk and Alston Jones. A number of students had guzzled at least a six-pack of beer or a pint of moonshine even before arriving at the banquet. For a dry state, beer and moonshine were in abundance at our banquet. Students congregated by their cars in the parking lot and had their drinks, girls as well as boys, before entering the party feeling quite happy. You just had to know where to buy it across the state line or from a buddy who made it himself. Driving drunk?

Well, the friendly police officer guided you home. "Good ole boys" took care of each other at all times.

As the banquet wound down, a girl announced plans to continue the party at someone's house.

One of the boys asked me, "Ella, how did you get here?"

"My dad brought me."

"Can I take you home?"

"Yes," I replied.

On the way out he told his friends, "I'll see you later, I'm taking Ella home."

He drove past my house.

"Where are you going?"

"We are going to park awhile. We'll continue the celebration."

"I don't think I want to." I said.

He turned into the out-of-service cotton gin at the end of Salem Street, just about half a block from my house. No sooner did he cut the motor off than he grabbed me full force and dragged me across the front seat, planting a hard kiss on my lips. I could not escape. My hair, which was sprayed stiff and glued to my head, was coming undone.

"Please, stop! You're drunk and tomorrow you'll be sorry, I'm sure."

He assured me that he would not tell anyone if we went all the way.

I told him, "No! Don't you understand English?"

Finally, he came to his senses and apologized for his behavior.

"You made me crazy," he said.

He cranked up his car and drove me home.

* * *

Our yearbook, the *Tiger*, was handed out. Everybody ran around getting signatures from each other. Most of the students wrote in mine: "It was nice knowing you," "To a sweet girl," "It has been fun going to school with you," and "Good luck." The seniors wrote a last will and testament in the annual. Martha Davis, one of the most beautiful girls in the class, leaves her discarded lovers to Ella Schneider. Sadness and pain gripped my heart.

Summer of 1954. As a prerequisite for graduation, I had to take Latin under a kind and gentle teacher, Mrs. Lester. Here I was, trying to deal with English verbs, adverbs, and adjectives, with various additional school subjects and now I had to take Latin. I failed it.

All of that summer was taken up with six weeks of summer school in order to graduate with my class of 1955 next year. I quit my job at the drugstore for a better-paying one at the Dairy Queen on Highway 78. Having a pronounced German accent, I always had customers to talk with. The girl I worked with invited me to her house for weekend visits. One Saturday night Judy announced she was having a party at her house.

"My parents are out of town. Will you come?"

"Yes indeed."

Three sailors were waiting at her house. They were in training at the Millington Naval Air Station near Memphis. One more girl joined us. At first things were pretty nice. Then the drinking started and the separation into the different bedrooms. I had not bargained for this.

"No, I don't want to neck . . . Yes, I want to go home."

My biggest fear was to shame or embarrass my parents. I would not let them down for anything in the world. The sailor reluctantly drove me home.

* * *

My senior year began with Mrs. Olson, our English teacher, encouraging me to start writing my life story. I kept telling her, "I don't know enough English words."

"Worry about words later," she kept saying.

The boys were not very kind to the elderly Mrs. Olson. One incident I recall in particular. It was wintertime. Some of the boys urinated in her classroom on the hot radiator. It really upset her. Herr Lehrer Mohr, back in Camp Hofstetten, probably would have killed the participants. Here the boys were "talked to" by Mr. McKenzie, our principal. They did not pull that stunt again.

Our home-room teacher, Mrs. Lee, was a tall, skinny, no-nonsense teacher. After the Pledge of Allegiance and someone reading the Bible, followed by a short prayer, strict silence was enforced in her classroom. I tried to avoid her as much as possible. Our music teacher, Mrs. Doxey, was a very beautiful woman and always had a smile on her face. Would she please give me piano lessons? Yes, at $2 per hour. I didn't have a piano. She arranged for me to use the piano in the high school auditorium after school. The lessons didn't last long because we needed the money more at home.

1955

April of 1955. Such excitement in school. The Holly Springs Pilgrimage was about to take place. The whole town began to clean and spruce up for the event. Sadness rose in my heart. Last year, almost every girl was somehow involved in the promotion of this display of southern history and hospitality. No one asked me to do anything.

The town looked like a picture postcard. Azaleas, dogwoods, tulips, and lilacs in bloom, mixing with all kinds of other flowers. This was the time when people with antebellum homes opened their houses and yards for tourists. This was the Old South being relived. The town tripled in size. People came from as far away as Ohio and Virginia.

It was an especially festive and exciting time for the girls of Holly Springs. Some lucky ones lived in antebellum homes that were on exhibit, or they were invited to be present in their friends' homes. They wore the most beautiful formal dresses from that period. Hoops were used under the dresses, a beautiful cameo around the neck; antebellum-style hairdos and very expensive custom-made hats completed the authentic look. At every opportunity girls congregated in the school hallways and discussed where they would serve, what to wear, how to do their hair; they even polished up on the War between the States. I was not aware that there ever was a war in America. Didn't even know where to start to read about it. I finally talked to Mrs. Lee, my home-room teacher, who suggested that I check out some books on the Civil War. I did.

Another surprise: "Southerners" were the people who didn't want to belong to the Union with the northern states, but to be a country unto themselves. Suddenly it was a mystery no more. These homes were built before the "late unpleasantness," as some old ladies referred to it. (Some unreconstructed rebels called it the "Second War for Independence" or "The War of Northern Aggression." Most authors referred to the war as the "Civil War.") These were the homes of families who actually had family members fight during the war, whose homes were taken over by the Yankees on their way south. The South suffered because of the "Damn Yankees." Vicksburg would never have been taken if they had not run out of rats. Each state and locality had its own story to tell of the hardships and suffering during that time in history. I only read about Mississippi's part. Even though it was so long ago, people still talked about it, especially the old, unforgiving ones. Now, I knew why there was such animosity toward Yankees. It was because they did away with slavery. Now these southern farmers had to pay to get their cotton crops in, little though it may be.

No one asked me to be part of this occasion. Many girls were scheduled to participate. Most of them were in my senior class. I was left out. But even if someone had thought to ask me, I could not afford to have a dress made.

Most of my time after school and on weekends was spent working. I always babysat in the evenings. Bills had to be paid. We had to pay rent, food, gas, insurance, and day-to-day living expenses. We were always living from hand to mouth, pooling our money every week to meet expenses. A family of seven needs a lot of money.

Mrs. Armor was a thin, tall, very soft-spoken southern lady, who never had much to say to me at her store. She asked me to visit her one afternoon at her home after work. It was about one week before this grand event of the Pilgrimage. Her house was beautiful, with very high ceilings and windows. We sat in the living room, which was furnished with antiques. It was very dark because graceful old magnolia trees blocked the sun. A black woman served us tea and cookies on beautiful china.

"Ella, I just want you to know how much we appreciate your help and positive attitude in our store. If you continue on as you have been, it will serve you well in America. Now, I've been meaning to ask you, would you like to be in the Pilgrimage?"

"Who, me, Mrs. Armor?"

"Yes, you."

"I would love to, but—"

"I'm glad. I'm the chairman for the Holly Springs Women's Club, which sponsors the Pilgrimage. I thought it would be nice for you to be in this year's Pilgrimage."

I was thunderstruck. She would take care of all I needed and I would serve at Gray Gables, where General Grant spent a few nights on his way south.

My instructions: "Don't talk about the War between the States. You have a German accent, and it would raise eyebrows to have someone in the Pilgrimage who had just come off the boat, so to speak. Just mill around outside for people to take your picture standing by the magnolia trees or the flower beds." God must have heard my heart to give me the opportunity to be like my classmates.

"Lets see, I have a dress," said Mrs. Armor. "Let me get it for you to try on."

She came back with the most beautiful off-the-shoulder pink dress. It had a hoop skirt, with a black scalloped ribbon wrapped around the waist and held by a small bouquet of violets pinned on the left side. I slipped out of my thin secondhand dress and into the gown with Mrs. Armor's help. It was a perfect fit. She handed me a cameo, with earrings to match. In my imagination I was now in *Gone with the Wind*. I looked at myself in her guest-room mirror and was thinking, if this is a dream, don't let me wake up. Mrs. Armor took care of everything, for which I was eternally thankful. I made an appointment at the hairdressers.

Coming into home room at school the following day, I announced to the cluster of girls standing around that I would be serving at Gray Gables. A chill came over the group, nothing was said. I thought the news would be greeted with happiness and laughter. Nothing. One of the girls finally said, "We're so happy for you."

The day arrived. I was all dressed up and standing on the ornate front porch of Gray Gables when the first busload of tourists arrived. Elderly men and women exited, cameras in hand, and headed through the black-painted wrought-iron gate toward the main building. Almost all the old ladies had their hair dyed blue, with a lot of makeup and red fingernails. I thought that these women didn't know how to grow old gracefully. Women at that age would never paint themselves like that in Germany.

I was asked to pose time and time again. One elderly lady asked me, "Did your great-grandfather fight in the war?"

"Yes, he did."

"Where in the South did he fight?"

"All over," I said.

I didn't lie, really. I am sure my real great-grandfather fought in some kind of war in southern Russia.

In my antebellum dress, I felt like I was somebody, somebody important. It was very difficult to answer questions with only a "Yes, ma'am," or a "No, ma'am."

"Miss, could you tell me something about Holly Springs?" a lady asked. "What is the population?"

Without giving it a second thought, I blurted out, "Thirty thousand."

She looked at me kind of funny then said, "Somehow, I must have missed it."

"Miss," someone behind me called.

I turned just in time to have another picture taken. Saved! I avoided any further conversations with people who came to the Pilgrimage. My main objective was to pose for pictures.

Each evening I sprayed my hair with so much hairspray it was like spraying it with glue, then wrapped a roll of toilet paper around it to preserve its look, in order for it to be presentable the next day. The hairdo had to last three days. When I finally combed it, I pulled out half my hair.

My parents were proud of my part in the festival. In fact, my whole family was beaming with happiness. Those three days of stardom ended far too soon.

* * *

Right after the Pilgrimage our landlady informed me that we had to move. Her sister was coming to live with her and they needed the extra room. The responsibility of taking care of my family rested heavily on my shoulders. Checking the newspaper and talking to acquaintances, I finally turned up a few houses and apartments for rent. The drawback was that they all were too expensive. I paid a visit to our sheriff and told him of our predicament.

"Mr. Coopwood, we need to move. I've been checking out apartments around town. There are apartments available, but we don't have enough money to pay for the rent. Being the sheriff, you probably know someone who has a house. We will even fix it up. We would appreciate it if you could find someone who will rent us something we can afford."

"I'll look around, honey," he said.

A couple of days later he came to Armor's Drugstore, told me he had found a place for us, and handed me the keys to his pickup.

"Honey, keep it as long as you need it to move your family."

We could not get over how trusting he was. We loaded all our earthly belongings and moved into a spanking clean, new, beautiful three-bedroom apartment. Mama was walking on cloud nine. Heaven had come to earth for her. She had a beautiful baby daughter, a beautiful home, her kids were getting an education, and Papa had a job. Mama completely missed the fact that this was government housing, a recently completed "project." I didn't realize the stigma attached to someone who lived in government housing (even though all our neighbors were white). The two American girlfriends I had made in Holly Springs immediately distanced themselves, wouldn't call, and didn't invite me over anymore. With high school graduation only two months away, parties were in full swing, but not for me. There was nothing I could say or do to remedy the situation. Instead of plummeting into despair, I resolved to keep a sunny attitude. I knew I could not change my situation, but I could always have a happy outlook on life. Surely God had other plans for me.

I summoned up the courage to talk to Papa and Mama about my going to college. My concern was that they would not be able to make ends meet, and I was feeling guilty about leaving the family while they were still struggling. Papa assured me they would be OK. He had brought us to America so that we would be able to make something out of ourselves, and education was the only way. Sister Erika, only one year behind me, would now interpret for the family.

I had been babysitting regularly for Katherine Mackie ever since we moved to Holly Springs. She tutored me in the American way of life, lessons which were beneficial to me in years to come. She explained idioms—for instance, the "green-eyed monster" (jealousy), among others. I was delighted whenever her sister, Corrine Russell, came to visit from Jackson with her husband, Lawrence, and their loveable daughter, Sue. Corrine was a beautiful, gracious, loving, and warm woman who became my American role model.

A few weeks before graduation, Katherine asked, "Ella what are you going to do after high school? What's your dream? America is a land where if you want something bad enough and you are willing to work hard enough, you will attain your dream."

"I don't want to live like this forever," I replied. "I want to go to college. We don't have any money, cannot save any money, so there is no chance of my going."

"This is America," she continued. "If you want to do something in your life bad enough, there are always ways and people who will help. We'll see what we can work out. I'll talk things over with Corrine. Maybe we can come up with something."

She called her sister in Jackson. Corrine and Lawrence decided that I could live with them free for one year. My parents marveled that complete strangers, people who were not family, would take someone in to live with them, paying for food, transportation, even clothing and college books. God was beginning to answer my prayers and take an interest in me. I cried for happiness. My day of deliverance was at hand. Katherine helped me compose a letter to the admissions office at Belhaven College, a Presbyterian women's college in Jackson. To the absolute shock and amazement of my classmates, I received a reply. Yes, yes, yes. I was offered a full scholarship, without even having straight-A grades. My feet didn't touch the ground until graduation day. Needless to say, my whole family rejoiced in my good fortune and were very proud of me.

One of my classmates, Betty Dale Buford, was to attend Belhaven. Two others from my graduating class were going to be a few blocks away at Millsaps College. I visualized how great it would be to have friends from home. That never happened. The gulf between the "haves" and the "have-nots" could not be bridged.

Graduation day has finally arrived, June of 1955. I am all dressed for the ceremony. The whole family is dressed up for this occasion.

"Ella, you look so pretty in your cap and gown. I am proud of you," Mama said.

The whole family piled into our unreliable car, and Papa drove us to the high school. After the ceremonies were concluded, all of my classmates paired off to attend parties in different homes. I was not invited. I folded my cap and gown, ready to return them the following day. Then I started to pack my few belonging for my trip to Jackson. My parents had mixed emotions, pride and sadness. Pride in my accomplishment and sadness over losing me. But as Papa would say, "Life must go on."

On June 23, 1955, my nineteenth birthday, I arrived at the Trailways Bus Station in Jackson after an all-day ride through the kudzu-covered countryside. I was warmly met by the whole Russell family. On the way to their home we stopped at a restaurant. After we ate, Corrine gave me a beautifully wrapped box, with a warm smile and "Happy Birthday, Ella." I opened the box. It displayed a beautiful wristwatch. My gratefulness spilled over into tears. Within a few days, Corrine found me a part-time job at Southern Farm Bureau Life Insurance Company in downtown Jackson. During my interview, she waited for me in the lobby. I got the job, part-time during the school year and full-time in the summer. Belhaven College here I come.

Epilogue

In 1955, life at Belhaven College, a Presbyterian school predominately for women, brought new adventures every day, but sharing these experiences with my family was impossible. I felt guilty leaving my family because they were having such a hard time just making ends meet. Mama and Papa could not understand the American culture. They completely disapproved of what little they did grasp. I felt my sisters and brother would resent my newfound independence. Letters, cards, phone calls, and nine-hour rides on the Trailways bus to Holly Springs were rare.

Moving to Jackson, I expected to be able to spend more time with Janis, my boyfriend. However, as soon as I shared the good news, he said that his parents had decided we were getting too serious and he was going to transfer to the University of California in the fall. With a broken heart, I kept his picture but gave back his class ring.

My salvation was church, which I faithfully attended. Most Sundays I went to either the Methodist or the Presbyterian church, but eventually joined the Lutheran church. To make some money I worked part-time as a clerk at Southern Farm Bureau Life Insurance Company. My freshman year I lived with Lawrence, Corrine, and Sue Russell.

I was impressed by how the campus looked. All of the girls were in beautiful dresses, smiling and walking in twosomes. Some who were going downtown wore hats, stockings, high heels, and gloves. Everyone was very friendly. My appointed big sister, Betty Quinn, met me and accompanied me to registration, guided me through buying books from the bookstore, and helped me locate my classrooms. I knew I would be happy here. Before I caught the bus home to Corrine's house, Betty said, "Ella, tomorrow you are to come to class dressed as a roach."

"Why would anyone want to dress like a roach?"

"It is a tradition at Belhaven that freshmen dress like roaches the first day and do everything upperclassmen tell them to do."

When I arrived home, I told Corrine that I needed to look like a roach. Could she please help me? She came up with black shorts, black tennis shoes, and a black T-shirt with all kinds of things sewn to it; a crust of bread, a piece of garlic, a candy wrapper, and various other food articles. My hair was parted down the middle and two ponytails were sticking straight up on top of my head. She used black shoe polish to make up my face. My new friend Ruby Jewell, who lived down the street, picked me up in the morning. She didn't look much better than I did. After many orders, running errands in every direction and doing things for upperclassmen, the day finally ended. I was sure that now I was truly accepted at Belhaven.

The next day we were told to bring overnight clothes because we were having a bonfire with singing and hotdogs that evening. I spent the night in a dormitory room on campus. Around noon the following day, I was summoned to see the dean of women, Miss Bess Caldwell. I dashed over to the main building by the fountain. The secretary asked me to wait and added that Miss Caldwell would see me in a few minutes. My heart beat wildly. God only knows what I had done or left undone. I was finally ushered in. Once I was seated, she began, "Miss Schneider, please look out of my window and tell me what you see."

"The steps leading to the fountain. I see green grass. I see trees. I see a flagpole."

Then it hit me. My black-and-white-striped pajamas were fluttering in the breeze instead of the American flag.

She said, "Miss Schneider, here in America we respect our flag very much. We do not take the flag down and raise in its place someone's pajamas. Would you please find the janitor to retrieve your pajamas?"

I was in complete shock. The only things I could stammer were "I'm sorry" and "Yes, ma'am." After some time, I found the janitor. As we approached the flagpole, a few of the girls were assembled and laughing so hard that some of them were crying. I was terribly embarrassed. The traditional "hazing" continued for days.

Corrine taught me all the do's and don'ts of the American culture. Her motto was to "never wear runners in your stockings or chipped fingernail polish on your nails."

As soon as I started classes, one of the girls from the Baptist Training Union asked me if I would like to go with them to Ridgecrest, North Carolina, for a week during the upcoming school break. I was somewhat dumbfounded. I was a Lutheran attending a Presbyterian college invited to a Baptist retreat. I told her I could not afford to go. She said, "Ella, we'll sponsor you, all expenses paid."

A couple of weeks into the school year I was approached to join the Tau Gamma organization. I was thrilled. The group promoted friendship among the girls who lived off-campus with the purpose of service to Belhaven.

During the fall break, a busload of BTU kids and I went to Ridgecrest. The singing, praising God, praying, eating, and sleeping were wonderful. My first experience at a religious retreat was marvelous.

Every day at Belhaven College, I was coming closer to being an "All-American Girl." I struggled to lose my German accent, but I was never able to duplicate the southern drawl. Instead, I perfected neutral pronunciations. Eventually, I succeeded in sounding American. I dated boys from the surrounding colleges and churches who attended swap dances, swim parties, picnics, and plays at Belhaven.

My second year in college Sister Erika moved down to Jackson and we lived together at Miss Blackburn's house. She was my biology teacher at Belhaven. I joined the school thespian organization "Sock & Buskin" and performed in a school play.

Tom Hilton and I started dating. I had seen him in Sunday school, but he was shy and rarely spoke to me the first year I was in Jackson. Tom had graduated from Central High School, class of '54. He and his friends were attending Mississippi State College in Starkville (still an all-male school in 1956) and were home for Christmas looking for dates. Tom asked Sister Erika out, but she turned him down. I was second choice. Later, he told me he had flipped a coin to decide whom to ask first. We went to a rock-and-roll dance at the Wagon Wheel. An all-black band called the Red Tops played for an all-white audience. Moonshine was brought in bottles and kept in paper bags under the table. Tom did not drink. He was a teetotaler.

Tom became my steady boyfriend. We had long, interesting conversations, and to my astonishment I learned that his birthday was April 27. I had dreamed of that date years ago back in Germany. He was a smart, sensitive, caring, and lovable man. He accompanied me to all the formal dances at Belhaven. I still had to borrow formal clothes from my girlfriends, but Tom always brought a sweet-smelling white camellia corsage for my wrist. He looked so handsome in his white sport coat with a pink carnation. The highlight of my year was attending the ROTC Ball at Mississippi State College. All of the cadets wore their green army uniforms and looked impressive. Tom and I became engaged.

We had met in '55, dated for a year, and had been engaged for six months before we drove up to Holly Springs for him to meet my parents. I had waited until the last possible minute—just two months before the wedding—to introduce him to them. Shortly after I left for college, my folks had been evicted from the government housing project because they were not American citizens and therefore didn't qualify to live there. The apartment they moved into was in a two-story brick railroad building that dated back to the Civil War. The wallpaper was peeling from the fourteen-foot ceiling and walls. I just knew that any man who saw the run-down conditions my family lived in would never marry me. Nevertheless, love prevailed. Tom didn't focus on the poor surroundings. He was impressed by the way Mama treated Papa.

It is dinnertime:

Papa says, "Elsa, bring me a beer."

Mama gets the beer. Mama sits.

Papa: "How am I going to open this can with my fingers?"

Mama gets the opener. Mama sits.

Papa opens the can and beer spews out onto the table.

Papa: "Elsa, wipe the table."

Mama gets a towel and wipes the table. Mama sits.

Papa: "I need a glass. You know I don't like to drink beer out of the can."

Mama gets a glass. Mama sits.

Papa: "Tom drink beer?"

Tom: "No thanks. I don't like beer."

Papa: "That's OK. One beer OK. You family."

Tom: "No thanks."

Mama says to me, "Und so was willst du heiraten?" (And such you want to marry?) Mama could not believe I would marry a man who would not drink beer. She also thought he was too skinny.

My first meeting with Tom's folks was not much better. His mother, Alice Rushing Hilton thought I was too sophisticated for her adopted son and told him so. (They were both born and raised in Mississippi.) She was also not happy that he wanted to marry a foreigner. His dad, Monroe Hilton, worked in a factory making steel-and-wood counters used in restaurants, kitchens, and cafeterias. They rented their house and drove an old car. They had an older son, Monroe (nicknamed "Money"), who was already married and an architect in Jackson. Tom's father came to love me and call me "Sugar," but his mother never approved.

We married in Jackson during the Christmas break in 1957. Only Sister

Lida attended from Holly Springs, since the rest of the family could not afford the trip. Sister Erika was my maid-of-honor.

Tom graduated in June. He was commissioned as a 2nd lieutenant in the U.S. Army Quartermaster Corps. We moved to Fort Lee, Virginia, for his training. Our first daughter, Erika, was born there in 1959. Both of us fell in love with the structure of army life and the travel opportunities. Tom decided to make the army his lifelong career.

I read all kinds of books on what was expected of me as a 2nd lieutenant's wife, and I entertained "by the book." Tom was a brilliant logistics officer. We were a popular couple and always a welcome addition to any dinner or cocktail party. The officers who had fought in Germany in WWII found me a knowledgeable conversationalist about the places where they had been. I had a new identity again, but this one I loved. I was now Ella Hilton, "You know, Lieutenant Hilton's wife."

Looking at myself in a full-length mirror, I was amazed at my transformation. Wearing a brand new, store-bought, green silk, strapless, long evening gown with elbow-length white gloves, long rhinestone earrings dangling from my ears, and a beehive hairdo centered on top of my head, I resemble the perfect American society wife of the late 1950s. Tom wore his formal army blue uniform with highly polished brass insignia. It reflected the sparkle of crystal chandeliers as we went down receiving lines and greeted VIPs—generals and ambassadors from all over the world. The sheer splendor would bring tears to my eyes. Oh, how I wished Mama could see me now! She never did.

Mama and Papa did not fare very well. Papa had a variety of menial jobs. The family lived a hand-to-mouth existence in substandard housing. It was all they could afford. Mama never left Holly Springs. Her life revolved around raising the children, watching Lawrence Welk, washing clothes, and crocheting. She never learned English. Mama relied on her children to keep her informed. Her sole friend was Mrs. Ositis, and Papa's only friend was Mr. Ositis. They spoke Russian with the Ositises and German at home with their children.

Mama and Papa struggled to accept the American way of raising children, which was still quite foreign to them. After Sister Erika left home, Sister Lida took over translating. When she left for college, Brother Otto and then Sister Susan took their turns caring for the family. Papa's lifetime of carpentry skills he now taught his son.

In 1960, after we had transferred to Fort Lewis, Washington, our second daughter, Angela, was born. Later, Tom was assigned a short tour of duty, one year, unaccompanied, to Korea, and I spent the year in Virginia with the girls. While in Korea he was promoted to captain. The salary increase allowed us to send $25 a month to Mama and Papa. His next post was Virginia, where we remained until 1966.

One day I had a phone call from Papa.

"Papa, what's the matter?"

"Mama got a letter today from someone in Hamburg, Germany, asking for help. He wants her to send some money."

"Who is the letter from?"

"I don't know," Papa said. "It is written in perfect German in a beautiful script from a man claiming to be her brother Emil."

"Does Mama have a brother named Emil?" I asked.

"She says she does, but the only thing is that he cannot read or write." Papa continued, "I told Mama not to send money or even answer the letter. Mama is very upset. I think the Communists have found us."

"Really, Papa," I said, "even if they found you, how will they ever make you go back? But, Papa, you did the right thing."

When Mama got on the phone, she kept saying, "What if it *is* my brother? I will never forgive myself for not helping him."

But Papa didn't want his family compromised.

With deep sadness in her voice, she said, "I will never know."

When Tom came home from work, as was our custom, we retired to our bedroom. The children knew not to disturb us when the bedroom door was closed. This was our time alone together, while he undressed, to talk about the day.

"Tom, would you believe, Papa called today to say that Mama—mind you, Mama—received an interesting letter." I repeated the story.

After listening he said, "Ella, Theodor is not all that daft. Maybe the Communists really are looking for him. Somebody has found your mother's married name and is trying to take advantage of them somehow."

After that incident, I always wondered, *why* would the Communists be looking for him?

* * *

In 1966, Tom was transferred to Ankara, Turkey. We rented a beautiful second-floor apartment in the best part of town, Çankaya Hill, right below the presidential palace and surrounded by a variety of embassies, including the

U.S. embassy. Interestingly, we were advised to bring a U.S.-made toilet, which we installed in our apartment and left there when we rotated back to the States. The Turkish version of bathroom facilities consisted of a hole in the floor and a water tap. Both of us learned Turkish by attending classes. In 1966, the exchange rate was 14 Turkish lira to the dollar. Because labor was inexpensive, I hired a Turkish maid, Hiteeja (whose husband had two wives and five kids), for $2 a day, once a week. American dependents were forbidden to work, so I attended oil-painting classes and the officers' wives' luncheons, played bridge, and enjoyed shopping downtown in Ulus, the oldest part of the city. We turned the Ankara Officers' Club into a big celebration party when Tom was promoted to major. Now we were able to send $50 a month home to Mama and Papa. We lived off Tom's monthly income and budgeted our travels. One summer we visited: five of the seven churches Saint Paul wrote to in the New Testament; the tomb of the Virgin Mary (which may or may not be her actual resting place) ten miles from Ephesus at Panaghia Kapulu; the site of Alexander the Great's prayer to the goddess at the strategic pass known as the Cilician Gates in the Taurus Mountains; and the Tarsus harbor gate where Antony met Cleopatra in 41 B.C. Turkey has a most marvelous history. We also vacationed in Greece, Italy, Austria, and Germany.

My friends were making Christmas travel plans. Some were going to Germany, traveling by car through Soviet satellite countries to get there. Others who had made the trip were fascinated with the countryside.

"Tom, I want us to drive to Germany for Christmas."

"You should really stay away from the Officers' Wives' Club luncheons, they're giving you all kind of ideas. I think, before we make any plans, you need to go the U.S. embassy and see if you can travel through the Soviet Union, considering that you were born in Kiev and that is stamped in your passport. All of your friends were born in the USA."

Next day I dressed up, had my hair done, and headed straight to the embassy. I met with the U.S. attaché and told him what I had planned for Christmas. He looked at my passport and smiled.

"Mrs. Hilton, I can understand your wanting to go back to Germany after so many years. However, we will not allow you to make the trip by car. Your husband is an officer with a top secret security clearance. Hungary and Czechoslovakia are Communist countries. If you enter any Soviet country, you will be taken hostage. They will claim you are a Soviet Citizen and will not grant you an exit visa. Most likely you will be sent back to

Kiev, and the U.S. government will be powerless to obtain your release. Then your husband will be compromised and do whatever he can to get you back."

Almost in tears I said, "Why would they want me? I was only a child when we left Kiev. I don't know anything anyway."

"How long have you been married, Mrs. Hilton?"

"Almost ten years," I said.

"Do you sleep together?"

"Of course we do."

"Then you know a heck of a lot more than you realize."

On the way out, he told me how sorry he was. It was his job to protect Americans, and I was a naturalized American.

"This embassy is American soil. Do me a favor and don't go to the Russian embassy. *Ever.* Because once you step onto their property, you are legally in the USSR."

We spent Christmas in Ankara with a borrowed aluminum Christmas tree that I decorated with electric lights. We could not afford to buy one, since Turkey is an arid land and all the trees had to be imported. I must say, it was the most magnificent tree we ever had. We made plans for a trip to Germany for the following year by way of military air transport.

In 1968, Tom received orders to Vietnam. I wanted to buy a few Turkish rugs, handmade brass tables, candleholders, and knickknacks because they were inexpensive. However, "friendly finance" was unavailable and money was in short supply. Plan B went into effect. Each morning after Tom left for work, I opened the apartment window and waited to hear "Eskagee" shouted from the street. The secondhand dealer would make his way up Sehit Ersan Çaddesi Street yelling that he would buy anything you would want to sell. "Burda" (Over here) I'd yell, and he would come up to our apartment. Unbeknownst to Tom, little by little, I sold all of his civilian clothes except for his underwear and socks. The secondhand dealer paid a lot of money because Tom's clothes were Western men's apparel, a very hot resale item. With that money, I bought rugs and brass. I figured that Tom wouldn't need any civilian clothes in Vietnam.

When it came time to move, I faced a big decision. The army would move us anywhere in the world we wanted to go. Virginia was my first choice.

I liked Fort Lee. I wanted to return to where my friends lived while Tom served his unaccompanied tour overseas. We took the cruise ship SS *Consti-*

tution home across the Atlantic. The trip took eleven days. I was seasick for most of the crossing, but the kids loved it. When we arrived in Virginia, Tom had only four days to get us moved in and settled before reporting to his new duty station. We tried to rent, but the equal housing laws were in effect and every rental space was blacklisted by the army as off limits to military personnel because the local Virginians were unwilling to rent to minorities. Tom had no choice but to buy a house. Even so, both of us had to meet the realtor to assure him we were white. Within the four-day period, Tom purchased a house, moved our household goods in, and left for Vietnam.

My loving Tom had set me up in an upscale neighborhood with a new house, new car, and money in the bank. But then September, October, November came and went with no paycheck from the army. I depleted our savings and our checking accounts. The Red Cross, as well as the Army Community Service, would not help me because I was an officer's wife and it was Tom's responsibility to take care of his family. Sending Tom recordings on miniature tapes telling him how unhappy I was only added to his frustration while serving in a combat zone. He could not understand what was happening to his paychecks. I met with the postmaster in town and explained the situation. He had our mailbox staked out by police officers and put the mailman under surveillance as well.

My next step was to visit the finance center at Fort Lee. A very nice young captain assured me he would do everything he could to get our problem straightened out. He called the main finance center at Fort Benjamin Harrison and was told that if I didn't get a check by the end of December, they would automatically stop payment on the old checks and issue a new check for all the back pay. At this point Tom became angry, which was one thing the army orientation officer told us wives of soldiers fighting in Vietnam we should not do: "Don't upset your husbands, and don't send bad news from home." I had no choice but to start working. Since I had finished only two years of college, I worked as a substitute teacher at my children's elementary school. December came. I wanted to spend Christmas with my family in Mississippi, but I was broke. Late one Saturday night, with an idea to cash in a savings bond to finance the trip, I opened the brown envelopes of government mail that I had deposited directly into our home safety deposit box unopened. The first envelope I opened sent me into shock. To my utter amazement it contained the December check. The next was November. All of the checks were there clear back to September, plus all the saving bonds as well. After my joy, the next thought I had was, "How am I going to get out of this situation gracefully?"

I did.

In September of 1969, Tom returned home. Opening his closet he wanted to know, "Ella, where are all my clothes?"

"You're standing on them," I said.

In disbelief, he looked down at a gorgeous Turkish rug. The situation grew worse when he discovered that I had not reconciled the checkbook the entire time he was away. Not only did he not own any civilian clothes, he didn't know if he had any money to buy any. For two days Tom locked himself in the study, in his underwear, auditing our bank statements. Somehow we managed to avoid a divorce. I was relieved to learn that we did have the money for him to purchase new clothes.

New York City here we come! In 1969, we moved into army housing at Fort Totten. Tom worked in Manhattan in the Federal Building. Every day he traveled from Long Island on the subway in his major's uniform. That policy changed when a hippie spit on his commanding general one day. An edict went out to all military personnel to report to work in civilian attire and change into their uniforms after they arrived at the office. We enjoyed living in New York from 1969 until 1972.

We saw thirty Broadway plays in those three and a half years. Both of our girls were in school. Over Tom's objection, I got a job as an assistant chemical buyer in Flushing. I was hired because I knew how many grams made an ounce.

One day at work I met the Russian attaché. I had previously set up appointments for him with my boss over the phone. He came by my desk and I said hello in Russian. He stopped and we talked a few minutes.

"Where are you from?" he asked.

"Kiev," I said.

"Your husband?"

"He's in the army."

"Really," he said.

He continued into my boss's office. On the way out he said, "By the way, how much are these people paying you to work here?"

I said, "$125 a week."

"Oh, that's not much. Would you like to come to work for us? We'll double the money and send a car for you."

"I don't know. I need to talk to my husband."

"Good," he said. "I'll call you tomorrow."

When I got home and told Tom, he went into orbit. This was 1971 and the cold war was raging.

"Ella, have you lost your cotton-picking mind talking to the Communists? If Theodor finds out you even consider working for the Russians, he'll come up here and shoot you! Besides, can you imagine what will happen to my military career and my security clearance?"

"No, I hadn't considered all that."

I kept my job at the chemical company.

Papa called and said they were moving out of the dilapidated Civil War building by the railroad tracks into a small house near a lake. Sister Erika and her husband had bought them the house, just outside of Holly Springs. After all those years of hardship and sacrifice, Mama and Papa finally had a home of their own. Their American dream for a piece of American soil had come true. They were so happy and proud.

Mama reported, "Theodor plays the accordion sometimes, which he hasn't done in years."

Papa would not have a modern heater in his house. He built a stove below the house similar to the one he had in Russia. He said, "I cannot understand why it keeps smoking up the house so much. I built it just like in Russia, and those didn't smoke."

He never could fix it. Papa was becoming "Americanized." He had his own house and his own pickup truck. Still, any time the truck wouldn't start, it was always "the Communists' fault."

I received long letters handwritten by Papa in the old gothic German style. Though I wanted to hear news from home, they primarily contained explanations of God's Holy Word. Papa read only the Bible. His letters would begin with, "Dear Ella and Tom. We are fine. Have you read the second chapter of Revelation? Here is what I think it really means," followed by pages and pages of in-depth analysis. He invested a tremendous amount of time and effort to writing his thoughts. Mama never wrote.

One day I opened a letter and read that Mama was in a nursing home. She had suffered a stroke. She went directly from the hospital to the nursing home. I was very happy that she had survived and was in a place where she would receive good medical care.

Tom, the girls, and I made the two-day drive home. The nursing home smelled like urine. Mama was clean and well groomed, but she didn't say much. It was difficult for her to talk. She wanted me to take her outside in the wheelchair so that she could see the sky and the grass.

"Mama, do you like it here?"

"No. I want to go home."

"What is it you don't like?"

With much difficulty she said, "It's too clean. Whenever they want to bathe me or put me in my chair, they talk to me in English. I don't understand what they want me to do. They pinch me, slap me, sit me down too hard in my chair, or pull my hair. I am abused daily. What kind of life is that for me in my old age? Theodor, please get me out of here and take me home."

Papa didn't say anything.

I pulled up her dress and saw black and blue finger marks on her milk white legs. Her arms didn't look much better. I made my way to the director's office. I told him what was going on, which, of course, was news to him. He assured me that the mistreatment would stop. This visit was very upsetting, but I left believing that her care would improve with the director taking a personal interest in her well-being.

Within a month, Papa called to tell me that he went to see Mama. Her tears and begging overwhelmed him. He picked her up, carried her out to his pickup truck, and brought her home.

I said, "You know, Papa, you won't be able to take her back. They won't take her."

"I don't care. I prayed to God that if He will spare her, with His help, I will take care of her."

Mama lived a couple of years under his loving care. She was completely bedridden. Washing sheets and bedding never ended for Papa. He never complained.

* * *

Tom's next change of station was to the Defense Language Institute in California to learn German. We would be going to Germany after he completed the course. In 1972 we drove across the U.S. from the East Coast of New York to the West Coast of California. The trip took two weeks. We stopped in Mississippi to visit, drove through the ice storm of the century in Texas, watched a sandstorm develop in the desert and took in Meteor Crater, the Painted Desert, and the Grand Canyon. In just nine months, Tom became fluent in German. I took advantage of the Russian Department and was given permission to audit the course. I wanted to acquaint myself somewhat with the written Russian language.

Tom received orders to report for duty in Germany in 1973. While I was waiting for transit visas for myself and the children, Sister Erika and I visited Mama. She smelled so bad that we decided to give her a bath. Papa could not wash her or the bedding every day. He would simply hang the wet sheets out on the line to dry then reuse them until they were so soiled that they had to be washed. Between the three of us we half-carried, half-dragged Mama to the bathroom and placed her in the warm water. Sister Erika and I stood in the tub washing her. Suddenly she had an unexpected bowel movement. At that point, both of us were exhausted. All we did was stand in that mess, laughing until we cried. Somehow we got Mama outside on the front porch. Papa washed her plump body down with the garden hose.

Looking in the kitchen cupboard, I discovered only canned beans with fatback.

"Papa, what do you and Mama eat?"

"Beans," he said, "I just open a can and feed it to Mama. I eat the same thing."

I bought enough groceries to last them a month. I told Papa that all he had to do was put the chicken in a pot of water and cook it until the flesh fell off the bones. He could refrigerate it and eat it over a few days, stock and all.

I cried a lot on the way back to Jackson. My heart was breaking to see my parents, who sacrificed so much to bring us to America and give us a better life, spend their autumn years in such dire conditions.

In November of 1973, we arrived in Germany. Shortly thereafter, Mama died. I could not attend her funeral because I could not get a flight out of Germany due to the oil embargo.

We lived in Nürnberg, a beautiful walled city of the old mediaeval world. In the middle ages Germany consisted of separate small nation states, each with its own prince and culture. The people who live in the state of Bavaria, the South, still consider everyone else in Germany to be Prussian. The saying, "If you are not Bavarian, you are Prussian," means they have no use for you if you are not from Bavaria. They have their own dialect, food, dress code, songs, and holidays. Almost every town and hamlet makes its own beer. The monks not only make their own beer, they even make their own brandy. Since Bavarians are predominately Roman Catholic, there are many holidays that are observed only in Bavaria and not the rest of Germany.

They are a hard-working and fun-loving people, but they don't like foreigners, and "foreigners" are all who are not from Bavaria. Bavarians are the Real Germans.

Returning to live in Bavaria, this time as a middle-class American, I found the same little everyday discriminations as before. For example, in a Gasthaus, the menu comes in English or German. The English version is more expensive. The German is reasonably priced. It doesn't matter that I now drive an expensive American car (shipped over by the armed forces) or live in an American-built house. I still speak Volga Deutsch and the Bavarians are still the Real Germans.

Nürnberg has the distinction of being Hitler's choice as the center of his New World Order. We toured Zeppelinfeld, where once the Nazis filmed their torchlight parades, and Dutzendteich Lake near the coliseum. Now kids from Nürnberg American High School played football at Zeppelinfeld—renamed Soldiers Field by the American occupying forces—and all of the military facilities had the swastikas removed or covered and were being utilized by the U.S. Army. The former S.S. Kaserne was known as Merrill Barracks, and Tom worked there. I found Bavaria beautifully rebuilt. In the smaller towns, the Bavarian building codes are strictly enforced.

I was hired by the military to teach our soldiers a simplified conversational German and used the same techniques in teaching the language that I learned at the Defense Language Institute while auditing the Russian course. Two years later Tom was promoted to lieutenant colonel and reassigned to Stuttgart, Germany, the home of Mercedes-Benz. This modern city had been completely rebuilt after it was totally destroyed during WWII.

We spent four wonderful years in Germany. Erika and Angela were both in high school and both learned German. As a family, we would participate in "Volksmarches," group hikes, on the weekends. Each little town would host a 10-kilometer or a 20-kilometer walk on different weekends. For completing the Volksmarches we received medals. Over time, we logged more than 500 kilometers (300 miles). Tom and I were guests at the German 5th Corps Fasching (Mardi Gras) party. Our holidays and vacations were spent all over Europe. We toured Amsterdam, London, Paris, Verdun, Rome, Pisa, Salzburg, and Zurich, to name only a few places. Once more I tried my hand at skiing, though this time with my daughters in the Alps.

Our family made the trip to Passau to see what was left of the camp. The monastery is still standing and occupied by priests. Then to Straubing to find that Camp Hofstetten had been replaced by a grocery storage company.

I visited with many of my former Camp Hofstetten friends but shared very little with them because they considered everything I had and did as bragging. Only one friend, Herta, ever came to visit me. My friends who stayed in Germany are still considered Flüchtlinge (known by their speech pattern) and treated like second-class citizens. Their children have all adopted the Bavarian dialect.

The feelings of being unwelcome in Bavaria also stemmed from the political situation. America, Britain, France, and the Soviet Union split Germany into four sectors after WWII, and each had an occupying army on German land. Bavaria was occupied by the Americans. Almost all of the military installations which the Nazis used were now utilized by the Americans. The war had ended twenty-eight years earlier, but Germany was still an occupied country, and that alone was cause for resentment.

My family and I went to the concentration camp at Dachau and saw the barbed-wire fences, gas chamber "showers," and crematory ovens. It was important to me that my family see not only the beautiful Germany as it is now, but also what it was like during Hitler's reign and the horrors that were perpetuated during WWII.

My Tom was a workaholic. He seemed always having to work long hours, from 7 A.M. to 7 P.M.. I wanted us, as a family, to see and experience as much of Europe as possible. The place I wanted to go as a family was Italy. When I approached Tom, I got his standard answer.

"I don't think I can make it."

Many trips I just took the girls, who were both teenagers, and Tom stayed home and worked.

"Tom, I want for us to visit Italy, because the girls want to get a suntan."

"They don't need it."

"Well then, I'm going without you, and I'll bring back a grandfather clock. They're very inexpensive there."

I already had accumulated six antique wall clocks.

"How are you going to get it home?"

"I'll take the station wagon and have it strapped onto the top."

My poor Tom could just picture that scene. I'm sure he had nightmares. Nevertheless, he took off the time from work and did the driving.

We always listened to the Armed Forces Radio Station. As we neared the Italian border, we heard that there was an election in Italy the next day and the Communist Party was predicted to win. We checked into a bed and breakfast and waited. The Communists lost. We went to Pisa.

My daughter Erika graduated from Stuttgart American High School in 1977 (she was presented her diploma by Herr Manfred Rommel, the mayor of Stuttgart and son of Field Marshal Erwin Rommel). She stayed in Germany to begin college, studying at the University of Maryland's extension campus in Munich. The rest of us were headed for Chicago.

I took a job in the personnel department with the Department of the Army at Fort Sheridan, Illinois.

Papa and Brother Otto began construction on Otto's house in 1978. It is an A-frame building built completely by hand. They completed it in 1982. My whole family was very impressed while touring the two-story house. They did an outstanding job.

Tom retired from the army in 1982, and we moved back to Virginia. I transferred to the personnel department of the Adjutant General Division at Fort Lee. Tom accepted employment with the Commonwealth of Virginia doing the same thing he had done in the army. Our daughter Erika graduated from Mississippi State University with a bachelor of arts in political science that same year.

Papa died in 1985. Both Mama and Papa are buried in the hot, humid, kudzu-covered Mississippi red clay.

Our daughter Angela graduated from Mississippi State University later in 1985 with a double-major Bachelor of Arts degree in English literature and philosophy. She went to the University of Southern Mississippi for her master's degree in philosophy and the University of Kansas to work on her Ph.D.

I keep busy with gardening, traveling to different parts of the world (from Australia to Alaska), and participating in a German-speaking Damen club. We celebrate holidays such as Christmas, Oktoberfest, and Fasching with singing, dancing, and feasting. German is our mother tongue, which we try not to forget. Our club meetings are very festive, with presentations of poems or short stories and German songs.

I attend many church functions; serving as an elder in the local Presbyterian church, singing in the choir, participating in Bible study groups and the DeColores movement (known as the Pilgrimage of the James in Richmond). I volunteer at the Fort Lee Thrift Shop and serve in the Petersburg Soup Kitchen. Occasionally I speak to different clubs and organizations about my life.

All of my siblings married and had children.

All owned a piece of American soil.